PATRICK KENNEDY

Real Politics in America

Series Editor: Paul S. Herrnson, *University of Maryland*

The books in this series bridge the gap between academic scholarship and the popular demand for knowledge about politics. They illustrate empirically supported generalizations from original research and the academic literature using examples taken from the legislative process, executive branch decision making, court rulings, lobbying efforts, election campaigns, political movements, and other areas of American politics. The goal of the series is to convey the best contemporary political science research has to offer in ways that will engage individuals who want to know about real politics in America.

PATRICK KENNEDY
The Rise to Power

Darrell M. West
Brown University

UPPER SADDLE RIVER, NEW JERSEY 07458

Library of Congress Cataloging-in-Publication Data

West, Darrell M.
  Patrick Kennedy: The rise to power / Darrell M. West
    p. cm. — (Real politics in America Series)
    Includes bibliographical references (p.) and index.
    ISBN 0-13-017694-X
    1. Kennedy, Patrick J. (Patrick Joseph), 1967-2. Legislators—United States—Biography, 3. United States.
  Congress. House—Biography. I. Title. II. Series.

E840.8.K358 W47 2001
328.73'092—dc21
[B]   00-039202

To Tracey, Gail, and Roberta,
for keeping me sane throughout this project

VP, Editorial Director: Laura Pearson
Executive Editor: Beth Gillett Mejia
Editorial Assistant: Beth Murtha
Director of Marketing: Gina Sluss
Interior Design and Project Manager: Serena Hoffman
Prepress and Manufacturing Buyer: Benjamin Smith
Copy Editor: Ann Hofstra Grogg
Cover Art Director: Jayne Conte
Cover Designer: Bruce Kenselaar
Cover Photo: The Providence Journal Company

This book was set in 10/12 Times New Roman
by Progressive Information Technologies
and was printed and bound by Courier Companies, Inc.
The cover was printed by Phoenix Color Corp.

Real Politics in America Series
Paul S. Herrnson, Series Editor

©2001 by Darrell M. West
Prentice Hall, Inc.
A Division of Pearson Education
Upper Saddle River, New Jersey 07458

Printed in the United States of America
10 9 8 7 6 5 4 3 2 1

ISBN 0-13-017694-X

Prentice-Hall International (UK) Limited, *London*
Prentice-Hall of Australia Pty. Limited, *Sydney*
Prentice-Hall Canada Inc., *Toronto*
Prentice-Hall Hispanoamericana, S.A., *Mexico*
Prentice-Hall of India Private Limited, *New Delhi*
Prentice-Hall of Japan, Inc., *Tokyo*
Pearson Education Asia Pte. Ltd., *Singapore*
Editora Prentice-Hall do Brasil, Ltda., *Rio de Janeiro*

Contents

Preface

It was the height of the U.S. House Republican impeachment effort against President William Jefferson Clinton. Speaking in the legislative chamber on December 18, 1998, conservative Bob Barr (Rep.-Ga.), the first member to introduce an impeachment resolution on Clinton over the Monica Lewinsky sex scandal, quoted President John F. Kennedy to buttress his point that no one was above the law. Using language from Kennedy's famous 1956 book *Profiles in Courage*, Barr moralized, "Americans are free to disagree with the law but not to disobey it. For a government of laws and not of men, no man however prominent and powerful, no mob however unruly or boisterous is entitled to defy a court of law."[1]

Seething quietly as he heard the speech was Representative Patrick Kennedy, youngest son of Senator Edward Kennedy, nephew to President John Kennedy and former U.S. Senator Robert Kennedy, and cousin to a slew of young Kennedys. The 31-year-old legislator, who had been elected to the House from Rhode Island in 1994, could not believe the outrage he was hearing. Barr was using Kennedy's beloved uncle to criticize a Democratic president whom Patrick supported! Kennedy was not going to take that lying down.

Exploding out of his seat, Kennedy headed for the House Speaker's lobby just a few feet away from the floor. Spying Barr coming off the floor talking to reporters, Kennedy screamed at him, "How dare you! Anybody who has been to a racist group has no right invoking my uncle's memory." The charge was a reference to Barr's appearance at a meeting of the Council of Conservative Citizens, a white supremacy group. "Young man," Barr started to respond, "you are wrong. Young man, you are showing a lack of decorum." Kennedy immediately fired back, "I'm a duly elected representative of my state." The encounter ended with Barr sarcastically replying, "I'm impressed. I'm duly impressed."[2]

The outspokenness Kennedy demonstrated that day came naturally to the young man. After all, he was raised in one of the most famous families in America. Ever since his grandfather Joseph Kennedy's emergence on the national political scene in the 1920s and 1930s, the Kennedy name has been synonymous with wealth, power, and celebrity. His uncle's rise to the presidency in 1960 and efforts to energize government ushered in an era of political activism personified by the Peace Corps, the space program, and a call for civil rights. John F. Kennedy inspired a new generation into public service, including a young Bill Clinton.

JFK's tragic assassination in 1963 truncated the nation's hopes, but soon a new legacy was born. Jackie Kennedy's graceful mourning during her husband's funeral — the first time such an event had been televised live nationally — deepened public respect for the Kennedys. Before long, the Camelot legend was flourishing, helped along by a sympathetic *Life* magazine article by Theodore White. The 1968 assassination of Robert Kennedy and the subsequent ups and downs of Senator Ted Kennedy's career reinforced America's fascination with the family. Fueled by the tabloidization of the country's press and the emergence of new television shows such as *A Current Affair*, *Hard Copy*, and *Inside Edition*, Americans followed the trials and tribulations of the Kennedy family with unparalleled interest.

Now a new group of Kennedys has come along to extend the dynasty to a new generation. If the Kennedys are America's royal family, then Patrick Kennedy is the political crown prince. Within a decade, he has risen from a reformer in the Rhode Island legislature to being a leader in Congress. A passionate spokesperson for the less fortunate, he is one of his party's top fund-raisers as chair of the Democratic Congressional Campaign Committee. Over the last three elections, he has raised millions of dollars for himself and his party. He ranks fifth in the House Democratic leadership and is a close protégé of Democratic leader Richard Gephardt. With cousin Joseph Kennedy's retirement in November 1998, Patrick is the highest elected Kennedy of his generation.

Kennedy is the latest in a long line of rich and famous Americans who have made it into Congress. In recent decades celebrities such as Bill Bradley, Jack Kemp, Steve Largent, J. C. Watts, John Glenn, and Sonny Bono have become successful politicians. The rapid rise of these individuals in national politics is testimony to the tremendous advantages of fame. In previous centuries, the halls of Congress were packed with farmers, merchants, and local ward-heelers who worked their way up from poverty. It was the American Dream to better yourself by going into politics. Indeed, for those born without economic or social advantage, politics was the traditional route to upward mobility. Today the combination of high campaign costs, weak political parties, citizen cynicism, and media domination of the political process places a premium on personal fame and wealth. It is no surprise that one-third of the U.S. Senate is comprised of millionaires, and that candidates with famous last names such as Kennedy, Bush, Bradley, and Gore run for office. "Celebrityhood" is a major path to political power in America.[3]

If celebrity is reshaping American politics, there is no better example than Patrick Kennedy. Wealthy and famous, he is the archetype of legacy politics that has become common in America. A detailed study of Kennedy's rise to prominence provides important lessons about how our political system functions. This book uses the story of Kennedy's political emergence to explore what works in election campaigns, how the media cover famous politicians, and the manner in which political institutions are used by adroit politicians.

Kennedy's rise to prominence was almost derailed by his cousin William Smith's Palm Beach sexual assault trial in 1991. That event divided the Kennedys and ushered in a new media era that would set the standard for tabloid coverage of later celebrity court cases, such as those of Michael Jackson and O. J. Simpson. The case had all the ingredients of a highly rated miniseries: sex, drinking, and famous Kennedy names. The press went wild. Why had Senator Ted Kennedy awakened his young son and cousin to go to a bar late at night? What had happened in the early morning hours at the compound? Although Smith was eventually acquitted, the experience drained Patrick and nearly drove him to renounce public service.

The most recent episode in Kennedy's life—his election to the U.S. Congress—introduced a new cast of compelling characters, such as Bill Clinton, Dick Gephardt, and Newt Gingrich. When Kennedy entered Congress, he faced the new Republican majority committed to dismantling the very programs identified with the Kennedy name. For two years, Patrick Kennedy walked a tightrope between attacking Republican extremism on domestic policy and working closely with the Republican majority on the National Security Committee to bring military contracts back to his state. It was not the only time that Kennedy used Republican connections to advance his career.

Kennedy's political emergence is illuminating in its own right, but his story also is a personal drama about the struggle of dealing with fame in a media era. The fame associated with the Kennedy family has had a tremendous impact on the lives of the Kennedy cousins. For some of the "third generation," as they are called, it has been a terrible burden. Never able to overcome the trauma of his father Robert's assassination, David Kennedy died the victim of a drug overdose in 1984. John Kennedy, Jr., was killed in a 1999 airplane accident. Several others have been treated for alcohol and drug abuse. Patrick Kennedy himself was treated for cocaine abuse as a teenager and was accused in 2000 of pushing an airport security guard while rushing to catch a plane. No family in America has labored under more unrealistic stereotypes than the Kennedys. This book shows how Patrick Kennedy built a successful career during one of the most tumultuous political times in American history.

As a close follower of Patrick Kennedy's career, I have had a number of opportunities to observe Kennedy firsthand. I first met him on February 27, 1991, over lunch at the Brown University Faculty Club. He has addressed my political science classes at Brown University, and I have moderated television debates in his campaign. As a pollster at Brown University, I have monitored the ups and downs of his political fortunes. For research on this book, I conducted 94 interviews, including conversations with Patrick Kennedy, family members, top political advisers, business associates, priests, and political adversaries. I have read thousands of newspaper and magazine articles about Kennedy from his childhood to the present time and seen many television stories about him. I have reviewed confidential strategy memos, unpublished interviews, private journals kept by friends, polling data, and documents dealing with his voting record, campaign finance records, and testimony in the Palm Beach trial of his cousin William Smith. This information allows me to present new insights into how the Kennedy family functions and how the next generation of Kennedy cousins has made the transition to prominence.

I am grateful to many people for their assistance on this project. A number of individuals took time out of their busy schedules to share their thoughts about Patrick Kennedy. I could not have written this book without them. M. Charles Bakst of the *Providence Journal* deserves a special thanks for lending me a tape of an indepth interview he conducted with Patrick Kennedy. I also appreciate the helpfulness of people at the Brown University Library, Providence College Library, Georgetown University Library, and Boston Public Library who helped me locate material on the Kennedys. Paul Herrnson of the University of Maryland read an early draft and gave me very helpful comments. Beth Gillett Mejia of Prentice Hall made a number of suggestions that improved the book's organization. Serena Hoffman shepherded the book through the production process, and Ann Grogg did an excellent job of copy-editing the manuscript. My biggest debt goes to my wife, Annie Schmitt, with whom I spent countless hours discussing this project and who provided detailed comments on the manuscript. Her keen eye and helpful suggestions made this a better book.

Darrell M. West

1 A Sense of Fragility

*P*atrick Kennedy was famous from the moment he was born — at 2:30 p.m., Friday, July 14, 1967, weight 8 pounds and 7 ounces. His birth made the front page of the *Boston Globe* with the headline, "2nd Son for Ted." Within two hours of his arrival, reporters quizzed Ted Kennedy at a press conference on his child's political future. "What if the new son has Presidential ambitions?" one reporter asked. "He'll have to clear that with his uncle," Senator Edward Kennedy replied referring to Uncle Robert Kennedy, the senator from New York and a prospective presidential candidate in 1968.[1] The parents were caught off-guard by the birth of a male child. They had been expecting a girl and had no name chosen for a son. "We had some leads on names if it had been a girl," the senator said. It would take several days before they would settle on the name of the child. At the hospital press conference announcing the birth, the father informed the gathered crowd, "I've called my father and my mother and Joan's parents and I'm trying to reach my sisters." Continuing, he said, "When I got Bob, I told him the baby was very well. He asked, 'How's Ethel?' Bobby thinks every baby born these days is one of his."[2]

Five days later, the baby slept through his very first news conference. Just before leaving St. Elizabeth's Hospital, his parents met the press and announced they had named the baby Patrick Joseph Kennedy. The name had come from the child's great-grandfather P.J., who had lived from 1858 to 1929 and served eight terms in the Massachusetts legislature. Patrick's namesake was a considerate and affectionate man who on his deathbed ordered the burning of IOUs from poor people for fear his son Joe would attempt to collect the debts.[3] Naming the baby was no easy task, Kennedy told the reporters. "We thought very hard about a name, but my brother Bobby has already used most of the familiar ones in our family. We finally thought it would be nice to name him Patrick Joseph after my grandfather." The forebear had been "quiet and soft-spoken," Kennedy said. "We hope his namesake will be the same in the months ahead, particularly as his room is very close to my own."[4]

On July 29, Patrick was christened by Cardinal Cushing of Boston, an old family friend, in St. Francis Xavier Church in Hyannis. Patrick, wearing a long white christening gown, was described as a "model of decorum" during the 12-minute cere-mony. He yawned a few times but did not cry. Two hundred relatives and friends were present for the ceremony, including cousin Caroline Kennedy and two aunts, Mrs. Eunice Shriver and Mrs. Patricia Lawford. His weight was up to 10 pounds. At the end of the service, Cardinal Cushing proclaimed, "You've got a beautiful baby, Ted. A wonderful kid."[5]

Patrick's childhood was not what one might expect of a future political leader. "Birthday parties were always a disaster," Patrick's mother recalled. "He would have a wonderful, wonderful time, but he would always end up having an asthma attack." His father echoed the point. "He had more time in the school infirmary than any other child. Even when he was healthy, I could say to Patrick 'Let's go out and play ball' or something, and the first play he'd run extra hard and that would trigger it, and he'd have to stop. And all the other kids would say, 'What's wrong with you, Patrick?'"[6]

Then there was the campaign incident. It started as a routine plane flight in Ted's losing presidential effort to derail the 1980 Democratic renomination of President Jimmy Carter. Desperate to turn things around, the Kennedy camp chartered a plane from Air New England, a bargain basement airliner from a company that soon would go defunct. The pressurization was terrible, but the campaign could not afford a better plane. The plan was to fly from Washington, D.C., to Wisconsin, with stops in West Virginia, Indiana, and Kansas. The race had started with grand hopes of defeating an incumbent president who in the eyes of Kennedy had betrayed his party's traditions. Inflation was double-digit, and the "misery index" was at an all-time high. But the campaign was not turning out the way supporters had anticipated. Ted was losing state after state, and not by small margins. The commentary was devastating. Kennedys were not supposed to lose. The plane had left Wichita for St. Louis on March 29 when passengers noticed that Ted's youngest son Patrick could not breathe. Ted turned to the doctor, Lawrence Horowitz, and nurse Ann Goshko, who always traveled with the presidential campaign. Horowitz examined the gasping youth and said he needed a hospital. Patrick was choking and coughing, with persistent breathing difficulties. Af-ter the plane landed in St. Louis, they went straight to a hospital. The diagnosis was a "mild to moderate" asthma attack. Ted called off the scheduled trip to Milwaukee even though the Wisconsin primary was three days away. He did not want Patrick to have to fly that night.[7]

Asthma deeply affected Patrick's childhood. The name of the disease comes from the Greek word for panting or breathlessness. It is a debilitating chronic illness that afflicts 6 percent of all children and 12 million Americans overall. Four thousand die from it each year.[8] Asthma blocks the flow of air into the lungs and squeezes the exchange of oxygen. One minute a child is well, and the next he is wheezing like an old horse. The disease left a clear imprint on Patrick's life. "It forced me to have to use a ventilator practically every night when I went to bed," Patrick remembered. "I had to have adrenaline shots and susphrine [also known as epinephrine] shots if not every week, then every couple of weeks."[9] During the third grade, he missed so many days of school he had to repeat the year. Even in adulthood, he had to use a Ventolin inhaler to ward off attacks.

With his frequent bouts of asthma, Patrick did not grow up like other youngsters. He was shy, polite, and deferential—not a typical Kennedy male. The Kennedy men were hail-fellow and well-met—gregarious, outgoing, and boisterous. Patrick was small for his age and vulnerable. He did not engage in the rough-and-tumble for which many of his cousins were famous. There was a sense of fragility about him. His father recalled, "Because of the health thing, he wasn't able to keep up and wasn't as robust. He had to conserve energy, and that did impact his personality." Patrick himself could remember only one fist fight in his life. As a young boy, he hit a bully at an ice skating rink who was taking advantage of others.[10] Unlike most members of the extended Kennedy clan, Patrick was content to be by himself. He constructed cities with building blocks and erector sets. It was a solitary activity that took great patience, qualities for which most Kennedys were not renowned. Around the family compound when the cousins were together, there were organized activities like football games or water sports. Patrick participated when he could, but often was not able to do so for very long, especially when he was very young. "I was never athletic. I would always drop the ball," he later recalled.[11] The asthma created in him a strong sense of empathy and introspection. He could understand what it meant to be different and not to be able to do things other kids took for granted. His father felt that "his medical problems sensitized him to people's needs and sufferings, and toughened him in his own struggle to establish himself as an individual."[12]

Many people mistook Patrick's shyness and deferential manner for lack of ambition. But his cousin Douglas, the son of Robert Kennedy, who was close friends with Patrick when they were growing up, detected broader goals. Their homes were just down the road from each other, and the two had been born just a few months apart. Like most young boys his age, all Douglas cared about was sports. "I wanted to be a football player when I grew up," he said. Once he asked Patrick if he could choose one thing to be the best in the world, what would it be. Assuming the obvious answer for most little kids would be the best athlete, he was startled when Patrick replied "if he could have one thing that he was the best at in the world, it would be a debater. He wanted to be able to debate issues."[13]

For children born to fame, Patrick and his siblings, Kara and Teddy, were remarkably unspoiled. They lived in a French country-style mansion in the tony suburb of McLean, Virginia, just outside of Washington, D.C. Set on 6.5 acres, it was a one-story, 16-room house overlooking the Potomac River. In one wing of the home were bedrooms for Kara, Teddy, and Patrick. The other wing featured a large master bedroom with a spectacular view of the Potomac. Each child had an allowance and was expected to live within it. Teddy was six years older than Patrick. He was gregarious like his father, with the same stocky build. Since Ted didn't want his children growing up snobbish or with a rich person's sense of entitlement, one summer Teddy earned $2.35 an hour directing cars as a parking attendant for the Wood's Hole, Martha's Vineyard, and Nantucket Steamship Authority.[14] Kara was the oldest of the kids, seven years older than Patrick. In Gaelic, her name stood for "dear little one."[15] She was more irreverent and had a totally unaffected manner. Being the youngest had its advantages. Patrick said, "I was always around an older crowd," which helped him grow up fast and gave him a maturity far beyond his years. But the interactions were not always positive. "I'd always be the one everybody got a laugh out of, because they ended up making me cry or run from the room."[16]

Politics was the center of Patrick's father's life. Thrust unwillingly onto political center-stage by the assassinations of his brothers Jack in 1963 and Robert in 1968, Ted Kennedy was the patriarch for a large extended family. There were John and Caroline Kennedy, and Robert's 11 kids to look after, not to mention the brood of cousins from his sister's marriages: 5 Shrivers, 4 Smiths, and 4 Lawfords. Because Ted was a powerful senator from Massachusetts who had a lot of seniority, political people always were present at the McLean estate. Several times a month, Ted would organize expert briefings on the issues. The kids were expected to listen, and occasionally Ted would put his youngest son on the spot by yelling, "What do you think, Patrick?" before the startled group of experts.[17] The experience did not endear the political world to Patrick. At an early age, Patrick concluded that he never wanted to enter politics. "Politics to me didn't seem to make sense. My father was away a lot, and politics was just people rushing in and out of the house."[18] His father's 1980 presidential campaign had created an absolute zoo at his home. "There were three network television stations almost camped out daily at our house," Patrick recalled. "Whenever I would pick up the bus to go to school, it was just strange." The campaign was "surreal" and demonstrated to Patrick that "there is an absurdity about the political process" with all the traveling to distant states, the chartered 727s, and the press hanging on the candidate's every word.[19]

Despite these distractions, Patrick was proud of his father and understanding of the personal pain he had endured from numerous family tragedies. He respected his father's perseverance in the face of tremendous obstacles, such as the assassination of Jack and Robert and the tragedy at Chappaquiddick, where a young woman had drowned in a car Ted was driving. His father had spoken to Patrick about Chappaquiddick around one of the anniversaries "when the media," according to Patrick "made it a media circus." Patrick remembered, "My father was obviously very sensitive to the way I learned about it and how I responded."[20] There was a personal tie between Ted and Patrick, sometimes accompanied by "bruising joshing."[21] Ted had helped administer asthma shots, which prompted Patrick to give his Dad a cartoon of Nurse Gooch from an English magazine. She had a horrible expression on her face and was carrying a big needle. Patrick autographed the picture "to my Daddy and my night-nurse."[22] For one of his father's birthdays, Patrick wrote and sang a song for his Dad in front of a big crowd. Longtime friends of the Kennedy family said that the quickest way to get Patrick ticked off was to go after his father.

Patrick's mother, Joan, represented another aspect of life for her son, the artistic side. She was a "reserved private person," according to her youngest son.[23] "Music was one of their languages for communication. She was the artistic self that politics does not give you much of an arena to express," explained Brown University Professor Barbara Tannenbaum, a close friend of Patrick's during his college years. Once as a teenager, he had learned a whole piece of piano music to surprise Joan on her birthday—Louis Armstrong's song "Satin Doll." Even though he was ill with the flu, he came down to her party at 9:00 p.m., dressed up with a bow tie. He went over to the piano, talked to the band leader, and played the song for her in front of the assembled guests. "Knowing that I'm a pianist, that was the loveliest thing he could do for my birthday," Joan remarked, crying as she recounted the story later to a reporter. When he turned twenty-one, she returned the favor, insisting on having a piano at the party so she could play "Happy Birthday" for him.[24]

According to family members, Patrick learned different things from his parents. From his mother, Patrick developed the need for independent grounding. Joan kept her distance from the Kennedy myth. More than anyone else in the family, she understood its elusiveness. One cousin noted, "She is much lighter in her dealings with life. . . . That is where he gets his not buying into our whole family stuff, which is very easy to buy into." From his father, Patrick developed the quality of living life actively. "His Dad insists on experiencing life to its fullest. That is why they share that bond of love which is so great. This is here, you have to experience it."[25]

People who know Patrick feel he is a unique combination of both parents. "His Dad expects a lot from him," said close friend Jack McConnell. "His Mom is a Mom that has no expectation except the best for her son for whom Patrick could do anything and she would be supportive and proud as could be." According to McConnell, Kennedy believed that not enough credit has been given to the influence of his Mom. "He is very much his mother's son. When you talk to him and listen to him, when Patrick gets real when he talks, it's about his Mom. His relationship with his Dad seems far more professional."[26] To a reporter, Patrick once said when he felt like he wasn't "Kennedy enough, it's not the end of the road for me. I remember I'm part of two different people."[27]

Part of growing up a Kennedy involved having famous relatives. His "Aunt Jackie" was Jacqueline Kennedy Onassis, the celebrated widow of the assassinated president and shipping magnate Aristotle Onassis. Thinking back on her years later, Patrick described Jackie as a normal person who "was very natural and human" and "very common in her approach." He appreciated the way she had "reached a level that is almost like my uncle. Bobby and my uncle President Kennedy"—that of a living legend. What he admired most about her was that "she managed to shield herself from so much of the publicity and hype that if she had exposed herself to that, she may have been a very different person."[28] At the other end of the spectrum was his "Aunt Rosie," the mentally retarded Rosemary about whom virtually nothing had been written. Every year, he had seen her when she came to spend time with Eunice Shriver and his father. Conversations were not easy. For example, you couldn't conduct a conversation with her as two people normally would talk, but "we can communicate with one another," Patrick said. Her suffering had produced a legacy that was one of the proudest in the family, the Special Olympics, in which the families of the mentally retarded can get together and celebrate their common bonds.[29]

When Patrick was 6, in November 1973, a crisis developed that engulfed the entire family. His brother Teddy, then 12 years old, noticed a bruise on his right knee while a student at St. Albans in Washington, D.C. Worried that it would interfere with his making the football team, his parents had it examined. The tissue was biopsied at Georgetown Hospital, and the news that came back was grim. It was not a youngster's normal bruise. It was rhabdomyosarcoma, a rare and virulent bone cartilage cancer. The estimated survival rate was 25 percent, and death could come within 18 months.[30]

His father broke the information to Teddy, telling him that he was "going to lose part of [his] leg due to cancer." Not understanding the severity, Teddy at first thought the news meant "the doctors would simply have to cut out the swollen part in [his] kneecap." But Ted replied, "Not exactly. It's from the knee down."[31] The discovery shook the foundations of the household. After his Dad learned the news and informed Teddy, Patrick remembered being summoned to his father's room. "We knew it was serious to be called into his room. He told us that Teddy had cancer. All I felt was fear. I didn't know whether we could go near him, whether we'd catch it. I didn't know what to say, what to do, how to respond, who to talk to. And I wondered: How did he catch it? Was it anything I did?"[32]

Doctors recommended an immediate amputation of the right leg, just above the knee. The surgery was scheduled right away, with little time for the family to comprehend the news. Following the surgery, Ted slept in the hospital room at night while Joan visited during the day. But there were arguments over how to handle the recovery. Joan recalled, "Ted brought in famous athletes to amuse Teddy in his room. We argued a lot about this. It was a circus all the time and I thought Teddy should be quiet."[33] For 18 months, there was painful chemotherapy to ensure that the cancer did not spread. Once every three weekends, Teddy flew to Boston on the Eastern shuttle as the fourth participant in a new experimental treatment involving a drug combination of methotreaxate and leucovorin. The first drug was given in doses 40 times higher than usual in order to kill the cancer. The latter then was administered to keep the methotreaxate from killing the patient. Teddy suffered waves of nausea from intravenous administration of the drug designed to combat the cancer. He developed painful mouth sores that made it nearly impossible to keep anything down. He lost most of his hair and worried about whether he ever would father children given the toxic effect of the drugs. The medical treatment proved successful. Within four months, Teddy was skiing at Vail on one leg with special poles for support.

But for the family, it was a traumatic experience. According to Patrick, there was a feeling of "Don't talk about it. But that's disruptive and can further add to the stress of the family. . . . Stress and confusion manifest themselves in many ways."[34] For his father, there was work and career, which he threw himself into. Since Kennedy was one of the chief spokespersons of the liberal wing of the Democratic party, there were always speaking engagements, which took his father away from home. And there was alcohol for his mother. By spring 1974, just four months after her eldest son's surgery, Joan was treated for mental strain and physical fatigue at Silver Hill in New Canaan, Connecticut, a luxurious treatment center set on a rolling landscape. That fall, she was arrested on a drunk driving charge in Fairfax County, Virginia, after her car hit another auto. What had been rumored for some time was confirmed. Joan Kennedy was an alcoholic. The pressures had been building for years. In a 1978 *McCall's* interview, she recalled her problems finding a niche in the Kennedy family. "I drank socially at first, and then I began to drink alcoholically. . . . It doesn't happen overnight; it just creeps up. Little by little." "I tried to talk about it," she said, "but I was embarrassed and Ted was embarrassed about it. Everybody was embarrassed about it. Even my best friend would tiptoe around it." The rumors about her husband's affairs with other women hurt. "I began thinking, 'Well, maybe I'm just not attractive enough or whatever,' and it was awfully easy to then say, 'Well after all you know if that's the way it is, I might as well have a drink.'"[35]

When Teddy had his leg amputated, she didn't drink. "I was in okay shape while he was in the hospital. I was the mother by the bedside. But as soon as he was well and back in school, I just collapsed. I needed some relief from having to be so damn brave all the time."[36] Her problems with alcohol would affect everyone in the family. There was shame and silence. Joan shuttled from treatment center to center in a ceaseless bid to find help. Asked how he handled growing up with an alcoholic parent, Patrick said, "You start very early turning within yourself to figure out where things are coming from, because things get pretty skewed."[37] He developed a fearlessness that gave him great personal freedom. Accustomed to rumors about each of his parents, Patrick didn't care as much as most children growing up what others thought. "I'm not living my life for what other people think of me."[38]

But there was one thing that did concern him—his father's safety. During the 1980 presidential campaign, when his Dad constantly was on the road, Patrick worried about security. His family was a lightning rod for crazy people all over the country. There were unpublicized incidents on the campaign trail, according to Patrick, where "someone would stab [his father] with a pen or something like that and his hand would be bloody and Secret Service wouldn't know whether they had poisoned him."[39] Strangers would stop by the house unannounced. Patrick was spending time with Robert Kennedy's kids, who lived just down the road at Hickory Hill, and could see how devastating their father's assassination was personally to his cousins. "I'm very lucky to have my father alive," he said. "I know it must be a lot more difficult for my cousins to live with the name they've been given without having their fathers there to help them understand and separate the myth from the reality."[40]

When his father traveled, Ted worried the most about Patrick. The other kids were old enough to be on their own; Kara attended Tufts, and Teddy was headed for Wesleyan University. Patrick was 12 years old and vulnerable. To reassure his son, his Dad called Patrick every night from the campaign trail. According to Bob Shrum, the senator's press secretary, "We would just stop. We would campaign after the call. He just stopped. He would be in a holding room and he would call him." Continuing, Shrum said, "Sometimes they were two minutes and sometimes no matter what the schedule said, they were 25 or 30 minutes because there was something Patrick wanted to talk about. They were kid calls. They could be about homework, they could be about what happened in school that day. Kennedy would talk about what happened on the campaign trail. Patrick was really hurt when his father lost too. We did some losing in that campaign."[41]

Ronald Reagan beat Jimmy Carter and was inaugurated in 1981. Two months into his presidency, John Hinckley shot Reagan and his press secretary, James Brady. Douglas Kennedy was with Patrick at the time. "I remember Patrick and I were alone. We had heard about it when we were at McDonalds. We drove back to his house and watched a bit of it on the news. We were alone in his father's room." Cognizant of what might have been had his father been elected president in 1980, Patrick turned to Douglas and said, "I'm going to say a prayer." He knelt down and said a bunch of Hail Marys. Reflecting back on it, the prayer struck Douglas as an unusual gesture for a junior high kid to make. Patrick wasn't worried how he looked or that he was doing something that might look weird to his cousin. Douglas was impressed that Patrick did not care how someone his own age thought about it.[42]

The next year over Thanksgiving weekend at the Kennedy compound in Hyannisport, the family gathered to consider another presidential run for Ted in 1984. Senate aide Lawrence Horowitz, the doctor who treated Patrick's asthma attack in 1980, made the case for running. The kids argued strongly against it. "I need you and I want you around," Patrick proclaimed to his father. Each had participated in the 1980 contest and come face to face with Kennedy haters from around the country. In New York, Kara was accosted by a stranger who reminded her that her father at Chappaquiddick in 1969 had "killed a young girl about your age." There were Jimmy Carter's campaign ads about "family values" and open digs at Ted's unsettled marriage. Bumper stickers were distributed proclaiming, "Vote for Jimmy Carter. Free Joan Kennedy."[43]

For Patrick, the campaign was not a very good first impression of electoral politics. Recalling the presidential campaign, he said, "That was a tough time. I was only 12 years old, and I was very timid." It was not something any of the children wanted their father to repeat.[44] After hearing his kids out, Ted declined the race. "It was the conversations with his kids, and especially when he drew out the depths of Patrick's feelings, that was decisive," an aide explained. Later, when others urged him to reconsider, Ted joked that he could rethink the decision only if "Patrick changes his mind." In 1982, Ted publicly announced his decision not to run. With his three children seated in front of him—Patrick, age 15, Teddy, age 21, and Kara, age 22, the senator informed reporters, "For the members of my family the 1980 campaign was sometimes a difficult experience. It is very soon to ask them to go through it all again." Ted then made it official. "I would not be a candidate in 1984, nor would I accept a draft in 1984 for the presidency or the vice presidency."[45]

Ted also announced that Joan and he were formally divorcing. They had lived apart since 1977, when she had moved to Boston to pursue an education degree at Lesley College.[46] The marriage had been miscast from the very beginning. She was a warm and sensitive soul, someone more comfortable in the world of music and art. He was tough and analytical, and completely immersed in politics. There were details to work out—the settlement, division of assets, and custody of Patrick. At the official divorce hearing in Barnstable, Massachusetts, in December 1982, the couple declared there had been an "irretrievable breakdown" of their 24-year marriage. Under the settlement, Joan got annual alimony of $175,000, child support, a lump-sum cash settlement, their seven-room condominium on Boston's Beacon Street, and their gray-shingled Hyannisport home on a bluff a mile from the Kennedy compound. Overall, the settlement was worth an estimated $4 million of Ted's $20 million total.[47] The divorce meant a major change for Patrick. Between 1977 and 1982, he had spent a lot of time by himself at the family residence. "I was left all alone at the house," he said. "My father was very busy in his political life. My mother had moved out."[48] After five years on his own with his father, Patrick moved in with his mother in Boston.

2 On the Brink

*A*fter the divorce proceedings, Joan took Patrick on a Christmas trip of the Holy Land, where they met Israeli Prime Minister Menachem Begin and toured Bethlehem. From there, it was on to Italy, where they had a private audience with Pope John Paul II. The pontiff "asked about the family. He was wonderful," reported Joan. This trip culminated in a January 19, 1983, appearance by Patrick and his mother on ABC's *Good Morning America.*[1] For Patrick, the trip was a chance to get to know his mother again after several years away from her. Speaking on *Good Morning America*, he said "We've been getting to know each other in a way that I couldn't when things were worse. Now it's just like the old days. We've caught up on a lot. . . . My mother and I kind of discovered each other on that trip."[2] Between the family's celebrityhood and his mother's alcoholism, his social isolation and his parent's divorce, Patrick's childhood had not been easy. "Living where I was living [in McLean], you couldn't walk next door and be with your friends. You had to be driven everywhere, and that wasn't always that easy to do," he noted. Other children razzed him about being a Kennedy, although he "had grown accustomed to people treating [him] just a little bit differently. . . . There really wasn't much that I wasn't used to," he said. Recalling that time later in life, he felt "things weren't easy and I don't make them out to be easy. But I don't think they are easy for anybody. I don't think that anyone lives the kind of life that is free from the kinds of problems that my family's faced."[3]

Around the time of Ted and Joan's divorce, Patrick was hitting the teenage years, a time that is hard for any youngster, let alone someone whose last name is Kennedy. As a result of the custody decision, he moved from his father's McLean estate to his mother's Boston condominium. That meant a new school, new friends, and a new life. "When you're going through a divorce, you really have to spend a lot of time with the youngest one—it's a full-time job," Joan explained.[4] Subtly, she tried to steer him away from politics and a public life.[5] Joan realized that Kennedy men faced particular problems. They are "powerful, rich, social, important. With them life's very exciting," Joan said. "But there's nothing to fall back on when the clapping ends."[6] One of the things that helped Patrick was learning the value of faith as evidenced by his grandmother, Rose Kennedy. "Here was a woman who had lost her husband and four of her children, and she never made you feel that she was ever lonely because you always felt that she was with God. . . . You were able to feel her serenity and her peace of mind."[7]

After attending the Potomac School in Washington, Patrick transferred to Fessenden School in West Newton, Massachusetts. From Patrick's standpoint, going away to boarding school was a good move. His brother and sister were away at college. "It was a decision that I made that I didn't want to be the only person at the house. . . . By going to boarding school, it gave me an atmosphere where I could spend time with kids my own age. I could play sports after school," he said.[8] Sitting on 45 acres, Fessenden had 400 boys in kindergarten to ninth grade from all around the world. According to its mission statement, the school was designed "to instill moral character, a strong sense of good sportsmanship, and a love of learning."[9] In 1983, Patrick graduated ninth grade with honors. As he was awarded his diploma, his mother gushed, "That's my baby getting magna cum laude." His father, a Fessenden alumnus himself, told Patrick's classmates, "I was particularly delighted that Patrick's grades were a lot higher than mine, but after a while I said, 'I appreciate the grades, Patrick, but enough is enough.'"[10]

That fall, Patrick enrolled in Phillips Academy in Andover for the tenth grade. Located in Andover, Massachusetts, about 20 miles north of Boston, the Phillips Academy is one of the most prestigious secondary schools in America. The school's 1778 Constitution charged that "Goodness without knowledge is weak and feeble; yet knowledge without goodness is dangerous." Andover is a 500-acre residential high school whose stated mission included not just academic excellence but "aesthetic sensitivity, physical well-being, athletic prowess, and moral decisiveness." Almost immediately upon his enrollment, there was a health crisis. Patrick lived in one of the older dorms on campus and found that mold spores in the old building were exacerbating his asthma. His physical reaction was severe enough to necessitate a move to new housing. On campus, he kept to himself. He wasn't distinguished in academics, sports, music, or leadership. David Cobb, the dean of student life, described him as going through the school in "studied anonymity." Patrick wasn't well known other than his famous last name, but he was regarded "as a nice person who was somewhat introverted and shy."[11]

At Phillips, Patrick's personal problems began to escalate. In order to deal with the difficulties of adolescence, Patrick had started to experiment with drugs. Despite his family history of alcohol abuse, he also was drinking. The worries in his life had accumulated. During his three-week spring recess in March 1986, he decided to seek help at Spofford Hall, a drug and alcohol rehabilitation clinic on Lake Spofford in New Hampshire. The hospital had a 40-bed adolescent unit for teenagers at an average cost of $360 a day. With its gym, sauna, weight room, and nature walks, Spofford Hall was a model treatment center—new and commodious, with an alert staff. "You can't do much better than Spofford Hall," wrote one industry expert.[12]

At the time, Andover's dean of student life heard rumors that Kennedy used drugs but didn't believe them. "He was a frail kid and his health wasn't very good. He was asthmatic and had pretty serious respiratory difficulties. I knew him and he and I had conversations. I know that he was not a major user when he was here," indicated David Cobb, who gained notoriety in 1996 after being convicted for trying to molest a

12-year-old boy and possessing hundreds of child pornography photos. Cobb said, "I had my ear pretty close to the ground and knew what was going on. I got around a lot and talked to a lot of kids. I had no hesitation to get students into conversations off the record, and had a pretty good idea who was doing drugs and who was selling drugs. Patrick wasn't one of the people I was really worried about."[13]

But the rumors were true. Patrick had a substance abuse problem. "My problem was low self-esteem and loneliness and a sense of anxiety and a feeling that the world was overwhelming," he said. "I looked for ways to cope with those stresses through substances and chemicals and drugs and alcohol."[14] He was not the only one of his family to do so. His brother Teddy had spent three weeks at an alcohol treatment program in Connecticut in 1991. His cousins Robert and Michael, sons of Robert F. Kennedy, had been treated for substance abuse. David Kennedy had died of a drug overdose in May 1984. Reflecting on this episode, Patrick said, "I was lucky to get early intervention. I did have a problem. . . . As a teenager I started down the wrong path in dealing with the pressures of growing up. I mistakenly believed that experimenting with drugs and alcohol would alleviate them. I finally decided not to escape from those pressures but to confront them."[15] Continuing, he noted, "The Spofford Hall program, in addition to follow-up counseling, was the best step for me. I am grateful to my family for the strong support they gave me." Counselors trained Patrick with simple aphorisms: Make lemonades out of lemons. Keep it simple. Fake it till you make it.[16] To combat the periodic depression he would experience throughout his life, he began regular visits to a psychiatrist and started to take anti-depressant medication. "Support groups are very helpful," he noted. "I have been very lucky to get the kind of professional counseling and support that I have needed as well. Again, I am better off for having received that help because it has helped me put these problems in the contest of life and I think it has made me a stronger person for it." When news of his psychiatric treatment became public in 2000, he explained, "In my life as a public figure, it's not always easy. . .for me to spill the beans, if you will, with someone that I have to worry about telling other folks. So for me, it really helps to have someone who is protected by professional confidence. . . . If I started telling my friends what I was worried about and what I was thinking about this and that, it may end up in the tabloid newspaper."[17]

Patrick's problems were not over. He flunked a math course spring semester at Andover and did not graduate with his class.[18] The day of commencement, he was AWOL, with the commencement program listing him with "the almost grads" due to insufficient credits. Later talking to a reporter, he admitted, "I had taken some summer classes there, prior to matriculating at Georgetown," but hadn't revealed the reason why he was enrolled in summer school in 1986.[19] The previous months had been a blur between his drug rehabilitation and graduation embarrassment. No one at this point knew about Patrick's drug treatment, but the story about the flunked math class and graduation snafu had made the gossip column of the *Boston Herald* on July 15. Owned by arch-conservative Rupert Murdoch, the tabloid always was on the lookout for anti-Kennedy stories. The *Herald* showed a picture of Patrick with the caption, "Doesn't add up." The story was headlined "1 & 1 Is What?"[20] It was not the type of publicity you wanted in your hometown newspaper, especially right before the wedding of Caroline Kennedy and Edwin Schlossberg, which almost everyone in his extended family attended.

Patrick's fall arrival at Georgetown University only escalated the personal pressures. *The Hoya*, Georgetown's student newspaper, pointed out that Maria Shriver had just been elected to the university's board of regents, after having graduated from Georgetown in 1977. The issue also advised freshmen, "Remember that A's don't come as easily in college as they did in high school."[21] The entering class at Georgetown in 1986 was considered the "most select ever." Applications for the class of 1990 were up 11.5 percent to a record 12,400 applicants, with only 20 percent accepted to the university. Of the 1,305 students who enrolled, the average Scholastic Aptitude Test score out of 800 was 628 verbal and 659 math, making Georgetown one of the most academically competitive schools in the country. Nearly half of the class of 1990 ranked in the top 5 percent of their high school graduation class. Four hundred and ninety-five were National Honor Society members.[22] Three hundred and five of the students, including freshman Patrick Kennedy, were enrolled in the Edmund A. Walsh School of Foreign Service, where the typical course of study the first semester included political theory, Western civilization, microeconomics, English, and a foreign language.

Patrick dropped out of school after two weeks on campus. He explained that he felt "threatened by the overwhelming presence of my family in Washington. I wasn't there on my own ticket." Referring to his family heritage, he added, "There is a fine line between being consumed by it and wrapping yourself around it and using it and being positive about it. There's a fine line between having it become a negative albatross on your back and having it become a lift and support to back you up. . . . It could have been a destructive factor in my life as it was a positive factor. In fact, in various periods in my life, it's been both."[23] The proximity of the school to the nation's capital posed a major problem. Patrick wanted to leave the "craziness in that political world that was still so close that I was unhappy. I wanted to get to know people on my own, as opposed to through my father or my family."[24] When he broke the news to his father, Ted instantly objected. "You've already committed to Georgetown; you ought to complete the year." Then with the frugality of a rich man, he pointed out a pragmatic reason to finish the term. "Tuition is paid," he argued. But Patrick refused to budge. "You can take it out of my allowance, but I'm not going to go." Ted was disappointed. "I thought it would be good if he stayed. It would be nearer home, where a lot of interesting things are going on." But Patrick's decision could not be changed. "I needed a time to think about who I was and what I wanted to be and how I wanted to live my life."[25] He considered going to college on the West Coast until his mother persuaded him that independence was not a matter of geography. He could not escape the celebrated Kennedy name.

With time on his hands following his abrupt exit from Georgetown, Patrick volunteered for his cousin Joe's 1986 congressional race. Joe was the oldest son of Robert Kennedy. The campaign was nearby in the Eighth District around Cambridge, Massachusetts, for the seat originally won by John F. Kennedy in 1946, which opened through the retirement of House Speaker Thomas "Tip" O'Neill. Initially, there had been speculation that Teddy Kennedy would run for the seat. Shortly after Teddy's graduation from Wesleyan, his father had arranged for him to address the 1984 Democratic national nominating convention regarding the need for the elimination of "stifling barriers" to the handicapped. Elsewhere, he had spoken about the trauma of losing his leg at age 12 and his fears that girls his age would not want to go out with a one-legged boy. NBC had even scheduled the broadcast of a documentary, *The Teddy Kennedy Story*, about his childhood cancer, around the time of the 1986 election. With his natural gregariousness and forceful speaking manner, Teddy seemed the natural candidate. The Kennedys always had followed the rule of primogeniture in politics. Fate seemed to be on Teddy's side as well. In 1982, he had been booked on Air Florida Flight 90, which had crashed into the Potomac River, but missed it by 10 minutes after Kara, who was driving him to the airport, arrived late because of treacherous ice on the highways.[26]

Ted had been grooming his eldest son to enter politics for several years. Along with several dignitaries, the senator had taken Teddy to South Africa in 1984 and early 1985 for a Christmas trip. The visit was organized by Bishop Desmond Tutu and designed to build support for a multiracial United Democratic Front opposed to the apartheid regime. When flying back from South Africa, the traveling party had split into two. Ted, Teddy, and Robert Shrum ended up in adjacent seats. Ted raised the possibility of his son running for Congress from the Bay State in 1986. "It's there and you have to think about whether you want to do it," Ted told Teddy. "What do you think about it? Do you want to do it?" Teddy wasn't sure he wanted to do it. "I'm starting this other stuff on disability that I want to do. Maybe the opportunity will come at some other time in my life," he replied.[27]

Teddy's decision about running was complicated by the fact that his cousin Joe wanted to announce for the seat. Joe had gained a favorable public reputation as the savvy manager of Citizens Energy Corporation, a nonprofit company founded in 1979 that supplied low-cost heating fuel to the poor and elderly. The press dubbed Joe the "Robin Hood of the petroleum set" for his ability to buy crude oil at discount prices from oil-producing sheiks and resell it at bargain levels to those in need.[28] He was a businessman's Kennedy, one who was compassionate about the downtrodden but moderate in his political views. It was not the job of government to solve every social problem, he proclaimed. The private sector needed to act as well.

Public speculation over a Kennedy run for the Eighth District persisted over 1985. Newspapers openly discussed a rivalry between the two wings of the Kennedy clan—Ted's and Robert's—over who would get to run. The *Washington Post's* story, "Which Kennedy's First?" cited family tensions over who among the next generation should be the first to run for office. One unnamed source told the paper, "Teddy Jr.'s decision last spring to take a look at his own chances in the 8th District surprised Joe. And that surprise caused some tension within the family." The *Los Angeles Times* reported that a political rivalry between the Kennedys was brewing.[29] The *Boston Herald* wrote that "Joe was upset. He knew you couldn't have two Kennedys running in the same state in the same year, with one already in the Senate."[30] Eventually, there was a family powwow on the Cape. Despite his father's open encouragement, Teddy was not that keen on running, so the way was cleared for Joe.

The Massachusetts Democrat, however, had some clear negatives. As a young man, he had been the driver in a 1973 jeep accident that left a female passenger, Pamela Kelley, paralyzed. Yet in an open-seat election with no incumbent on the ballot, a novice challenger had a good chance of winning.[31] Joe officially kicked off his campaign January 19, 1986, at the packed Mount Auburn Veterans of Foreign Wars Post

8818 in Cambridge, surrounded by celebrities. There was his mother Ethel and uncle Sargent Shriver, along with siblings Courtney, Kerry, Rory, Kathleen, Michael, Robert Jr., Maxwell, and Douglas and cousins John, Teddy, and Patrick. There were sports celebrities, such as Bill Walton of the Boston Celtics and Mike Eruzione, captain of the 1980 U.S. Olympic hockey team that won a gold medal. In his announcement speech, Joe attacked the national debt, defense spending, the tax system, America's fading economic strength in the world, and the Strategic Defense Initiative and positioned himself as more moderate than his other liberal rivals.[32] He also extended a debate challenge. "I hear my opponents can't wait to debate me on the issues," he said. "Let me tell you I can hardly wait for that occasion to occur. Bring them on one at a time or all at once." Kennedy's most serious opponent was George Bachrach, a liberal state senator. At Bachrach's announcement, he unveiled his slogan, "A Congressman for the Rest of Us," and reminded voters he was different from the "candidates with big bucks and big names." He also made available to the press a three-page listing of his legislative accomplishments and detailed issue papers.[33]

Throughout the campaign, Joe Kennedy made frequent use of family celebrities. Commenting ruefully on this strategy, Bachrach concluded, "Kennedys are largely fungible. It doesn't matter which one you're talking about, there's a large reservoir of good will for all of them. I can recollect making political stops and Joe might not be there, but his sister Kerry might be there or Courtney or Rory or Michael. And the response was as good for any one of them as it was for Joe. People just wanted to be close to or touch a Kennedy."[34] Joe brought in other big names. Andy Warhol did a celebrity fundraiser for him where guests had Polaroid pictures taken with a cutout of Warhol and then received a personal autograph from the artist. Martin Luther King III held a fundraising party in Atlanta. At another, members of the Boston Celtics were the star attractions. Dizzy Gillespie held a $250 per person fund-raiser. There was the Joe Kennedy Concert Series, five fund-raisers held at the Great Woods Performance Center. It would be "a beer with Bill Cosby," at $150 a person and drinks with Peter Allen, Willie Nelson, and James Taylor for $100. Pictures of contributors and the celebrity would be taken and given to the donor. Overall, Joe raised $1.3 million to Bachrach's $536,000.[35]

The initial spring poll of the 11 candidates in the race showed Kennedy leading Bachrach by 38 to 17 percent. Kennedy ran well among senior citizens, a large voting bloc that had a high likelihood of turning out to vote. Reporters joked, "Joe Kennedy has been in so many homes for the elderly, he qualified for Medicare."[36] But as the race wore on, his advisers were troubled. Their candidate was having difficulties rising above 40 percent in any of the polls. It was one of the dilemmas of being a Kennedy. Many voters loved them, but family members also had high negatives that guaranteed a sizable anti-Kennedy sentiment. The time had come for Joe to activate his secret weapon, an endorsement from outgoing Speaker Tip O'Neill. After a Cape Cod meeting, O'Neill announced that he saw Joe "agreed with my philosophy more than anyone else in the fight that had a chance to win, and it had actually narrowed down to two people. . . . I truthfully didn't think Bachrach could get the things done I want for the district."[37] O'Neill filmed a 30-second spot for Kennedy that aired right before the September 16 primary and ran ads in the *Boston Globe* and *Herald* the day before the primary.

Joe Kennedy had delayed his own advertising until the month before the primary, when voters started to pay close attention to the race. One ad featured pictures of the candidate at the Kennedy Library dedication in 1979, the founding of Citizens Energy, and his congressional announcement speech. Another showed Kennedy seated among a group of ordinary voters talking about the problems people were having making a living.[38] Joe ended up winning the primary by 52 to 30 percent over Bachrach and coasted to victory in the general election. He was the first of the Kennedy younger generation to win elective office. The victory illustrated a valuable political lesson for the family. In a crowded field, not everyone in the district had to like you. As Christopher Kennedy put it, "There's 500,000 people in the congressional district. Only 250,000 are registered to vote, and only 125,000 of them will probably vote. To win, if there's only five guys running, you only need 25,000 votes. So you don't need everybody out there to become a fan."[39] The race also showed the Kennedy cousins they were up to the challenge. Recalling his more famous opponent, Bachrach said: "He entered the race unsure of himself and pretty rough. But in the course of the campaign, he grew and developed into what he is today, which is a very good and effective advocate for the causes that a number of us care about."[40]

For Patrick, the race was a crucial turning point in his life. He had been down on politics for some time. Elections were pressure-packed for his family because of the "worry and feeling of success and rejection" that comes from participation in national life. Too often in his family, success had been defined in terms of the public arena. Yet despite all the negatives, his cousin's campaign whetted Patrick's appetite for public service. He recalled that the campaign "was a major marshaling of family attention and resources. . . . There wasn't any kind of family, political, or resource that wasn't marshaled in a concerted effort to see him elected. I remember all the members of my family at one stage or another really were involved. All the members of his family were on a day-to-day basis involved in his campaign. I just remember the size of it and financially the commitment made was huge in terms of putting it together."[41] He told a reporter, "That [campaign] was really exciting. I realized it was time for the torch to pass to our generation."[42]

Coming on the heels of a tumultuous childhood, drug abuse, and school problems, Patrick's political interests shocked his mother. "I was just surprised," she confessed. "I thought if anybody was going to go into politics, it would be my older son, Teddy."[43] But the news was true. Patrick explained, "I would not have been able to have coped to the extent that Joe had so much riding on his being the first one out there from my generation. . . . Since he had made it, it took the pressure off of me. I wasn't carrying the torch for the entire generation."[44] Patrick fared most poorly when there was no clear focus to his life. As he later revealed to a newspaper columnist, "I don't think I'm the kind of person that wanted to just stand still and sort of let myself enjoy being a young person. . . . I'm not comfortable without having direction and purpose."[45] For all its personal risks to him, politics had one virtue that Patrick found desirable. It provided structure and gave him people who organized his life. As his friend Barbara Tannenbaum pointed out in regard to Patrick, this realization helped Patrick turn Kennedy disadvantages into advantages. "Politics gives him a focus. It is totally your life," she said.[46] The youngest Kennedy finally was learning to turn lemons into lemonade.

3 Running for Convention Delegate

With the campaign over and his cousin safely ensconced in Congress, Patrick set about finding his own way in life. An old friend of his father's, Senator Christopher Dodd of Connecticut, who had graduated from Providence College and was on the college board, recommended the small Catholic school in Rhode Island. Patrick checked it out and enrolled the next year. At PC, he felt "I could make my own friends, live my own life."[1] Providence College was a cozy, close-knit community founded by Dominican Friars, an order of the Roman Catholic Church. The sect shaped the very essence of the college—devotion to scholarship and service, and allegiance to community and values.[2] The curriculum featured a two-year required course, "Development of Western Civilization," which covered Mesopotamia to the 21st century, and had recommended chapel and required ethics and theology courses. With 3,500 undergraduates, it was just larger than a metropolitan high school. Ninety percent of the students were white, almost all were Catholic, and three-quarters were from New England. Around 70 percent of those applying to the school were accepted each year, with average SAT scores of 502 for verbal and 559 for math, well below those of Georgetown.[3]

Catholicism hung over the campus like a thick fog. Priests taught the religion classes and held the chief administrative positions. For some students, the emphasis on ethics, religion, and moral reasoning stimulated their own thinking. Chris Shaban, an undergraduate from Connecticut at the same time as Patrick, recalled: "I don't think there is any attempt to force feed religion on people. Providence College does a good job of allowing individuals to develop their own religious foundation and beliefs."[4] But not all students shared that feeling. Scott Avedisian was a lifelong Republican and Episcopalian who later was elected mayor of Warwick. On the first day of his required ethics class, all the students stood up and started praying when the priest walked in. Because Scott didn't know the prayer, he did not join in. After everyone sat down, the priest announced, "Fourth row, third seat." Much to his chagrin, Scott realized the priest was talking to him. The priest said, "You weren't praying along with all of us." Scott replied, "I don't know the words." The priest said, "You're not a good Catholic."[5]

School officials were loud advocates of a traditional Catholic education. Shortly after Patrick arrived on campus, the student newspaper *The Cowl* ran a column by Father Joseph Lennon, vice-president of community affairs, on "The Worth of Catholic Education." Lennon argued forcefully that Catholicism provided an antidote to the vicissitudes of modernity: "Today, in a milieu of kaleidoscopic change, it is essential that students embrace a philosophy of life, a scale of values, that will enable them to maintain psychological and moral balance in a world of external flux. Otherwise, they will end up being a restless, shallow, rootless and anxious people."[6]

It was a philosophy that Patrick must have found comforting in light of his own personal odyssey over the previous years. In the space of a short time, he had seen his parents divorce, undergone treatment for an alcohol and drug problem, and made an abysmal start to his collegiate career at Georgetown. He craved structure and guidance, and the PC philosophy of heavy thinking about philosophic matters appealed to him. By the end of his first year at PC, Patrick reported that the courses he had most enjoyed were philosophy and religion. His grades were so-so, mostly Bs and Cs, with an occasional A.[7] Later, he would register as a social studies major, which had a reputation on campus as an easy course of study.

The downside of the heavy Catholic presence on campus for a political liberal was a well-defined Catholic position on abortion. Once at a Young Democrats and Young Republicans debate on campus, abortion dominated the discussion. Even though the panel had debated education, affirmative action, South Africa, taxes, and homelessness, nearly all of the questions from the audience concerned abortion. Unlike the situation on most college campuses near the end of the 20th century, many students openly accepted that "abortion is murder" and believed there should be a constitutional amendment outlawing it.[8] Priests were relentless in their support of church doctrine, using guilt and repetition as their keys. In the required ethics class, for example, the first assignment presented students with a moral dilemma: "Susie finds out that she is pregnant. It is going to interfere with her job. She is not ready to settle down and have a family. What do you suggest that she do?" Answers proposing, "That's a decision Susie has to make on her own," would come back ungraded with a remark from the priest, "Maybe we should talk."[9]

Not surprisingly for such a small school, Patrick's arrival on campus was accompanied by lots of attention. "People knew him," one student said, "like he was Dickie Simpkins," the PC basketball star who went on to play for the Chicago Bulls.[10] One of the people Patrick got to know during his first semester was Jim Vallee, a senior who was the student body president. Vallee had known Patrick in his early teens through sailing because Vallee's family used to summer near the Kennedys on Cape Cod. When Patrick arrived at Providence College in 1987, Vallee remembers Patrick as very low key. "He liked that it was a middle class, working class type of town, the city of Providence. He felt very comfortable there. . . . He was able to make his own friends and establish his own life there. That's what he wanted. He didn't want to use his position to get himself anywhere. He wanted to establish himself as his own person. That's important for anybody growing up, but it's even more important to him because people tend to judge Kennedys by the fact they are Kennedys." Patrick had liked hanging around an older crowd. "He is a pretty mature guy," Vallee said.[11] The two later roomed together. All his contemporaries remember Patrick as quiet and unassuming: "timid like a little rabbit," Avedisian said, and "awkward with people," according to Shaban. Avedisian observed, "It seemed with older people, he was okay but with people his own age, he was very insecure and unsure of himself."[12]

Unbeknownst to his classmates and family, there was another side of Patrick. He went to Providence College determined to make something of his life. Raymond Sickinger, assistant dean of undergraduates, was one of the first advisers Patrick met at the school. "After we talked about courses," Sickinger recalls, "I asked him if there was anything he wanted to ask me. He said yes: Was there any organization in which he could do some service work?" Sickinger suggested the Catholic diocese. Three weeks later, he was surprised to find Kennedy at a diocesan workshop talking about social justice and the legislative process.[13] There also was "Patrick 507." During his first year at PC, Patrick spent hours on a suicide hotline with his secret numeric code, waiting for telephone calls from people contemplating suicide. "I can see the enormous difference that government can make in support of causes such as this, but there is nothing that can make the kind of difference that people, as individuals, can make day to day," he said.[14] His mother recalls when she found out Patrick was volunteering for the suicide hotline. Driving to Hyannisport one day with him, she noticed the Samaritans' suicide prevention sign on one of the bridges to the Cape. He told her he had been a Samaritans' volunteer at least once a week for six months.[15] It was not an idle job for him. According to his roommate Vallee, "He was very committed to it. He would drop whatever he was doing to go serve his time at the Samaritans."[16]

At the same time Patrick was easing into campus life, he was making contacts in the Rhode Island political world. His cousin Joe had shown him the formula for turning the Kennedy name into electoral success—a strong organization, dedicated volunteers, generous spending, favorable media coverage, and a heavy emphasis on celebrityhood. One of the first individuals he met in the summer of 1987 was John Tabella, the energetic young executive director of the Rhode Island Public Interest Group (RIPIRG). Patrick came into Tabella's office one day and said he wanted to do door-to-door canvassing. He told Tabella his name was Patrick Kennedy, but Tabella had no idea he was the senator's son. "It was ironic," Tabella recalled, "because I had a framed Andrew Wyeth print of John Kennedy on the wall of our offices." Kennedy commented that it was a nice print, but didn't say it was his uncle. Patrick did door-to-door canvassing for RIPIRG. A few months later, Tabella saw Patrick at the Statehouse working as a page running errands for legislators and a researcher at the Legislative Council, the research agency of the General Assembly. "I was surprised when I discovered he was the Senator's son. He had not mentioned it before," Tabella explained.[17]

In the fall, Patrick worked as a volunteer on Lieutenant Governor Richard Licht's campaign against Senator John Chafee. That earned Patrick an October 4, 1987, mention in the *Providence Journal*, the state's leading daily, his first since arriving in Rhode Island as a college student. The newspaper writer was Charlie Bakst, a reporter famous for his hard-nosed grilling of local politicians. Bakst was always on the lookout for new talent. Covering a $30 benefit for a local political operative who had suffered a stroke, he was introduced to Patrick by Licht. Bakst was not familiar with the guest so he pulled Licht aside and asked, "Is he the Senator's son?" and learned that Patrick had just enrolled at Providence College. Immediately sensing a good story, Charlie conducted his first interview with Patrick as to why he was hanging out with Licht. Patrick's not-very-memorable response was, "I just like to be with him."[18]

At PC, Patrick revived an old political organization, the Young Democrats, which had been dormant before he arrived on campus.[19] He also decided to run as a 1988 convention delegate pledged to Michael Dukakis, the governor of neighboring Massachusetts, who was seeking the Democratic nomination against Congressman Richard Gephardt, Senator Al Gore Jr., and civil rights leader Jesse Jackson, among others.[20] For Patrick to become an elected delegate, Governor Dukakis had to win at least 15 percent of the state's Democratic primary vote in order to qualify for any delegates, and Patrick had to receive enough individual votes on the ballot that he was chosen as one of the 14 Dukakis delegates over the other people seeking the positions. Patrick spoke out publicly on behalf of Dukakis, saying, "Governor Dukakis understands Rhode Island's history. Rhode Island's history is very much like Massachusetts history."[21]

With primary day nearing, Patrick picked up the pace of his campaign. He addressed the Democratic state committee and had his father send a letter to elected Democrats. Patrick relied on a "big volunteer pool from Providence College."[22] For his delegate run, he became the only person in state history to use lawn signs touting his candidacy. In Rhode Island, this was a cheap form of advertising that allowed the targeting of particular neighborhoods. An active campaign for delegate was unusual in the state. According to Avedisian, "I couldn't believe someone would actually campaign to be a delegate. It was always one of those things that was bestowed on certain people in the party to go to the convention. You didn't actually go out and campaign for it."[23]

On March 3, just five days before the primary, there was a rally for Governor Dukakis with Senator Ted Kennedy as the featured speaker. When Patrick's father appeared, the crowd "oohed and aahed and squealed as if a movie star was in their midst." The two Kennedys attended a St. Patrick's Day party afterward at the Sandy Lane Knights of Columbus Hall. As the senator entered the hall, the band, surrounded by green decorations, was playing "Heart of My Heart." The senator took the microphone and told the crowd he was there to support the Dukakis candidacy. But what he really wanted to talk to them about, he said, was St. Patrick's Day. Taking some liberties with the truth, he joked, "I love St. Patrick so much that I named my youngest son Patrick!" "Keep your eye on the Number 13 ballot position," the senator continued. He wanted the number to be lucky for his son since Patrick occupied the 13th slot on the primary ballot. Side by side, the two Kennedys then sang "When Irish Eyes Are Smiling" for the assembled guests.[24]

This visit was followed by a glowing feature column right before the primary about Patrick and Ted by Charlie Bakst in the Sunday *Providence Journal*. The *Journal* had a Sunday circulation of around 135,000 households, which meant that the column entitled "Kennedy Touts Dukakis Bid with No Regrets" reached a huge share of eligible voters in the state. The column reviewed the senator's career and gave the father an opportunity to tout the family legend. Asked about the Irish music on St. Patrick's Day,

Ted explained, "Usually when we're home, on the weekends, particularly in the evenings, 6 to 7, there's a neighbor that comes over and plays the piano, and we have all the old Irish songs mimeographed up and distribute them to members of the family, all the nieces and nephews, and they all sing." Charlie had visited Patrick's home the morning after the St. Patrick's Day celebration for an exclusive personal interview with the Kennedys. According to the columnist, Ted did nearly all the talking, while his son sat quietly, "sort of like a piece of furniture." Bakst later rode to the state airport with the two as Ted rushed to another campaign event. In the car, Charlie broached a rumor he had heard: Was Patrick "eyeing a run" against a local representative later that year? Patrick responded, "I'm running for delegate right now. Obviously, I'd be interested in holding elective office at some time, but I haven't made any decision as to when and where."[25] It was the first press mention of Patrick's longer-term political ambitions.

When the results of the primary came in, Patrick had succeeded beyond his wildest dreams. Not only had he earned a delegate seat but he had received 6,184 votes, second only to the 7,684 votes for Joe Paolino, the mayor of Providence. Indeed, in the Mt. Pleasant area around Providence College, Patrick had gotten more votes than Mayor Paolino. Not only had Patrick scored well, he had bested older and much more prominent politicians, such as sitting members of the General Assembly. He also beat political contemporaries at Providence College. For example, Patrick's co-founder of PC Young Democrats, Angela Petras, with 1,344 votes, finished dead last of the 18 candidates for Dukakis delegate in the Second District.[26]

To Patrick, the outcome confirmed his personal hopes. "Even though [the delegate race] was not a public office, I was so fortunate to have that [come] in between me and my first election as a state rep in the primary. It gave me some unspoken credibility because it wasn't the first time." Continuing, he pointed out that voters "had the comfort of knowing my standing and I had been tested before and withstood the test. . . . I wasn't asking people to do anything other than to send me down as a delegate, a committed delegate at that, to the Democratic convention." In Kennedy's mind, the victory "had taken the rough edge off of being so young."[27] Patrick's expenditure of $11,700 was an extraordinary amount of money for a delegate run. Typically, candidates for delegate in Rhode Island spent a few hundred dollars; Patrick had averaged around $1.80 per vote, considerably higher than the 5 cents a vote spent by one of the other delegate winners, Susan Erno. Erno was a secretarial supervisor for a Providence law firm, and she won nearly 4,000 votes while spending $216 for her delegate seat.[28]

That night, Patrick went to the Providence Civic Center for a Democratic victory celebration. Party leaders were thrilled that Dukakis had won big. Many of them would be going to the Democratic convention as Dukakis delegates. Tabella was elated. He had organized the rally right before the primary at which Ted Kennedy spoke and had written the flyer for the delegate campaign. To him, Patrick's victory was no surprise. Delegate contests, he reasoned, "are driven almost entirely by name identification. We were helped by stories in the news that Ted Kennedy's son was running for delegate. Ted Kennedy came in to speak on his behalf and that helped." Tabella recalled, "Patrick was excited and thrilled at his big victory. . . . I got a call the next morning from Ted congratulating me on the great job I had done. It was ironic because it was

Ted's 1980 presidential campaign that had gotten me involved with politics." Democratic stalwarts, however, weren't so keen. Speaking of the Civic Center celebration, Tabella noticed that party bigwigs were polite but reserved toward Patrick. "There was some wariness in the room that night toward Patrick. He was a young guy and people weren't sure what to make of him," Tabella said.[29] Their anxiety soon would escalate. Shortly thereafter, Kennedy would make a move that would mobilize nearly all of those leaders against him.

4 Running for the Rhode Island General Assembly

Jack Skeffington was sitting in his funeral home at 925 Chalkstone Avenue, Providence, in spring 1988 when the phone rang. An earnest but easygoing man known for his bright-colored sports jackets and loyalty to the Democratic party leadership, Skeffington was the deputy majority leader in the Rhode Island House of Representatives, serving the Mt. Pleasant area around Providence College for 10 years. Since his graduation from high school in 1957, Skeffington had been a funeral director. During his 31 years in the funeral business, he had buried more than 4,000 Rhode Islanders. Being a funeral home director gave Skeffington instant recognition throughout the district. "If you had a party at your house for graduation or a confirmation, you would go to your funeral director to borrow chairs for the party and you'd get them for nothing," he explained. "If your daughter got married in the older days, you even got a free car" for the day. People remembered those small touches, he said. "Whether it is chair rental, looking for positions, looking to have parking tickets looked into, water bills looked at, electric bills, telephone bills, help with non-payment extensions, license plates, . . . you're pretty well known."[1]

The phone call was from his good friend and political ally, Joseph DeAngelis, Speaker of the Rhode Island House. "I got some bad news for you," DeAngelis announced. Skeffington replied, "What's up?" DeAngelis said, "You're going to have a primary and Patrick Kennedy is going to run against you." Nonchalantly, Skeffington asked, "Who's Patrick Kennedy? Is it a big deal?" DeAngelis explained, "He's Senator Kennedy's son." The realization suddenly dawned on the representative. He had heard the senator's son had enrolled in Providence College. Skeffington quizzed the Speaker, "How disastrous do you think that's going to be?" With a somber sigh, DeAngelis replied, "I'm going to tell you one thing. I wouldn't want him running in Smithfield after me." At that point, Skeffington thought to himself, "I'm in deep trouble. . . . I knew I had a fight on my hands."[2]

Skeffington was an old-style politician whose mission was to "help secure jobs through politics for local people" and "being here when [people] feel they need someone to give them a push" for a political job. The leadership made it easy to be a team player. Legislative bills were phrased in such a way that a vote for the leadership was always a green button for yes. Amendments by dissidents were easy to kill. Legislators just voted red on them. Once, though, a leadership opponent offered a reverse amendment that required a red button vote. When it came time for the vote, the Speaker tried to warn the legislators. "If you want to vote for Rodney Driver's [amendment], you have to vote yes. If you want to vote the way the Majority Leader thinks you should, you are going to have to vote no." Since he had been off the floor, Skeffington was not paying close attention to the discussion, and voted green as always. To everyone's surprise, the amendment passed 48 to 47, making it one of the rare times the leadership lost a vote on the floor. Another legislator leaned over to Skeffington. "Jack," he said, "you just voted against the leadership." Without being recognized, Skeffington immediately jumped up and started yelling, "Mister Speaker, Mister Speaker. I didn't want to vote against you. I wanted to vote with you. I'm confused. Can we have another vote?" The General Assembly took a second vote, and this time, Driver's amendment lost overwhelmingly.[3]

Patrick Kennedy had decided to run against Skeffington a few weeks earlier while in the hospital for an operation. All spring, he had severe headaches and back pain and was experiencing difficulty walking. He had been examined by doctors, who were not sure what the problem was. On April 18, Patrick was hospitalized at Massachusetts General Hospital in Boston. Using a new imaging technique, doctors discovered he had a tumor 2 centimeters by 1.25 centimeters growing on the front of his spinal cord, just below the neck.[4] Three days later, in a delicate 12-hour procedure, doctors operated. Led by Doctor Nicholas Zervas, chief of neurosurgery, the medical team discovered that the tumor was benign, but that unless the operation had taken place, Patrick could have become a quadriplegic. As Kennedy left the hospital May 7 wearing a neck brace and leaning on a cane, the press swarmed over him. Patrick described the operation as "a long ordeal, but I'm thankful to the doctors and nurses." His Dad said, "He's been through a great deal on it, but he's back on his feet."[5] Skeffington had kept track of Patrick from a distance and even had gone so far as sending him a card with a Mass offering while the young man was in the hospital. For a two-dollar contribution, a priest would say a Mass in the individual's honor and wish the infirm a speedy recovery.[6]

Unbeknownst to Skeffington or to reporters at the time, the period in the hospital had been a time of decision for Patrick. "One thing that does is shake you into a sense that every day counts," he said about the operation.[7] He had decided to run for the General Assembly. While recovering in the hospital, he broke the news to his father, who was not pleased. The senator's longtime friend and press spokesperson Robert Shrum said, "His father was worried initially. . . . He was young and [Ted] wanted him to finish school."[8] Jim Vallee was present for the conversation when Patrick informed his father about his plan. "I've made my decision. I'm definitely going to run," Patrick announced. Ted was worried about his son's health and insistent that Patrick finish school. "Don't overdo it," he said. "Don't ruin your health as a result." Patrick's father peppered his son with questions. What are the dynamics of the district? Who is serving? Why do you think you could run and win? He told his son, "You are new to the neighborhood, new to the city, and new to the state. What makes you think you can win this seat?" Every time Ted raised an objection, Patrick came back with reasons he could win. Vallee recalled, "Patrick had done his homework on his own, not with consultants or anyone else. . . . He knew the political actors and he knew the area."[9]

Skeffington had been advised that as a Democrat in a heavily Democratic district, he never would have to worry about the general election. But Skeffington remembered the last-minute caution from his predecessor Billy Babin: The thing you have to watch is a primary, Babin warned. Babin had had a couple of close primaries before he left, which was the reason he had given up his $300 per year seat for a $30,000 sinecure at the Board of Elections. Skeffington had almost lost his 1986 primary to an opponent named Brian Reddy, a 22-year-old from the Olneyville end of the Ninth District. Because of Skeffington's voting record, the teachers union and truck drivers had refused to support him.[10]

After that close primary brush, Skeffington had worried that Reddy would run again. Behind the scenes, with help from Mayor Paolino, Skeffington arranged a city job helping the elderly for Reddy and a job in the Providence Police Department for Reddy's brother. But a much larger obstacle was looming: Patrick Kennedy. One week after leaving the hospital, Patrick announced he was challenging Skeffington.[11] According to Patrick, the hardest thing about his race against Skeffington was "hanging out there as far as I was in the public limelight and knowing how much I had riding on it. I don't think I ever let myself really kind of brood over how much I had riding on it in terms of personal reputation, family reputation, and all of the obvious financial and human resources, the number of people who were committed to me, helping me that had come to assist me, and feeling the obligation to make it worth their time." He explained, "There is a whole part of campaigning that doesn't immediately dawn on you until you're in it and you realize how much goes into something like this."[12] There is a public vulnerability about putting yourself on the line for judgment. Vallee was stunned by Patrick's decision. "I was shocked. Absolutely shocked. For the first year and a half I knew him, he had been talking about wanting to do something on his own, something that he could kind of lose himself in a little bit. I asked him, 'Why? Why are you running?' But sometimes it's hard to get answers from him, even if you're a close friend," Vallee said.[13]

Skeffington was even more shocked. "I can't believe the Kennedys are going to try to knock out a true Democrat," he said.[14] Of course, what he didn't realize was the Kennedy family had a history of taking on incumbents. Patrick's own father had tried to unseat a Democratic president of the United States in 1980. Skeffington set about trying to force Patrick out of the race. The undertaker went to see Salvatore Mancini, chair of the state Democratic party. "It was crazy," he told Mancini, "that we should fight against one another. I am the endorsed Democrat from this district who has done nothing wrong and who has worked very hard for his constituents." Mancini offered several alternatives to Patrick. "He was called on several occasions and even given some voting lists of a district that would be abutting the Providence, North Providence line. He was almost guaranteed by Sal Mancini that he could win that seat. He was offered districts where people were retiring that he could have gone in and taken over their particular seats and been the endorsed candidate."[15] Mancini offered Kennedy an appointment on the Democratic State Committee and announced publicly, "I think he should wait for a vacancy. If there was a vacancy or somebody retired, this wouldn't be a problem." But Patrick rejected the entreaties. "With all due respect, Chairman Mancini really irked me. I don't know where they get this idea that you wait your turn. Public office isn't something that is given to you for just hanging around; it's something you earn," he said. "I'm going to take my message to people door to door."[16]

The campaign kickoff was the hospital home-coming party on May 7. It was the Kennedy philosophy to turn even bad events to their advantage. Tabella, Patrick's old friend from RIPIRG and the Dukakis delegate campaign, was hired to organize "a little homecoming in the neighborhood when he got out of the hospital."[17] Tabella had Chris Nocera, a local liquor store owner, call one of Patrick's neighbors. Nocera asked, "Would you have a welcome home party for him?" The goal, according to Nocera, was to establish that when Patrick comes home, "he doesn't go to the Cape or to Boston or he doesn't go to Virginia; when he goes home, he comes into Mt. Pleasant." Nocera had a neighbor organize a "surprise" welcome home party. Nothing was left to chance, Nocera explained. "We staged it that he would walk, instead of dropping him off in front of the house, we had him go into his house so that he would have to walk five houses so the TV cameras would see him with the neck brace and the cane. He was surprised as he was going for a walk around the neighborhood that there was this surprise welcome home party for him, with all the TV cameras."[18] The plan worked perfectly. "We got some good press on that," Tabella noted. Shortly after that, Patrick announced he was running in the primary against Skeffington.[19]

The funeral director had not been sitting idly by. He hired Tony Pesaturo of Alpha Research Associates, a local polling firm, as his campaign manager. At the state Democratic convention, the party unanimously endorsed Skeffington over Kennedy. Nearly every party bigwig in the state lined up behind Skeffington: Speaker Joe DeAngelis, former Speaker Matthew Smith, House Majority Leader Thomas Lamb, Senate Majority Leader John Revens, State Party Chair Sal Mancini, Democratic Executive Director David Barricelli, Providence Mayor Joe Paolino, Attorney General Jim O'Neil, Secretary of State Kathleen Connell, and almost every Democratic member of the General Assembly. Even U.S. Senate candidate Richard Licht, for whom Kennedy had volunteered, supported Skeffington.[20] Patrick's two lone public endorsements came from Ray Rickman, a maverick liberal legislator from the Brown University neighborhood who had a contentious relationship with Speaker DeAngelis, and Shawn Donahue, the little-known president of Rhode Island Young Democrats.

In the first campaign finance report, Skeffington outraised Kennedy by 2 to 1. According to Tabella, who was managing Kennedy's campaign, "It was this macho thing. We are not going to get drowned by this Kennedy kid. We are going to raise a lot of money and we're going to spend a lot of money. We're going to show we are not going to take this thing lying down." However, Tabella felt "it had the opposite effect." Together with the flood of endorsements for Skeffington, "it made Kennedy the underdog."[21] The first polls in the district that summer confirmed that Skeffington was ahead. A survey by Kennedy's organization found Skeffington was the front-runner, but that a lot of new people had moved into the district and didn't know who Skeffington was. Skeffington had a problem, according to Tabella. "He hadn't kept a dialogue going with people in that district."[22] Skeffington's first poll on July 5–9 with 412 district voters painted a more detailed picture. He led Kennedy by 54 to 24 percent, with the remainder undecided. There was a huge gender gap. Skeffington's lead was 64 to 16 percent among men, but just 44 to 31 percent with women. Forty percent of the district was Italian, and one-third was elderly. Each candidate had high name recognition, Skeffington at 85 percent and Kennedy at 67 percent. By a 5 to 1 margin (71 to 14 percent), voters had a favorable opinion of Skeffington. Kennedy was viewed favorably by 48 to 20 percent. In terms of job performance, 43 percent rated the incumbent's performance as excellent or above average, 23 percent said it was average, and 14 percent thought it was below average or poor. The top issues on people's minds were drugs and crime (28 percent), followed by housing the homeless (23 percent), taxes (20 percent), the environment (14 percent), education (12 percent), roads and streets (7 percent), corruption (6 percent), and jobs (5 percent). Only 32 percent of voters felt Skeffington had kept in touch with his district, and many were unclear what the incumbent had accomplished in the House.[23]

This weakness was made clear to Pesaturo one day early in the campaign. Jim Skeffington, brother of the candidate, was a leading bond attorney at Edwards and Angell, one of the top law firms in the state. He had organized a meeting at his law firm attended by Jack Skeffington, Pesaturo, Bruce Melucci, an old Providence politician, and Jimmy Creamer, an aide to Speaker DeAngelis on loan to the campaign despite being a full-time state employee. The candidate's brother started by saying, "We've got to stop this Kennedy. The way you stop him is Jack's record." He turned to Jack and asked, "What have you done in the General Assembly?" Jack replied, "I don't know. Jimmy [Creamer], what have I done?" In deadpan fashion, Creamer responded, "How the fuck do I know what you've done." After attending this meeting and sifting through survey data, Pesaturo realized, "You can't bill Jack as a great substantive legislator. We all know he's not." Instead, Pesaturo came up with a slogan, "It Takes Years to Develop Friendship and Trust," which became the basis of the Skeffington's strategy.[24] The campaign would emphasize that "Jack Skeffington is a lifelong resident of the district he represents having strong ties and deep community roots."[25]

Kennedy's vulnerability was that voters felt he was most interested in his personal political career: he had lived in Rhode Island for just a year; 67 percent believed that Patrick would use the position as a stepping-stone to higher office; 29 percent feared that Ted Kennedy was buying a seat for his son. However, on the plus side, the Alpha survey revealed that voters liked the idea of someone new and felt Patrick was "independent and a fresh face." By 57 to 4 percent, voters agreed that Kennedy "is honest and can be trusted." Patrick's father was well known and well liked in the district. Even more ominous for the Skeffington campaign, the poll found that 50 percent of district voters who had cast ballots in the March presidential primary had voted for Kennedy as a Dukakis delegate. Based on these results, Pesaturo proposed a campaign plan. In a confidential July 1988 document called "A Campaign Plan for the Skeffing-ton Reelection Effort," Pesaturo outlined how sympathetic voters could be targeted through telephone canvassing, door-to-door canvassing, coffee hours, leafleting, and direct mail.[26]

Ten lines of secret phone banks were set up on the second floor of the funeral home, right above the room where wakes were held. The canvassing began in late July to identify favorable, unfavorable, and undecided voters. Undecided voters were mailed a personalized direct mail letter and brochure. One week prior to the primary, the telephone bank would initiate a get-out-the-vote effort targeting those individuals who indicated they were favorable about Skeffington. "Sometimes," Pesaturo reported, "we would be running our phone banks upstairs while a wake was taking place down-stairs. We put the phone banks in the funeral home so that the Kennedy people would not know how seriously we were taking the race and how much money we were putting into it." The plan proposed a committee consisting of community leaders "offended by the Kennedy candidacy." This group, whose suggested name was "A Committee of Concerned Citizens to Preserve Local Representation," "would do all the negative campaigning, freeing the candidate from this chore. Its first assignment could be to point out the socially liberal philosophy of candidate Kennedy on such matters as gun control, abortion, capital punishment, and crime."[27]

As the campaign got under way in July, everything was swinging in Skeffington's direction. Speaker DeAngelis had organized a $50 a person fund-raiser in July for Skeffington, and almost every major Democratic politician in the state attended. Nearly $30,000 was raised from that one event alone, a record amount for a state rep-resentative's campaign; such races in the state typically cost a few thousand dollars. The Speaker let it be known he was "going to do everything possible so that this guy [Kennedy] is not elected." Money was not a problem. DeAngelis provided all the per-sonnel that the campaign needed from his official staff. He assigned Jimmy Creamer nearly full-time to the campaign and had House Parliamentarian Elmer Cornwell write Skeffington's announcement speech. When Skeffington needed a dozen people to oper-ate the phone banks, Creamer "gets on the phone and they are there." After all, "they all have jobs and they were scared shit of the Speaker."[28]

The press started to gain interest in the race. As was happening nationally, talk radio was flourishing in Rhode Island, and one of the most skilled practitioners of the art was Vincent "Buddy" Cianci of WHJJ. Cianci was the former mayor of Providence who had resigned office in March 1984 after pleading "nolo contendere" to charges of assault linked to an affair he suspected his wife was having. A hot-blooded Italian male who brooded over personal slights, he defended the honor of his family in the only manner he knew how. With a Providence police officer present, according to the offi-cial two-count assault charge, Cianci had jabbed the man he believed was having the affair with his wife, accosted him with a lighted cigarette, hit him with an ashtray, and threatened him with a burning log from the fireplace. Near the same time, around two dozen city employees were indicted and convicted on charges that included bribery, extortion, and theft, although Cianci himself was never indicted on these crimes. After a few years out of the limelight, Cianci had resurrected himself by becoming a talk radio host for the biggest news station in the market. In 1990, he would make a political comeback as mayor, winning a three-way race with 37 percent of the vote. As a sign of his go-for-the-jugular instincts, he had unnerved his major opponent in that campaign by whispering to the man, a bachelor, right before the cameras came on for his opening television debate statement, "Don't raise the pension issue on me. Otherwise, I'll tell everyone you are a homo!"[29]

A contest for the state legislature by the youngest Kennedy, one who was timid and shy to boot, was perfect grist for Cianci. The host excoriated Patrick and his family over the air. What had Patrick's father known about Chappaquiddick? How had a young girl drowned in the car accident while Ted swam away? What about Ted's suspected affairs with women? Why did Ted drink so much? And then there was Patrick. He had grown up out of state and moved to Rhode Island very recently. Was he a carpetbagger? Where did he pay his taxes? Tabella had a policy of not listening to the talk shows. One day, however, he was getting his hair cut and the barber had Cianci on the radio. Patrick ended up going on Cianci's radio show. The lamb-shearing that ensued was devastating for the young man. Cianci was a street fighter—tough, smart, and fast on his feet. Patrick was none of those things. Buddy started to question Patrick about the carpetbagger accusation. "Where did he pay taxes?" Patrick patiently explained how he was paying taxes in the state. The trap swung closed. "Why should we believe you," Cianci inquired. "You haven't released your tax returns."[30] This was a delicate subject in the Kennedy family. Before Patrick had turned 21, his income had been modest, around $22,000 a year. But on his 21st birthday, July 14, 1988, Patrick became the beneficiary of a blind trust set up by his grandfather. With this change, Patrick's total assets rose to around $300,000, which produced income of around $50,000 to $70,000.[31] Patrick didn't want to release his personal tax returns, but on the spur of the moment, he promised Cianci he would release them. It was a decision that would come back to haunt Patrick during his later bid for Congress.

Cianci was not satisfied. "What makes you think you are qualified to serve in the General Assembly?" he asked. "You hardly know the district where you are running." Callers started to jam the phone lines of the radio show. Patrick had mentioned Veterans Hospital in his district. That was a problem. The district line ran right down Chalkstone Avenue. Roger Williams Hospital was in the district, but Veterans Hospital was not. Callers castigated Patrick. "My God," one said. "You don't know the streets that are in the district. You don't know what institutions are in the district and which ones aren't. There are families you don't know and haven't met," said the callers. "Do you know where Jasmine Street is?" one asked. Another chimed in, "Did he know the Mahoney family? Had he met them yet?" If he didn't know the people and didn't know the streets, they asked, "how can you represent us?"[32] The talk show was an unmitigated disaster for Patrick.

Tabella was knowledgeable about polling, direct mail, strategy, and the issues and was one of the best in the state on political communications, but more help was needed. The Kennedys met with Tabella. "John," they said, "we have a good campaign organization here, but you're from East Providence. You don't know the minutia of the district. Can you find somebody that can help run the campaign from a neighborhood perspective?"[33] In fact, Tabella was friends with Chris Nocera, owner of the most prominent liquor store in the area. Tabella had been the best man at Nocera's wedding, and Nocera had arranged the hospital home-coming party for Patrick. Nocera was brought onto the campaign to coordinate volunteers, arrange lawn signs, and organize coffee hours where Patrick could meet the voters.

Kennedy family members started to come in on a regular basis. "Someone [from the family] used to come in every weekend and go someplace with Patrick in the district," Nocera said. "Either they would go to eat or go to Mass or they'd go to a movie. The strategy was to try and make it like it wasn't a big deal to have Ted Kennedy in the district. . . . That made people feel closer to Patrick because these people weren't celebrities anymore. . . . We tried to fight that outsider image that Patrick didn't really belong here."[34] Nocera organized coffees where voters could meet Patrick. "When we organized our first coffee, no one wanted to show up. They were scared. We had 10 people there. I had to bring in people from outside the district so it wouldn't look bad," he said. He understood the fear. When he signed up to work with Patrick, "I was told my political career was going to be ruined. They broke the windows of my liquor store. It was real bad. . . . People would be calling my house and threatening my wife and threatening my baby. At one point, people from the Police Department were sitting outside my house."[35]

Barbara Tannenbaum, who taught a very popular public speaking course at Brown University, was given the job of strengthening Patrick's personal presentation. Patrick came across as a nice young man, but his speaking style generated no confidence in his ability. When he would introduce himself, he wouldn't look people in the eye, and his voice would rise at the end of a sentence. He would say, "Hello, I'm Patrick Kenn-e-dy?" Tannenbaum used to badger him, "Patrick, is that a question or a statement?"[36] From Tannenbaum's professional work, she knew nonverbal communication were crucial. Studies of political communications had found that the majority of the way an audience reacts to a speaker is based on nonverbal content. Whenever Patrick was invited on *10 News Conference*, the most widely watched local interview show, Tannenbaum, Tabella, and Nocera conducted practice interviews. The trio would badger Kennedy with questions and tell him how to perfect each response. Despite the help, Kennedy spent his first interview staring at the floor with a paralyzed look in his eyes. Eventually, the advisers got so good they were correctly able to predict 75 percent of the questions directed the candidate's way. Rarely did the media questions get into issues. "It was always family stuff, . . . how much money did he spend, and where are you going in the future," Nocera explained. The group also practiced going door to door. In a small district with a few thousand voters, candidates could personally meet most of the voters. People who hadn't met Patrick personally tended not to like him. But once they met him in person, they liked his quiet demeanor.[37]

For these visits, Tabella employed a system for identifying likely Kennedy voters. Patrick would walk the district with bar coded computer cards. He would go up to the door and say, "Hello, Mr. Smith. I'm Patrick Kennedy and I'm running for state representative." He would get as much information as he could, and after he left each house, he would code the individual's likelihood of supporting him, issues the voter cared about, and something personal from the conversation. The campaign would generate a personalized direct mail letter to the individual. It would say, for example, "Dear Mr. Smith. I know you are undecided right now. I hope during the course of the next few weeks we can convince you. Like you, I am concerned about education" (the policy issue the person had mentioned). Patrick would sign the letters, and, if the person had said he was about to go on vacation, Patrick would add a personal touch, "P.S. Have a great vacation." Throughout the summer, Patrick walked door to door. Tabella recalled, "It took a tremendous amount of discipline. It was the most influential factor in the campaign." Overall, Patrick knocked on 3,000 doors—about the entire district. He wouldn't leave the doorstep until he had material for his computer file. Those who were undecided often got a return visit.[38]

Patrick's personal motivator on these walks was George Hoey, a local undertaker who was a competitor of Skeffington's. According to Nocera, "George is the one who really motivated him. . . . John was doing the political consulting. I was doing the neighborhood stuff. George was the guy who really motivated him to walk everyday. He went out there walking with him. And when they were done walking, George would pump him up, get him in the pool, and tell him he was doing all right. . . . Without George, Patrick would not have walked as much as he did."[39]

Senator Kennedy was another matter. Ted had assigned one of his staffers, Jon Haber, to keep close tabs on the campaign. Both Ted and Haber would call Patrick's staff almost every day and ask "Is he working? How many homes did Patrick visit the night before?" No matter what the answer was, Ted would reply, "He's not walking enough. We have got to get him out walking more. He's not meeting enough people." Haber would offer advice, although much of it ran contrary to local political culture. Early in the campaign, Haber proposed a particular district walking technique. The campaign, he thought, should "have people with signs walking in front of Patrick." Then they would "have somebody go up to the door and say, Do you want to meet Patrick Kennedy? If so, they would bring that person out to the sidewalk so that Patrick could sweep the street." Tabella and Nocera vetoed that approach. Patrick had to be portrayed "as one of us and down to earth," Nocera explained. "It would not have been right to have him like the king walking down the street and asking the peasants to please come out on the sidewalk and maybe Patrick will come by and shake your hand." Despite the disagreements, the calls from Washington served an important function for the local staff. Nocera said, "We were all motivated because in the back of our minds, we said one of us is going to have to call Ted Kennedy and tell him that he lost. None of us wanted to make that call."[40]

In late July, a major event from outside the campaign transformed the entire race. One evening, there was a break-in at D-B Guns and D&B Electronics at 1284 North Main Street in Providence. Wayne Costa, armed with a pipe, drove a car into the front door of the store at 10:30 p.m. Tiring of the periodic break-ins that had plagued his store, shop owner Don DiBiasio was hiding in the back, and he shot and killed the intruder. After DiBiasio was arrested and charged with murder, the case was the talk of the town. Gun rights advocates were outraged. At Skeffington headquarters, campaign manager Pesaturo could not believe his good fortune. He thought, "This is a godsend!"

His candidate was campaigning as tough on crime against an opponent whose family was seen as soft on crime and opposed to the death penalty. He immediately contacted DiBiasio, the head of a local gun-owners association, and suggested a press conference. At the event, Skeffington talked tough. "I am just outraged that Mr. DiBiasio is being charged for protecting his business and his life. If a person is inside his home or business . . . he should have a right to defend himself," Skeffington argued.[41] To fight this assault on law-abiding citizens, Skeffington proposed an eight-point anti-crime package. He would reinstate the death penalty in Rhode Island, which Kennedy opposed. "I am sick and tired of crime," Skeffington emphasized. "It's not fair to society, and it's not fair to the taxpayer." He also called for granting tax breaks for burglar alarms and security systems, trying juveniles with more than three felony arrests as adults, eliminating parole for anyone convicted of heinous crimes, and offering grants to elderly who otherwise couldn't afford to install security systems. DiBiasio did not attend the press conference, but two of his sons did. With tears in his eyes, son Steven DiBiasio thanked Skeffington and said, "To the hundreds of people . . . that have voiced their concerns and have shown their support in unprecedented fashion, my Dad thanks you for your prayers and your encouragement." Skeffington then organized crime seminars in the Mt. Pleasant area. Pesaturo explained, "There were a lot of house breaks in the area. . . . There seemed to be a whole series of housebreaks and assaults. I just tied them all together and made it look even worse than it was. We invited the police to come. Jack would lead these crime seminars. . . . We established him as being a strong crime person."[42] Throughout the controversy, there was no response from Kennedy.

As the contest entered its closing days, a new issue altered the campaign. Kennedy's manager Tabella was puzzled by the large volume of returned mail. The Kennedy organization was sending out a tremendous amount of mailing, but the letters kept getting returned with a postal stamp marked "occupant unknown." Ted already was complaining about rising costs. "We were getting beaten up on mail costs because a lot of our mail was coming back," Tabella explained.[43] There was a related problem. When Patrick went door to door in the neighborhood, he kept finding voters listed on the official rolls who didn't live there. Something was amiss. By the middle of August, the entire district had been blanketed with personal visits and letters. According to campaign records, nearly 10 percent of the people listed on official voting rolls did not reside where they said they lived.

Even more troubling, every time the Kennedy campaign staff went to the Providence Board of Canvassers, the official body charged with maintaining voter lists open to the public, their requests were reported to the Speaker's office. Campaign staffers were told that "certain voter registration cards were kept in desks as opposed to the book where they are supposed to be kept by law."[44] Kennedy and his young staff realized that in every city it was a massive task to keep official lists up to date. But this arrangement seemed to be something different, possibly even old-fashioned Providence corruption. It was easy to rig the election in favor of those currently in office. Kennedy's fear was that illegal registrations would provide the incumbent with a way to stay in office no matter how the people who lived in the district voted.

The strangest discovery was the multifamily house at 926 Chalkstone Avenue, right across the street from Skeffington's funeral home. The voting rolls listed William R. Silva and Patricia Hunt as living there. But when Kennedy campaign workers visited the location, they found that none of the three tenants who actually lived there had heard of Silva or Hunt. It was an unusual coincidence because Silva and Hunt were Skeffington campaign workers whose registration forms were notarized by John J. DeMaula, also a Skeffington campaign worker who helped out at the funeral home. DeMaula did not fill out a section on the form indicating the type of identification used to verify the correct address.[45]

If the DiBiasio shooting had been a godsend for the incumbent's campaign, the charge of voter fraud leveled the playing field for Kennedy. On August 24, Nocera filed an affidavit complaining that two Skeffington campaign workers were fraudulently registered. A *Providence Journal* reporter quickly located Skeffington, who denied any wrongdoing. "I don't do anything that's improper," Skeffington claimed. "I'm a state representative and I raise my hand up there in the State House and I don't do anything wrong. . . . I think it must have been a mistake. I don't know why they used that address." When the 19-year-old DeMaula was interviewed, he said that he had "registered a lot of people" in the district for Skeffington. He could not explain why the identification section on the two forms was left blank. "I'm sure I seen [proper identification]," he claimed. "Maybe I missed a few."[46]

As he filed the affidavit with the Board of Canvassers, Nocera announced, "There might be more here than meets the eye. What we're trying to say here is that we believe elected officials should come from the district, and we also believe that the people who elect them should come from the district." With just a few weeks left before the September 14 primary, the campaign was starting to turn ugly. Forty-eight of Kennedy's 50 lawn signs with the slogan "Its Your Vote. Make It Work!" were torn down.[47] Skeffington had 250 signs up, and almost none of them were damaged. Around the same time, Tabella's car got splattered with eggs, which corroded the paint. "It stained and I never got it off. It was par for the course," he philosophized.[48]

About this time at the Skeffington Funeral Home, campaign manager Pesaturo was gearing up his nightly phone bank operation. The money was plentiful, more than he ever had seen in a General Assembly race. He had all the volunteers he needed. There had been favorable coverage of Skeffington's anticrime press conference. The clock was ticking down on Kennedy's prospects, and the young man just was not scoring. The issues were being framed around topics like crime and drugs that helped Skeffington. Pesaturo desperately wanted to be a giant-killer. After six years of school teaching, he had gone into state government, working in the governor's emergency management office, where he had risen to supervisor. With a professor from Rhode Island College, he had started his own polling firm, Alpha Research Associates. But it was politics that he loved. It was like a drug, he once explained. Once it gets in your blood, it is hard to find anything else as exciting.

Pesaturo was getting ready to start the phone banks when the telephone rang. Jimmy Creamer answered the phone, and the conversation went back and forth with a *Providence Journal* reporter on the other end. Skef, as Pesaturo called him, got on the phone. Pesaturo was starting to get nervous. He wasn't sure what it was about, but it didn't sound good. Finally, he exploded: "What the fuck is going on?" No one would tell him right away. He was running the professional campaign, the one with polling, voter identification, phone banks, and glitzy brochures. But there was a second campaign below the surface that had just blown up in their faces, the one with illegal registrations and vote fraud. Kennedy was accusing them of irregularities, and the press was writing a story about it. Pesaturo couldn't believe it. He said, "You stupid fucks. What the hell are you doing something like that for? You don't have to do it, first of all. And second, that's all this kid is waiting for." He knew the press would seize on the issue, for the activities smacked of corrupt politics. His team would be characterized as politicians who could not be trusted. The issue played to every strength Kennedy had. He was the outsider running against the entrenched old boys. He had the independence and personal integrity to reform the system. More than anything else, according to Pesaturo, the fraud issue "got Kennedy on the front page and kept him there for awhile," just as the election was nearing. Rather than being on the defensive, the tide turned in Kennedy's direction. From Pesaturo's vantage point, "They could say, 'see, I told you so. This guy [Skeffington] is part of the old boy network and ward politics and illegal voter registration, all the things that we need to put an end to in the 9th district.'"[49]

A week after the initial charge, the state Board of Elections declined to hold a hearing on Kennedy's allegations. Timothy Conlon, the lawyer for Friends of Kennedy, complained, "The response indicates an attempt to stall an open public inquiry until after the upcoming election. We have raised serious allegations which call into question the ability of the Providence Board of Canvassers to fairly and impartially administer the election laws and to conduct a fair election." He went on to point out, "No one from the Board of Canvassers has stepped forward to deny what is fully obvious from the sworn statements filed this week with the Board of Elections, that is, over at least the last several weeks the Board of Canvassers has been assisting the Skeffington campaign."[50] Kennedy scheduled a press conference the next day to discuss his complaint. Leonard M. Bento, a temporary clerk at the Board of Canvassers who knew Patrick from the Young Democrats, had filed an affidavit supporting the Kennedy charges. Strange things were happening at the Canvassers Board late at night after the office was supposed to be closed.[51] Tabella explained that Bento "had been working down there and he sees all this stuff go on. Every time we go in, they place a call to the Speaker's office. He sees them keep voter registration cards in their desks as opposed to the books. [These were] people Skeffington's people had registered. So he contacted us and we contacted our legal counsel."[52] The next day, Bento was fired. Bento claimed Board Chair Laurence Flynn had purposely withheld William Silva's registration card when it was requested by the Kennedy campaign. The clerk also claimed he had overheard an argument between Flynn and another staffer, who questioned why Flynn called Skeffington and why he had made copies of Nocera's original affidavits shortly after they were filed.[53]

The Kennedy people feared the illegal voters were just the tip of the iceberg. They hired a Providence investigative firm called Intertect, which sent private investigators to suspicious addresses around the district. At this point, Skeffington got a lucky break. Skeffington, too, had been going door to door in the district, although not as diligently as Kennedy. Skef preferred to hang out at Player's Corner Pub, a local watering hole. One night, 10 days before the primary, Skef encountered a local firefighter he knew. The man informed Skeffington that Kennedy investigators had falsely accused a woman he knew of not being properly registered, and she was terribly upset. After getting her name and address, Skef called his campaign manager. The two immediately went over to the woman in question. She said, "Come in. You wouldn't believe what happened." A private investigator from the Kennedy camp had just knocked on her door a couple of hours earlier and he was challenging her right to vote, she said. The woman was angry. She said, "I live here and I'm registered to vote here. They challenged my vote."[54]

Skeffington complained to the press about Kennedy's intimidation tactics, which responded with a lengthy story and picture of the woman Maureen B. Messier, a meat wrapper at the Star Market in Olneyville. She had lived at Wisdom Avenue for 25 years and owned the house for 15 years. She had voted in almost every primary and election since she was 18. Since the post office had mistakenly returned some campaign literature from Kennedy addressed to "the Messier Family," the Kennedy staff thought she no longer lived there and should have her name removed from the voter registration lists. An Intertect man came to question her proof of residency. She showed him 12 documents attesting to her residency, and after he checked the tax rolls in City Hall, he accepted her argument. But Messier was still upset. She told a reporter, "As far as I'm concerned, they challenged my honor, which is the worst thing you can do. I'm more hurt than anything else." She added that she planned to vote for Skeffington.[55]

Pesaturo immediately established an election hotline that voters could call to report Kennedy intimidation tactics. Skeffington's manager put together a brochure featuring the woman who complained about Kennedy "challenging my honor." The brochure announced "Mt. Pleasant, Elmhurst, and Olneyville Residents Beware!" and said "Kennedy's high priced investigators, private detectives, and lawyers are threatening our honor and our most cherished right—THE RIGHT TO VOTE." It went on to claim, "Patrick Kennedy is conducting a negative campaign based on fear and intimidation. . . . Using the tremendous wealth and political power that this Massachusetts family has amassed, Patrick Kennedy doesn't care whose rights are trampled upon."[56] It was Skeffington's most effective move in the closing days of the campaign. Tabella immediately realized his campaign had made a mistake. "It became a bad decision because we could have made all those same points without the private investigators and we wouldn't have taken the hit that we took for hiring private investigators. That created an ugliness. We had run a very positive campaign."[57]

In the last week, the National Rifle Association weighed into the campaign with a $2,000 contribution to Skeffington, district mailings, and full-page ads in local papers. One ad informed voters that when DiBiasio stood up for his rights, Skeffington stood besides him. Skeffington was a man you can depend on when it's time to right a wrong, the ad claimed. Tabella was delighted. He said, "We couldn't have paid them to do what they did. They took out this ad and they got the date for the election wrong."[58]

The election was on Wednesday because of a Jewish holiday. "They ended up cutting the legs out from under themselves," Tabella said. "'Kennedy doesn't belong, he's from Massachusetts.' So they bring in the NRA from Washington, D.C., to write ads for them. So who is the outsider?" Ted Kennedy blasted the ad. At a campaign event for his son, the senator made an emotional appeal about the danger of gun violence and how his family had been victimized by guns.[59]

On the night before the election, Pesaturo and Creamer decide to pay their respects to the opposition. They walked down to Patrick's headquarters to wish him luck now that the campaign was over. As the two men neared Kennedy headquarters, they saw that it was unlit inside. Since the Kennedy headquarters had a glass plate window, Pesaturo looked in and saw a number of Polaroid cameras with boxes of film. Creamer turned to Pesaturo and with a puzzled expression asked, "What the fuck is that?" Pesaturo said, "You know what that is Jimmy? That son of a bitch, they're going to take pictures at the polls." Puzzled, Creamer asked, "Why are they going to do that?" Pesaturo guessed, "I bet you they have Kennedy members down here [tomorrow]. Look at those cameras. They're going to be taking pictures at the polls with voters and members of the Kennedy family.[60]

The next day was bright and sunny, a beautiful fall day. The Kennedys were out in full force. Ted and Joan were there, as were brother Teddy and sister Kara and cousin Joe. Even John Kennedy Jr., who had just been proclaimed the "sexiest man alive" by *People* magazine, came to the polling place to campaign for Patrick. There were four polling places in the district. At the various locations, hired photographers took Polaroid snapshots of voters with famous Kennedy relatives. Each family member worked a two-hour shift. Pesaturo went to see what was happening. The Kennedy campaign had two people at Nathaniel Greene School who served as advance staff. "Would you like to have your picture taken with Congressman Joe Kennedy?" they inquired. Behind them was Joe with a photographer. Figuring he might as well have a souvenir, Pesaturo said sure. The congressman put his arm around him not knowing he was the opponent's campaign manager. Before Pesaturo knew it, the photo had been taken. "As soon as that picture was snapped, that man's eyes, energies, and affection went zoom right to the next person." "They don't care who you are," he explained. "He did what he had to do. I watched that throughout the day. All of them are good, efficient, [and] very mechanical." Pesaturo saw little old ladies coming up to vote who didn't expect to see Joan, Ted, Joe, Teddy, Kara, or John. The advance people would direct them to the nearest Kennedy. After each shot was taken, voters had 50 feet to walk to the polls while the Polaroid picture was developing. Voters didn't want to smudge the photo by putting it in their pocket or purse. Just about the time they entered the voting booth, the picture was fully developed. "The night before when I saw those cameras, I knew that we were in for a long day," Pesaturo remembered.[61]

When Skeffington went to greet voters at the polls, he ran into John Kennedy Jr. It was a hot day, and Kennedy was sitting on the stairs drinking a Coke. The advance man would set up the picture. Kennedy would haphazardly go over, put his arm around the person, have the picture taken, and then go back and sit down. "They had to prod him to do this," Skeffington remembered. After half an hour, Kennedy went up to

Skeffington. He said, "Jack." Skeffington replied, "Yeah." Kennedy said, "I'm John Kennedy." Skeffington told him, "I know who you are John." What John Kennedy said next surprised Skeffington, "Jack, I'm going to tell you something. I don't like being here. I don't think it's fair for me to be here. I want you to know the only reason I'm here is for my cousin. But I don't believe in it. I don't want to be here, and I don't think it's fair. This is your neighborhood." Kennedy closed the soliloquy by saying "Good luck to you" and sitting down. Skeffington was shocked at the comment, but pleased by the common touch that lay behind it. "John Kennedy was a nice, nice boy," he thought.[62]

That night, Patrick won the election by 1,324 to 1,009 votes, or 57 to 43 percent. The total of 2,333 votes cast represented an unexpectedly large turnout. Ted called everyone in his family, including Jackie and Rose Kennedy, and told them this was his "happiest election." Patrick later would give his father a framed picture of the celebration signed, "To Dad, my father & hero! Love, Patrick."[63] Shortly after 10:00 p.m., Patrick made his victory party appearance at Caruso's Restaurant. The young man was exuberant. "The message is clear today. They told me to wait my turn. Well, tonight, it's our turn," he proclaimed. Continuing, he said, "It's our turn for new ideas and the energy and commitment to make them work. It's our turn to give law enforcement officials the resources they need to fight crime. It's our turn to give senior citizens of our community the affordable home health care they deserve. And it's our turn for representation that listens to the needs of the people and not the demands of the party bosses." Then joking with the audience, he denied that "there were more Kennedys than voters" at the polls.[64]

Just after midnight, Patrick paid a personal call on the reporter who had been crucial in the campaign, Charlie Bakst of the *Providence Journal*. Kennedy told Bakst, "I think the people of the district demonstrated enormous confidence in me to represent them. My message has been clear from the beginning. It's been a message that they want representation that listens to the concerns of the community, not the demands of the party bosses." Bakst asked him if he would mend fences with those, such as Party Chair Mancini and U.S. Senate candidate Licht, who had opposed him. The response was not conciliatory. "Really, I was appalled at the way the Democratic Party felt that the endorsement was the last word on who was the representative in the 9th District. That was evident when Chairman Mancini said, 'Wait your turn,' and it's been evident through the lining up behind my opponent in an almost vindictive way." As for Licht, Kennedy said, "I was, quite frankly, dismayed with Lieutenant Governor Licht's endorsement of my opponent, because I had worked for him so hard and would like to model my career in the same progressive way that has exemplified his tenure in office." Finally, Kennedy added, "I don't owe anybody in the party leadership or the General Assembly anything except my efforts to speak out on behalf of my district." Coincidentally while they were talking, Speaker DeAngelis happened to call Bakst. Told that Patrick was present, the adversaries talked. Patrick said, "Mr. Speaker, fine, how are you? . . . Thank you . . . I hope I'd have the same loyalty that he had." The Speaker responded, "Mr. Skeffington had our loyalty because he was so loyal to us."[65]

The day of the election, Alpha Research Associates conducted an exit poll with 274 voters in the Ninth District. The poll found that Patrick had done much better among women (68 to 32 percent) than men (52 to 48 percent). His vote also was tilted toward young people. He ran better than Skeffington among those 18 to 34, while Skeffington ran stronger among those 50 and older. When asked what was most important for their vote, 29 percent of Kennedy voters named time for a change, followed by new ideas (27 percent), neighborhood involvement (11 percent), and job performance (9 percent). People who voted for Skeffington were most likely to name job performance (31 percent), neighborhood involvement (26 percent), and trust and respect (14 percent). Nearly a quarter of those questioned said they had made up their minds in the last two or three days before the election. Almost half indicated they had decided in the last two weeks of the campaign.[66]

Shortly after the election, Ted Kennedy was interviewed by Tom Brokaw of NBC News, who asked how the senator felt about his son Patrick winning a race by spending $73 per vote. Ted was stunned. No one had told him that the state representative's race had cost $93,000, which was unheard of for a representative's contest. All but $5,904 of Kennedy's spending had come in the form of loans from his own pocket. With free staff from the Speaker's office, Skeffington had spent just $36,000, but it was far more than the $5,000 spent on his 1986 reelection. Ted's aide Jon Haber, who was supposed to keep close tabs on the race, had been afraid to tell Ted about the escalating bill because of Kennedy's temper. The senator ended up hearing the amount in the most unfortunate setting for him, a public interview on national television. He sputtered through some answer. But afterward, he exploded at the staff. He couldn't believe how much the campaign had cost. Shortly thereafter, Haber was transferred to the Senate Agriculture Committee.[67]

5 Learning the Ropes

*P*atrick's first day in the General Assembly started with a national television appearance with his father on ABC's *Good Morning America*. Ray Rickman, the only sitting member of the General Assembly to have endorsed Patrick, recalled, "When Patrick came to the House, the national press came—*USA Today*, the *Boston Globe*, all the TV stations, and his father. It really was a big thing."[1] Referring to the *Good Morning America* interview, Speaker Joe DeAngelis said, "We all kind of chuckled at it. I don't think there were any hard feelings created by it. The general comment was, 'Look at this young fellow getting all this publicity when he is yet to introduce a bill.' Everyone understood his last name. It was funny. It was the kind of stuff we told a lot of stories and jokes about."[2] Patrick took the oath of office with his left hand on the Bible that his uncle, John F. Kennedy, had used at his 1961 presidential inauguration. In rapid order, Majority Leader Thomas Lamb nominated DeAngelis to be Speaker, with the choice seconded by Republican Brad Gorham and Democrats Nancy Benoit and Robert Bianchini. With no further nominations, the motion passed on a voice vote by the 83 Democrats and 17 Republicans.[3] The GOP did not even bother to nominate a candidate.

The General Assembly was a throwback to the old days. Much like legislatures around the country earlier in this century, it was a leadership-run institution. When the Speaker wanted a bill tabled, it was done so with dispatch. Bills were voted on soon after being distributed. No one who wanted action on proposals dared cross the leadership. One day in 1987, before Kennedy entered the Assembly, Rodney Driver, a maverick legislator who was a math professor at the University of Rhode Island, was sitting in the House. After a particular vote, he leaned forward and told Rickman, "That's not possible." Innocently, Rickman asked, "What's not possible?" Driver told him, "Seventy people just voted and there are only 60 people in the room."[4] Rickman looked around the hall and quickly solved the riddle. Some legislators had stuck a match cover over the green button so that they could vote yes on everything, just as the leadership wanted, without being in the room. The next day, at the Democratic caucus, Driver complained. In the ensuing argument, leadership allies yelled and screamed at Driver and balled up their fists. "It's none of your damn business," one said. "Who the hell are you anyway? You just got here." The caucus agreed that nothing would be done about this matter. "Don't you raise this again," Driver was warned. This was business as usual in the General Assembly.

Disagreements over policy were eased by material inducements in the budget. Since leaders controlled the passage of special bills granting money for various causes, cities and towns, and community organizations, it was like a big United Way with the leadership firmly in control. If you didn't play ball with leaders, no goodies came your way. According to Elmer Cornwell, parliamentarian of the House and a political science professor at Brown University, the bill approval process was very direct. "The leaders called in the chairman. He'd have a book with all the bills in it. They'd have a book with all the bills in it. They'd go through them. This one is a go and this other one is a no go. That would be the way it would go. It would be up to the chairman to go back to his committee and see to it that when those bills came up, they were dealt with in the manner the leadership wanted."[5]

Committees were the device through which leaders controlled the rank and file. Committee chairs and members were appointed by the Speaker and served at his pleasure. Every bill was assigned by the Speaker's staff to a particular committee, where it would sit until the leadership indicated which bills it wanted passed. Voting against the leadership was the cardinal sin in the General Assembly. Democrats overwhelmingly dominated the legislative body, often by as much as 80 to 20 seats in the House and comparable margins in the 50-member Senate. Leaders wanted to win big so as to demonstrate their firm control. If for some reason you had to vote against leadership wishes, you warned the leaders in advance so they wouldn't take it personally. The expectation was that "you are on the team," Cornwell explained. "Unless your vote is crucial, they're going to say okay [to voting no] as long as you don't go and take your bucket to the well too often." George Caruolo, a House member from East Providence on the outs with DeAngelis, detested this practice. Speaking of that time, he said, "People did not vote against bills. If there were 3 or 4 votes against a bill, you'd be called up to the front of the room and asked why you were doing such a thing. There was not tremendous amounts of debate."[6]

Caruolo and his friend John Harwood, a representative from Pawtucket, had been close allies of DeAngelis's predecessor, Speaker Matthew Smith. Indeed, Harwood had been Smith's golden boy but, after a disagreement with the leadership, became a "fallen angel."[7] The dispute occurred in 1985 over legislation in the Corporations Committee authorizing a 1,500-ton-a-day trash incinerator to be built at Quonset Point on Narragansett Bay. The initial cost was around $223 million and with bond payments over 20 years, the total cost was in excess of $1 billion. The bill was 3–4 inches thick, and it came out near the end of the session for surprise hearings. Harwood recalled, "A bill was given to us that was literally hot [off the press]. George and I had been around for a little bit, so we went to the back of the bill to find out what it was going to cost."[8] Much to their surprise, they discovered that the legislation, which would have funded the construction of the incinerator, would have indebted the state by $1.2 billion. House leaders told the assembled members the bill had to be passed that day.

Even in Rhode Island, it was unusual to have a bill of that magnitude passed on the last day of the session with no discussion. "We just felt we were indebting our children with that kind of debt. It was unconscionable," Harwood explained.[9] As the hearing was proceeding, the committee chair, Joe Casinelli, leaned over to his fellow committee members and whispered, "No questions guys, this bill is a go."[10] The leadership plan was to have the committee pass the bill, rush the legislation to the floor for quick approval, and adjourn the General Assembly for the year. It was a bald power grab that provoked a small group of Democratic legislators into dissidence. Why was this bill being rushed through, they demanded? Surprised at the resistance, Casinelli recessed the meeting. Eventually, a commission was formed that recommended an incinerator half the size of the original be built. But the damage to Harwood and Caruolo was done by their defiance. Not only were they kicked off the Corporations Committee and out of the formal party apparatus, the leadership humiliated them by taking away their choice parking spots, the ultimate symbol of demotion at the Statehouse.

In 1988, the year Patrick ran for the General Assembly, Speaker Smith retired to a lucrative job as court administrator and was succeeded by his former Majority Leader DeAngelis. If Smith was a backslapping and storytelling Irish politician, DeAngelis represented a new breed of leader. Cool, meticulous, and a very hard worker, he made it his goal to modernize the General Assembly. DeAngelis was an attorney for Licht and Semonoff, one of the premier law firms in the state. The new Speaker set about bringing a more businesslike approach to the work of the Assembly. Frustrated with the glacial pace of things, he started a policy team in the Speaker's office, a place that never before had employed policy experts. DeAngelis described his plan as wanting "to make the place run a little more efficiently, try and get sessions reduced in the sense of time, [and] get the committees working a little bit harder."[11] The budget was the tricky issue. Each year, in one piece of legislation, the General Assembly passed a bill that determined the funding level for every state agency. It was a mammoth bill that ordered the financial priorities for the state. Smith had not been timid about the budget. It was the one thing that moved fast in the Assembly, with passage typically taking just a single day.

In 1988, his first year as Speaker, DeAngelis had broken floor consideration of the budget into two days in order to appease dissident legislators. By letting the debate continue for one day more than customary, DeAngelis was trying to be more open, but he did not like the results. In his experience, extended floor debate was bad for public policy and bad for democracy. It was too much like the budget travesties that were making a mockery of the U.S. Congress. If too much floor debate took place, he felt, "special interest groups are going to grab the legislators and say you've got to put this in or you've got to take this out. The longer you let the budget hang out there [in public], you subject the members to a lot of pressure." The Finance Committee had spent months holding hearings and had come up with a bill that was balanced and that spread largesse among competing interests. The Speaker's perspective was that "the members should have trust in the Finance Committee and support them. That's the way it was done for decades and decades."[12]

DeAngelis's top two assistants were Majority Leader Tom Lamb and House Whip Chris Boyle. Lamb's style was laid back and pragmatic; he was imbued with the caution of a businessman, quiet and preferring to operate behind the scenes.[13] Boyle was more bold and assertive. An ambitious young man, he was street smart and looking to move up when the opportunity presented itself. His job was to handle the floor calendar, resolve disputes, and coordinate the leadership team. He listened closely to the concerns of the rank and file and communicated them to the Speaker so that there were "no surprises and that we had a sense of where people were coming from."[14] If there was a good cop/bad cop routine, Boyle was the enforcer. Cornwell thought Lamb was "a nice guy" but said DeAngelis relied on Boyle "to really run things. He managed the floor debate. He called things to order. He was the one who did the dirty work."[15]

With the election over, the leadership team tried to smooth things out with Kennedy. He had done the unthinkable—beaten the leadership—and now was an incumbent Democrat. In Boyle's view, Patrick's victory meant one thing: "Our rule is once you get elected, you're one of us. We are all together in this now. I recall Joe saying, 'Now we would support him in future elections.' That's just the way it worked."[16] A month after the primary, the Speaker had dinner with Kennedy and agreed to a request for an assignment on the Health, Education, and Welfare Committee. The leadership policy on Patrick was simple. "We never tried to freeze anyone out," Boyle explained. DeAngelis even attended a fund-raiser for the young man early in the first session. The relationship warmed up. Despite his reform-oriented campaign, in his initial days in the Rhode Island House, Patrick was a team player. Driver used to sit right behind Patrick on the Assembly floor. Driver recalled that on controversial votes in the first year, "I used to see his finger wavering between the red and green buttons, and eventually pushing the green one [for the leadership] even though he knew he ought to push the red one."[17] Another legislator, Linda Kushner, who served with Kennedy and sat next to him on the floor, felt the same way. "Patrick was treated with graciousness [by the leadership] and responded with graciousness. It wasn't clear where Patrick was. . . . There was no animosity [with the leadership]," she said.[18] On some issues, Patrick shared interests with the leadership. Lamb was known within the chamber as "Mr. Home Health Care," an issue Patrick cared very much about. Lamb's top legislative priority was "to get home health care established as a viable cost for health care." The majority leader felt it was ridiculous that insurance companies would not recognize home care as a reimbursable health cost. "They didn't want to have anything to do with that," Lamb said. Kennedy, Lamb recalled, "was 100 percent for all those things." The young man "was interested in the elderly and he knew that a lot of my legislation had to do with nursing homes, home health care, and things like that that he also was interested in."[19] Patrick's friend Caruolo recalled that at the beginning, "[Patrick] had not firmly cast his lot with us as dissidents. He had initially been able to meet with Joe DeAngelis on a footing which was more advanced than the average freshman legislators. Initially, the then Speaker had attempted to take to heart some of the things Patrick was pushing for." Caruolo said, "They attempted to mollify him in small ways, but there was never an embracing of [Patrick's] viewpoint."[20] For his part, Patrick tried hard not to upset the leadership. The strategy, according to Tabella, who was advising the legislator, was to "try to get some bills passed before you tick everybody off." Rickman said Kennedy "decided he would try to work with them or not tick them off."[21]

Kennedy set up his own district office. Unheard of for a freshman legislator, he was getting 300 letters a week. Some were congratulatory letters, but constituents were starting to make requests for help with Social Security and immigration. Chris Nocera and his wife Erin staffed the office and provided a 24-hour answering service for Kennedy.[22] At first experienced politicians laughed at Patrick for his district office. No one in the Assembly had a district office, not even the Speaker of the House. But the laughter died down when fellow legislators realized the office was a valuable constituency-building mechanism.[23]

One month into his term, Patrick wrote a short article for the *Providence Journal Magazine* on "five reasons to feel unashamed about being a liberal." The reasons were: (1) "being a liberal means having an optimistic view of government," (2) "liberal means being caring and compassionate," (3) "it means to be active and committed," (4) "to have vision, to anticipate problems and address them before they become crises," and (5) "to reject passivity in government, to reject the notion that manmade problems cannot be solved by man."[24]

Cognizant of his own personal limitations, the young man found mentors in the House who guided him: Kushner, who sat beside him; Rickman, who had endorsed him in 1988; and Driver, who understood the parliamentary rules better than anybody else. Kushner had a theory about the Kennedys. They "mature well," she thought and "surround themselves with good advisors." There were days when Kushner felt like Frederick's nurse in *Pirates of Penzance*. In a personal journal she kept, Kushner wrote, "I am probably sitting next to someone who will run for president, at least become a U.S. Senator so I should help develop his values."[25] Patrick understood his personal limitations and was eager to learn from others more experienced than himself. Reminiscent of his father's get-togethers, he organized monthly powwows with a circle of advisers: Rickman, Nocera, and Tabella. He videotaped speeches so he could go over them with Barbara Tannenbaum and improve his public speaking.

Patrick's first legislative test came on gun control. The National Rifle Association had targeted him for defeat in his first campaign, given $2,000 to his primary opponent, run newspaper ads against him, and written direct mail letters to people in the district. But when it came time to introduce gun control legislation in February 1989, during his first term, Kushner noticed that Patrick was "wobbling." There were several different bills in the hopper. Rene Menard had an antiassault weapon law, Kushner had a bill regulating "Saturday night specials," and Kennedy was thinking about legislation that would extend from three to seven days the waiting period for the purchase of handguns and establish a seven-day waiting period for rifles. At that time, there was no waiting period for the purchase of rifles.

In a February 8, 1989, entry in her personal journal about the gun legislation, Kushner wrote that Patrick "isn't sure he wants to be the prime sponsor. He says that it is the first bill he's putting in—he has no innocuous stuff." Patrick's fear was that "every one will jump him." Kushner had to encourage Kennedy to be the prime sponsor. "I who want the help of his automatic fame, urge him to do it. After all, anyone can put in innocuous bills I tell him—but it's something to put in strong bills."[26] Two days later, Patrick introduced the bill calling for a seven-day waiting period on purchases of rifles, shotguns, or pistols. Gun dealers would be required to notify law enforcement agencies about prospective buyers so that background checks could be performed. That day and the following one, there were stories in the *Providence Journal* publicizing Kennedy's initiative. At a press conference, Patrick explained his position. "We are not for restricting the use of guns by sportsmen and hunters and people who legitimately have an interest in protecting their home. But it's time that we had tough gun control regulations because of all the violence that our unrestricted gun laws have caused." Unlike later years, when he actively emphasized the personal effect guns had on his clan, he disavowed any personal motivation for the legislation: "My family is not the only family to experience the violence," he noted. Four days later, the newspaper wrote an editorial supporting Kennedy's gun control proposal.[27] Patrick brought Sarah Brady of Handgun Control, Inc. to testify about the need for effective gun control laws. On April 7, the Committee on Special Legislation passed Patrick's bill on a unanimous vote. A few days later, the legislation passed the full House on a 70 to 18 vote, with the leadership taking no position, saying it was a vote of conscience for members. But in May, the Senate Judiciary Committee killed the bill on a 7 to 6 vote, opting to form a study commission instead. This move torpedoed the bill's chances that session.[28]

The next year, another controversial issue percolated in the General Assembly. The Newbay Corp. proposed to construct a new power plant in East Providence, just across the river from the Providence East Side, one of the wealthiest neighborhoods in the state. Everyone from surrounding city councils to Republican Governor Edward DiPrete to the director of the state's Department of Economic Development favored the project. The project was of special interest to the Speaker since Newbay was represented by a law partner of Speaker DeAngelis named Bob Pitassi. The Department of Environmental Management had a reputation for being very tough on developers, and the Speaker was asked if he would set up a meeting between Newbay engineers and DEM, which he agreed to do.[29] As the engineers debated the fine points of plant construction, a citizens group organized. Not only were the citizens worried about the location of the plant, they were concerned about air and water pollution from the development. At a meeting of a neighborhood association, district residents complained to Kushner about Newbay. She said, "Listen, you are talking to the choir out here. What you need to do is get a wider reach. For instance, so and so says he hasn't heard from anyone on it."[30] That legislator soon got 50 or 60 letters from irate citizens.

At this point, Kennedy still was friendly with DeAngelis. The environment was an issue he cared about. As a chronic asthmatic, he was attuned to the way in which air quality affected people's lives. Past sessions had attempted to strengthen state oversight of new power plants, but the legislation always had been blocked by the leadership. Patrick wanted to get stronger siting regulations for future power plants. DeAngelis's policy aide Jeff Newman approached Patrick with a tantalizing offer. The leadership would agree to tough new siting regulations for future proposed power plants if Patrick agreed to sponsor an amendment exempting plants of less than 80 megawatts with applications pending. The Newbay proposal called for a 72.8-megawatt plant. In effect, the amendment exempted Newbay in return for tough legislation saying future power plants of more than 40 megawatts would have to be approved by the state's Energy Facilities Siting Board. Patrick accepted the deal. On May 23, 1990, he offered an amendment requiring new power plants with a generating power of at least 40 megawatts be reviewed by the state board, but that Newbay be excluded from this requirement. Kennedy said he felt "it would be unfair to subject plants already in the pipeline to the new regulation."[31]

Patrick's closest allies went ballistic. Kennedy was accused of cutting a deal with the Speaker. Majority Leader Lamb angrily took "personal offense" at that charge and announced, "The sponsor [Kennedy] has not been asked by anyone to accept anything he did not want to do."[32] Kushner's view of the situation was that Patrick had "worked out a deal to get [the amendment] to where it was." She stood up on the floor and gave a violent speech against it. "We really had it out," she recalled.[33] Paul Jabour, another legislative ally of Kennedy, denounced his friend's amendment. Kennedy said nothing during the tumultuous debate, but the controversy forced the leadership to pull the bill off the floor for redrafting. Rickman was good friends with Kennedy and Kushner. He felt the Newbay controversy was a classic political squeeze by the leadeship. House officials wrote the amendment and offered Patrick a choice. According to Rickman, "They said if you put this amendment in, we will let [the tougher future rules] pass. . . . Politically, it wasn't a good thing for him to do. It would have been better to put his legislation in and take a defeat."[34] Kennedy was learning the hard way how things worked in the legislature.

Outside the General Assembly, Patrick was in considerable demand by community organizations. Charitable organizations asked him to raise money for them, and groups requested that he speak at their events. The Kennedy name was magic in a small state not used to national celebrities. Paul Gournaris, the principal at Hope High School in Providence, was one of those who saw Patrick as an attractive draw for young people. Commencement was coming up at his high school, and he asked Patrick to be the main speaker at graduation ceremonies. Kennedy accepted. But on graduation day, Kennedy failed to show up. Gournaris was quoted in the newspaper as saying Kennedy did not inform him that he couldn't be the speaker until the afternoon of the graduation. "I'm sure there was no intent on his part to snub us or anything." the principal announced. The newspaper article pointed out that Kennedy was attending an event at the McGee Rehabilitation Unit of Hillcrest Hospital in Lenox, Massachusetts, near Pittsfield. The unit served drug and alcohol abusers and was named for former Massachusetts House Speaker Thomas McGee, a recovered alcoholic. The story blamed a "scheduling glitch by an aide [that] caused him [to] be slated to speak at the two events."[35] The real story, however, was less flattering to Kennedy. The event in Massachusetts was a golf tournament for the hospital, which had been scheduled to end in time to make the graduation ceremonies. At the conclusion of the rounds, however, one of his friends said, "We're all going to go out to this other place and eat. I want you to come with us." Torn between going out with his friends and speaking at the high school, Kennedy stayed in Massachusetts. He called up Nocera the day of the event and told him, "Tell them I can't make it. . . . Say it is a scheduling conflict." Like a dutiful aide, Nocera complied and publicly took the blame for the last-minute change in plans.[36]

6 Dealing with the Catholic Church

As he grappled with life in the legislature, Kennedy faced personal challenges from the Catholic Church. Catholicism had been a strong undercurrent throughout Patrick's life. The two colleges (Georgetown University and Providence College) Patrick had chosen were Catholic. Rhode Island was the most Catholic state in the union, with nearly two-thirds of its million residents saying they were Catholic. The religion permeated every nook and cranny of the state. Bishop Louis Gelineau, leader of the Providence Diocese, which covered the entire state, managed an empire of schools, social organizations, and charitable institutions that rivaled that of the government— 10 high schools, 52 elementary schools, 1 hospital, and 2 nursing homes. More than 17,000 children each year were educated at Catholic schools. The church's work force totaled more than 5,000, and its charitable arm served social welfare agencies through-out the state. Through an alliance with Matthew Smith, who had preceded DeAngelis as House Speaker, Gelineau had garnered large amounts of state aid for a Catholic-affiliated hospital and an assortment of charities. According to Scott MacKay, political reporter for the *Providence Journal*, "In the old days, if you weren't a Catholic in good standing, you didn't get elected."[1]

When Kennedy moved to Rhode Island, there were 156 parishes in the state. Three of them converged around the Providence College area: St. Augustine, St. Pius, and Blessed Sacrament. St. Augustine was the wealthiest parish in the area. St. Pius was the closest to Providence College, but Patrick's 1988 opponent, Jack Skeffington, was a parishioner there. Blessed Sacrament was the poorest of the three, but it had one virtue. It was the biggest of the three and therefore had the most votes.

Father Charles Maher was pastor at Blessed Sacrament. He remembered 1988 clearly because it was the centennial year for the church, and there were monthly events as part of the celebration. As the church planned commemorative events, Kennedy attended both evening and morning Masses and helped with centennial plan-ning. He even attended the church's annual picnic. With his family's well-known name,

Patrick stood out in the congregation. Except for Ted's abortion views, Father Maher considered himself "very much a Kennedy person." He appreciated the family's compassion and efforts at social justice even while he felt disillusioned by Ted's stance on abortion rights. But it was not just the celebrityhood that caught the eye of the priest. Patrick "was a very well-mannered young man," Maher said. That struck the priest because he thought good manners were so lacking today.[2]

It was a view Maher shared with the bishop. Gelineau's biggest frustration was the decay of basic values in society. "Christian values and religious values do not seem to be held in the esteem they used to be," he said. Father Maher and his fellow priest, Father Marcel, watched young Patrick. They talked among themselves and said, "Let's just see if he really is interested in belonging to Blessed Sacrament parish."[3] Each academic year, the church ran Confirmation classes, which sent two youngsters to a teacher's home for religious instruction. Children would study the Sacraments and learn about Catholicism. There were three sacraments of initiation into the church: Baptism, which takes place shortly after birth; Confirmation at the age of 15 or 16, when children have completed their initiation into the church; and the Eucharist or Holy Communion.

At one of the church events, Father Marcel approached Kennedy. Would he be interested in teaching a Confirmation class during the academic year 1987–88? Much to both priests' surprise, Patrick agreed. Since the program recently had changed from a classroom to home setting, two young boys used to go to Kennedy's house once a week for religious instruction. It continued throughout April 1988, at which point Patrick dropped out of the teaching program because of the time commitment of his impending campaign. Kennedy brought his mother to church events. On another occasion, Patrick showed up with his father. As Father Maher greeted the senator on the front steps, a flashbulb went off and the event was duly recorded for posterity.[4]

There was no discussion with the priest of Patrick's abortion views. In truth, Patrick felt tortured on this subject. He used to have long talks with Barbara Tannenbaum about abortion. According to her, Patrick had never been in a situation where he had impregnated someone. But he worried about the issue philosophically and morally. With Tannenbaum, Patrick worked through his abortion views. In his early career, he decided that "it should be a right of choice but what we needed to do was to strengthen other possibilities like adoption and remove barriers to that. It softened it a little bit for him."[5] The idea of abortion was hard for Patrick. His personal views and his sense of what was just for the rest of society were different. He was pro-choice, but saw abortion as the last option. Rickman, a pro-choice legislator, realized his friend was torn on this subject. Deep down, Rickman felt, Patrick "really is a Roman Catholic personally. The teachings of the church mean a lot to him. . . . I watched him struggle with [abortion] a lot."[6]

As the 1988 campaign got under way, abortion was an issue that could have been devastating for Patrick. It was a classic "wedge" issue that divided socially conservative, working-class Democrats from the progressive wing of the party. This was precisely the coalition Kennedy needed to assemble for his House race in one of the most Catholic districts in the country. Skeffington was pro-life and wanted to make abortion an issue in the election. After all, Ted Kennedy was going to Mass at Blessed Sacrament and was clearly pro-choice, and Skeffington thought the issue was a negative for Patrick in the heavily Catholic district. George Hoey, a local undertaker who lived across the street from the church and was active in the congregation, told Father Maher that Patrick "was a nice Catholic boy who went to PC and went to Mass every week" and that Kennedy's church-going was not just a political ploy."[7] It confirmed the priest's own view that Patrick was polite and well-mannered.

Skeffington, on the other hand, posed a problem for Father Maher. According to the priest, the two never had gotten along very well. Skeffington didn't pay his funeral bills on time, the only undertaker in the area who did not. Father Maher conducted 80 to 100 funerals a year and received a standard stipend from each funeral director to offset the costs of the funeral: $75 for the musician, $95 to the church, and $5 for the priest. Every other funeral director would hand Father Maher an envelope following the funeral, so it was easy to keep track of the money. With Skeffington, the priest had to badger the undertaker to pay the fee. The dispute finally had reached a point where Father Maher had issued an ultimatum. Either the money got paid up front or there would be no funerals. The two finally had worked out the problem, but it had left hard feelings.

Although he didn't realize it at the time, Father Maher was crucial in Patrick's 1988 campaign. As Kennedy's local priest, Maher had the power to signal acceptance. It was not something priests did publicly. Never did they preach against specific individuals. But priests moved around the community and talked to people. They were opinion leaders. Through the smile or the frown, they could confer legitimacy on others. It was a tactic long practiced by the bishop. For all his behind-the-scenes political clout, Bishop Gelineau was careful in his public statements. Interviewed one day in his sunny office overlooking Cathedral Square, Gelineau said, "I try to be careful not to comment publicly on specific politicians. I do not see that as my role."[8]

Father Maher never preached against Skeffington, nor did he make any public comments about the campaign that was roiling his parish. The race was in the paper every week. Kennedys were rolling in and out of the district. The priest did not feel it was appropriate for a local religious leader to get involved in the campaign. His job was to administer to his congregation's needs, not dictate political disputes. It was not his practice to ask new parishioners their stance on abortion. In fact, he was not even sure what Patrick's views were on the subject. Since Father Maher lived outside the district, he couldn't cast a ballot. This silence was all that Kennedy needed. The Kennedy staff goal was not to campaign for abortion rights, but to keep Skeffington from turning Patrick's pro-choice views into a political negative. Father Maher's neutrality helped Patrick immeasurably. Speaking of Father Maher and abortion, Nocera said, "By not saying anything, it just was never an issue. It could have legitimately become an issue. I think there were pressures placed on him [Father Maher] to make it an issue and he never did."[9] This silence defused the controversial subject and effectively removed abortion from the campaign.

Kennedy was not so fortunate in the General Assembly. Bills were filed on all sorts of matters related to abortion—waiting periods, parental notification, and funding for low-income women, among other things. As a representative who had to vote on each of these matters, he could not escape a public stance despite his private ambivalence. As the first year wore on, Patrick voted pro-choice on all the major abortion bills. He wasn't a legislative leader on this subject, preferring instead to focus his efforts on issues such as gun control and the environment. But he was a reliable pro-choice vote. Kushner remembered that she constantly had to prod Patrick on abortion. He co-sponsored every bill that was requested by abortion rights organizers but rarely initiated action in this area. "He had to be reminded that he was pro-choice," Kushner said. She occasionally had to tell him he had made a statement and "was he aware of it or did he really believe in it." At times, he "wobbled" on the issue.[10]

Early in the campaign, Nocera had warned Kennedy about the emotion surrounding religion in Rhode Island. Religion was not like other political issues, he noted. It was combustible and volatile, especially in a place with such a heavy Catholic presence. Nocera told him, "Patrick, don't ever use the church as a political ploy. If you're not the guy who goes to church every week, it's better not to go now than to use it and never go again."[11] But Kennedy wanted to get involved with Blessed Sacrament and had become close with Father Maher. The relationship was strong. Based on his personal observations, Father Maher had formed a very positive view of Patrick. The priest thought the young Kennedy "was sincere in his going to Mass," and he appreciated Patrick's teaching Confirmation classes.[12] But right after the election, Kennedy stopped going to church on a regular basis. The change in his behavior was obvious to all concerned. "Father Maher was very pissed," Nocera conceded.[13] Not only did his church attendance waver, but Kennedy was doing the unpardonable. He was voting for abortion rights as a state legislator. Father Maher was a strong supporter of the church's pro-life position on abortion. The bishop openly complained about the "Culture of Death" in American society. Neither priest understood how society could condone a practice so abhorrent to them. Father Maher started to get calls. He never heard directly from Bishop Gelineau, but he was hearing from other church officials, "priest friends may have commented or priests who knew that he was a parishioner here," Maher said. There continued to be press coverage of Kennedy's involvement at Blessed Sacrament in the *Providence Journal*. This coverage upset Father Maher, since it no longer was the case. The newspaper was "constantly harping on the fact that he was teaching religious education here."[14] It had been true in 1987–88, but that was before the priest knew of Patrick's stance on abortion.

One night in 1989, Maher saw Kennedy at a 5:00 o'clock Mass. When the service was over, Patrick and he talked with no one else present, and Father Maher said: "I am beginning to feel used and I don't like the feeling. I am disappointed with your stand on abortion." As his pastor, Father Maher felt it was his responsibility to say something. The young man had upset him with how he was voting in the General Assembly. He wasn't singling Patrick out. If another parishioner in a leadership position voted in support of abortion, he would have told him the same thing. In his mind, abortion was wrong, no matter who was casting the vote. He knew Rose Kennedy had not raised her children that way. Patrick's grandmother respected the sanctity of life. Maher couldn't understand this lapse in Kennedy upbringing. The Kennedy family had so many pluses, he thought. They didn't get bogged down in the money problems the way so many politicians did. They didn't look out just for themselves when they achieved a powerful position. The Kennedys did so many things that the priest supported, but on this one issue, he felt, "I can't support them and I feel betrayed by them."[15]

Kennedy calmly replied to the priest. He must have been upset, although he didn't show it to Maher. "It is the church's fault for being derelict in its duties," Patrick said. "The church was forcing politicians to take the stand that they were. It had not done all that it should to teach its people about abortion. The church was remiss in not teaching clearly its stand on abortion." Since abortion had emerged in 1973 as a political issue following Supreme Court legalization in the landmark *Roe v. Wade* decision, the church had taken an unambiguous stand. But it was too late in Kennedy's mind. By then, abortion had gotten defined as a political issue. Politicians had been forced to jump one way or the other. Either they were pro-choice or pro-life. A canyon had been created between the two sides that no politician could overcome. The crucial mistake, according to Kennedy, was that the church "should have been doing its teaching mission in the years before abortion had become such a political hot potato." With that, Kennedy left Blessed Sacrament, and Father Maher never saw him in religious services again. He ran into Patrick several years later when Kennedy came to the church to present a citation to one of the parishioners for her community service. On the way in, he saw Maher and was very polite. "Good evening, Father," he said as he was sliding into his seat. The priest was polite in return. When the ceremony was completed, Kennedy left right away with no mention of the earlier confrontation.[16]

Kennedy continued to vote abortion rights in the General Assembly but to have a quiet presence on the issue. One day in May 1990, Patrick was scheduled to give a speech at Prout Memorial High School in South Kingston at a mother-daughter breakfast. It was a Catholic high school, and the organizing committee was thrilled that someone of Kennedy's stature would address the event. Committee members even arranged a short mention in the May 2 edition of the *Providence Journal*. That morning, Brother Daniel F. Casey, school superintendent for the Providence Diocese, saw the notice in the paper. He went over to a file drawer in the Office of Family Life at the diocese. The file contained information about the positions public officials had taken on abortion. Seeing that Kennedy had voted pro-choice, Casey ordered the Prout administration to withdraw the invitation. Casey said, "It would be inappropriate that he speak. His position [on abortion] runs opposite to what the school is teaching."[17]

Patrick learned of the cancellation two days before the breakfast and said, "I understand that the Church is being very careful about who is invited to speak at these things. But I think the manner in which it was handled obviously was disturbing. I don't think anybody likes being disinvited."[18] Although this was the first time such a cancellation had made the paper, it was not the first time Patrick had difficulties with the Catholic Church. Another time, he was scheduled to address the Mt. Pleasant Senior Citizens group, which met at St. Augustine's Church. The priest threatened to cancel but eventually let Kennedy speak after he agreed not to talk about abortion.[19] It would not be his last run-in with church officials. Patrick's relationship with the Catholic Church would remain a continuing challenge in his life.

7 Challenging the Leadership

With no opponent in 1990, Kennedy's reelection was a breeze. His staff produced a 5-minute video entitled *Our Vote Is Working* that emphasized the efforts Patrick had made on behalf of the Ninth District. Starting with his "It's Our Turn" election night speech, the ad showed how Kennedy had fought to clear up a dangerous intersection, straightened out problems at the Department of Children and the Families, and stood up to the gun lobby. With some rewriting of history, the video also claimed Kennedy had helped defeat the Newbay coal-fired plant because of his concern over air pollution. The video closed with personal testimonies from two neighborhood residents, Elena Leonelli and Frank DiPaolo, about how Patrick had stayed in the neighborhood, and from his father, who talked about how important caring about people was to the Kennedy family.[1]

But despite the overwhelming electoral endorsement, Kennedy felt something was missing from his public service. He had sponsored a few bills attempting to get grants for his neighborhood, and there had been efforts on gun control and power plant siting. However, the more he thought about the first term, the more he concluded he was missing the big picture. It dawned on him that just as his uncle President Kennedy had inspired national confidence 30 years ago, he had to restore public confidence in state government.[2] It made little sense to tinker with individual bills if the whole system was flawed. Surveys showed that large numbers of state voters felt that "you couldn't trust public officials to do what is right." With the help of several allies, such as Rickman and Driver, Patrick started to speak out on government reform such as the rules and open records. During Kennedy's 1988 campaign, his staff had tried to get Skeffington's committee votes, but their efforts hit a brick wall. Tabella used to call the clerk for the committee votes, but he discovered "You just could not find out how Jack Skeffington voted in the House Judiciary Committee."[3] Kennedy also was bothered by the tactics he saw in the legislature. More information needed to be made available to legislators before they cast ballots. It was ridiculous to get the budget the day before voting on a document funding all of state government. Every time one of these complaints was raised, the leadership ignored them. "They had started abusing Rodney and I, and they just started with Patrick. . . . I'm talking about name-calling and balling up their fists and all sorts of things. . . . They would yell and scream at us and threaten to beat us up physically," Rickman said. Patrick was shocked at this treatment. According to Rickman, "Patrick was a kid then. He had his book bag. He was in college. He was kind of cute. He didn't always dress up." When other legislators yelled at him, he didn't know how to respond. "He didn't yell back, he was just shocked that they would behave that way."[4]

One day, there was a disagreement about House rules, so Patrick went to a page to get the rules passed out. But when the young person requested permission to do this, his supervisor said, "Oh no, you can't pass those out." At that point, Patrick exploded. "He went storming up to Chris Boyle and said, 'I want these passed out. They're the rules. What the hell is the problem? If I have to pass them out myself, I'm going to pass them out.'" The rules were distributed, but not without some jabs from DeAngelis.[5] The Speaker loved to tease Patrick about his vulnerabilities. But unlike men who had been athletes when they were growing up, Kennedy didn't respond positively to that style. Even the Speaker noticed the problem. "I would always try to rib him a little bit and he never knew how to take me. I could kind of see in his eye he thought I was being serious," said DeAngelis. Kennedy seemed uncomfortable with the social life of the Assembly. "There always was a side of the legislature that was social in nature, whether it was playing golf or just hanging around and having a pop after the session or just going to a local restaurant," DeAngelis noted. "I never saw that he participated in that aspect of it."[6]

A few people, however, were keeping their eye on Patrick. Ever since the infamous incinerator incident in 1985, Harwood and Caruolo had been on the outs with the leadership. As Kennedy's personal relationship with the Speaker deteriorated, the young representative drew closer to the two pariahs. Others around the Statehouse made fun of Kennedy for his poor public speaking. Associates of the Speaker used to ship recordings of Patrick's halting speeches to radio talk show host Howie Carr in Boston as well as other reporters. Carr would play them on the air and make fun of Kennedy's awkwardness.[7] Yet Caruolo could see that Patrick "had certain social skills which were overlooked by many people. His public speaking skills were less than they are today. Most people in this building focused on that, not his personal social skills. . . . He had skills that were far more advanced than anyone gave him credit for reading people and divining their intentions toward him and in dealing with people."[8]

Kennedy started to identify with the "troublemakers," as they were called. Rickman and Driver were the ringleaders, but Kushner was in that crowd, as were Harwood and Caruolo. The seating arrangement on the floor had Kennedy and Kushner side by side with Rickman and Driver in the row right behind them. Caruolo sat in front of Kennedy, and Harwood sat in front of Caruolo. The area was called the "Red Light" district because of the tendency of those legislators to vote against the leadership.[9] The budget became the focus of reform efforts. In a break with tradition, Rickman started to offer budget amendments. Typically, he would get 10 or 15 votes out of 100. But if he found the right issue, like more money for needy children, sometimes as many as 30 legislators voted his way.[10] The leadership started to get nervous about their margins. A victory of 90 to 10 made them look overwhelmingly powerful, but votes of 70 to 30 or 65 to 35 gave them the appearance of mere mortals. Perception is everything in politics, and the group of dissidents was growing. Even DeAngelis could sense the change. The 1990 budget debate had been acrimonious. The Speaker had been forced to pass the budget in a hurry to get it off the floor before "it got opened up and torn apart."[11]

After the 1990 session, DeAngelis appointed an ad hoc Rules Committee designed to see what procedural adjustments needed to be made. The Speaker's trusted lieutenant Boyle was put in charge of the committee, with Patrick as one of the members. DeAngelis was not keen on liberalizing the rules. He told fellow legislators, "You have to understand that the more you liberalize [the rules], it's going to make your job harder." The Rhode Island legislature was a citizen's legislature where members were paid $300 a year and had full-time jobs and outside businesses. Their task was to have a 60-day session, pass the budget, and forget about all of the crazy bills legislators wanted to pass. The state didn't need a full-time legislature staffed by professional politicians, thought DeAngelis. In his mind, "The more you fiddle with the rules, the more you make the rules more open, then you have to understand you are moving toward a full-time General Assembly."[12]

When the ad hoc Rules Committee had a meeting, the biggest point of contention was how long to leave the budget on the floor for discussion. In 1990, it had been on the floor for two days, and the leadership had seen the disaster that ensued. Reformers were arguing for a longer period; so members would have the budget for five full days before voting. Boyle agreed that there was "no reason in this day and age you can't have bills at least 24 hours in advance." But a period as long as five days was a problem. Boyle worried about powerful interest groups getting to the members. Too much discussion would give groups time to lobby legislators and would weaken leadership control. The House whip wanted to "balance the need to have a citizen's assembly where people have to work and have families against the need to respond to the type of openness that was and still is moving the debate along."[13]

At the beginning, Kennedy worked with the committee. His adviser Tabella had been interested in the rules subject for several years dating back to his work with RIPIRG. So had Driver and Rickman, each of whom understood that Kennedy's name would attract a lot of attention to the reform effort. Boyle made a point of calling Kennedy periodically to fill him in on what other members were suggesting and what Cornwell, who was acting as staff adviser, was doing with the proposals. Cornwell had been informed by the leaders that "there were not many things that the leadership or the party generally wanted changed. It was in part a little fine-tuning and maybe to vent some of the opposition and give people who were complaining about procedures a chance to get their ideas in shape and looked at, though with a pretty good certainty that they would be voted down in most cases."[14] When Kennedy's suggestions were submitted to the committee, the group turned down most of the proposals.

From the leadership standpoint, Kennedy's reforms shifted too much power to individual legislators. In Cornwell's mind, there was a constant "tug of war between the individual members and the leadership. The leadership wants to be able to lead effectively and determine legislative outputs. The members are very anxious to be able to make a name for themselves, which means introducing legislation that is in their own little package." DeAngelis was willing to open things up a little bit, but according to Cornwell, "The leadership was careful not to congressionalize the thing, not to lose the ultimate ability to control the major pieces of legislation and what came out. If you lose that, then the system becomes very difficult to operate at all in relation to the major issues that need to be dealt with."[15]

By December, committee recommendations were not ready, so Boyle suggested that when the General Assembly resumed at the beginning of January, the old rules be adopted as an interim measure while the committee continued its deliberations. This suggestion infuriated Kennedy to the point that he decided to take decisive action on his own. On December 31, 1990, he called a press conference in front of the House doors with the chamber locked shut and demanded that the rules be opened up. Good government could not be served, he said, unless there was adequate information available both to legislators and the public. Rank-and-file legislators needed reasonable time to study the state budget before having to vote on it. Under Kennedy's proposal, the budget could not be voted on until at least five days after members received copies of it. Kennedy also proposed to make it more difficult for committee chairs to kill a bill without a vote, and more difficult to suspend House rules and speed legislation through. In 1990, he complained, "The full House of Representatives passed a state budget of $1.5 billion after only one day of debate. The same has been true year after year. This is obviously not a process that inspires confidence." He said the ad hoc House Rules Committee was not taking seriously proposals to reform the House rules. He noted that the committee had held only one meeting and not proposed any significant changes. "To my disappointment," he said, "the rules committee never cast a single vote and never submitted a proposal in writing to change a single rule." A number of groups showed up at the press conference to support Kennedy's proposals, such as Common Cause, the League of Women Voters, the Audubon Society, and the Alliance for Lesbian and Gay Civil Rights.[16]

The day before, DeAngelis had heard about the impending press conference and was outraged. In his mind, Kennedy was striking off on his own. "If he was part of the committee that was working on the rules, it just seemed to us the fair thing for him would be to work within the committee and if there was any credit to be taken, he could take it within the committee since he had opted to be a member of that committee." Boyle publicly criticized Kennedy for "political grandstanding." The Speaker called Kennedy personally. Not only was DeAngelis upset about the press conference, but he understood that the next day, January 1, which was the opening day of the General Assembly, Kennedy planned to hold up floor proceedings on the rules. DeAngelis told Kennedy that his move "just was not done on opening day. People are there with their families and friends to be sworn in." Kennedy should at least wait until the following day, when there could be a debate on the rules. Kennedy acknowledged that point, but he said to DeAngelis, "You cannot, you will not be able to, I will not permit you to, or I'll fight you on the floor if you try to adopt your rules for even one day."

DeAngelis then gave Kennedy some friendly advice. The young man had asked to be on the Rules Committee and had been made a part of the team. Therefore, reasoned the Speaker, "he should work within the committee."[17]

Boyle talked to Kennedy. He had heard the news about the press conference literally five minutes before it happened. "What's the matter? Is there a problem?" Boyle asked Kennedy. It slowly dawned on Boyle that there was a transformation in Kennedy. "Everything was going to be as to what was beneficial to [Kennedy] politically. Everyone else be damned."[18] The next day, the Speaker read Patrick's critical comments in the newspaper and had another conversation with the young man. From the reported statements, the Speaker inferred that Kennedy had said things "derogatory toward the leadership." DeAngelis decided to call him on it since "we had had a pleasant discussion the previous day." At the end of that conversation, Kennedy told the Speaker, "I just want you to know Joe, this is nothing personal between us. I have enjoyed working with you. This is political and this is something I have to do. I hope you understand that."[19] It was the beginning of the end of Kennedy's relationship with the Speaker of the House.

While the rules debate was intensifying, a state crisis was brewing that would transform the political landscape. A new governor, Bruce Sundlun, had been elected in 1990 and was to be sworn into office on January 1, 1991. Sundlun was a brash millionaire, full of confidence. He had been the chief executive officer of the Outlet Company, which had owned a major department store and WJAR-TV, the most popular television station in the state. On December 19, as part of his transition, Sundlun had been called to a meeting at the Statehouse with federal banking officials and outgoing Governor DiPrete. Present were William Seidman, head of the Federal Deposit Insurance Corporation, former Senator Roger Jepson, head of the National Credit Union Association, and a man who was president of the Federal Reserve Bank of Boston. The men gave Sundlun some startling news. Seidman informed the new governor "he had a serious fiscal crisis on his hands." Banking officials had been inspecting the state's credit unions and found many could not qualify for federal insurance. The state agency known as RISDIC, the Rhode Island Share and Deposit Indemnity Corporation, was responsible for guaranteeing deposits at the credit unions, but it lacked sufficient financial resources. RISDIC had only $25 million to insure deposits, not nearly enough to cover the $475 million owed by institutions on the verge of default. In Seidman's opinion, "he didn't think that RISDIC was strong enough to survive." Senator Jepson was equally sharp in his criticisms of the state banking system. The Federal Reserve was prepared to step in with cash to help those credit unions that were solvent in order to avoid crippling runs, but beyond that there wasn't too much it could do.[20] What the officials were saying was that the state's banking system was on the verge of collapse, and the FDIC was not in a position to stop it.

It was a bittersweet moment for Sundlun. The 1990 election had been his third try for the governorship. He had lost overwhelmingly to DiPrete in 1986. In 1988, he had come very close, but lost by a few thousand votes. Now just a month earlier, he had beaten DiPrete by 75 to 25 percent. The state was mired in a severe economic downturn due to the collapse of a speculative bubble in the real estate market, and

DiPrete had become very unpopular. He later would plead guilty to extortion and bribery charges and serve time in jail. Ironically, in light of his ultimate victory, Sundlun had come very close to backing out of the 1990 race. One of his Democratic primary opponents, Providence Mayor Joe Paolino, the front-runner for the nomination, had through intermediaries broached a bald political swap. In return for not running in the primary, Sundlun would be named to the next vacancy on the Rhode Island Supreme Court. Sundlun agreed to the secret arrangement, only to find Paolino, confident over his own electoral prospects, nixing the deal at the last minute. In pique at Paolino's reneging on the agreement, Sundlun entered the primary as an underdog, beat Paolino decisively, and then won the general election.[21] The three combined races had cost Sundlun more than $6 million of his own money. The campaigns against DiPrete and Sundlun's own Democratic opponents had been hard fought. To beat Paolino, Sundlun had helped spread a scurrilous rumor that Paolino was a closet homosexual. There was no evidence to back up the charges, but in close-knit Rhode Island, the slanderous rumor was widely circulated and hurt Paolino politically with some undecided voters.[22] Sundlun himself had been the subject of scandalous rumors about his own personal life in his earlier races against DiPrete, who accused the Democrat of a swinging lifestyle. After all the personal abuse he had suffered, Sundlun was being told by authoritative men from Washington, D.C., that major financial institutions in the state were failing. It was not the way he had planned to start his governorship.

The governor-elect said, "I just got elected and this problem is going to be mine in two weeks. I want to know based on your experience what can a governor do in this situation." His initial opinion was that the credit union problem wasn't much different from the national savings and loan crisis. "I just want to know what are my options," Sundlun asked plaintively. Seidman said, "You have three choices." The first choice was, "You can pledge the full faith and credit of the state." The state would have to borrow money and put in whatever funds were required to bring the credit unions up to standard. Sundlun jumped in. "I don't want to start a political discussion. But the state doesn't have any full faith and credit to pledge at the moment because the biggest problem that I know I have is the deficit." Sundlun knew there was no spare money in the budget. "What's second?" Sundlun demanded. Seidman said, "Private sources." The governor-elect asked what that meant. Seidman explained, "Your banks. Go to your banks and ask them to put in money on some sort of basis." Sundlun replied, "Mr. Seidman, I don't know what you know about Rhode Island, but in my judgment in Rhode Island that means one bank and one man. His name is Terry Murray and the bank is Fleet." He turned to Governor DiPrete and announced, "Governor, I think you should set up a meeting with him immediately. If you don't mind, I'd like to attend." DiPrete whispered something to his policy aide Sally Dowling, who left the room, and came back holding up four fingers. The meeting was set for 4:00 that afternoon. The third choice was liquidating the bankrupt credit unions—selling off assets and seeing how much could be raised to pay off the depositors. Sundlun asked Seidman, "Based on your experience, what can you expect in liquidation?" Seidman said 35 percent. The credit unions had around $1.3 billion in assets. If the state was going to realize only a third of it, it would lose nearly a billion dollars and recover $400 to $500 million. The entire state budget wasn't much bigger than $1 billion.[23]

That afternoon, Sundlun went to Fleet Bank to see Murray. Neither DiPrete nor any of his staff showed up. As much as the crisis itself, that enraged the governor-elect and confirmed his poor impression of his predecessor. Murray disposed of Sundlun's request quickly. The bank didn't have $475 million sitting around, and even if it did, federal regulators wouldn't let him put the money in. Sundlun raised the issue of Marquette Credit Union, which was located in Woonsocket, Murray's hometown. "Take over Marquette," he implored. "You can be a hero there." But Murray had no interest in the troubled credit union.[24]

After leaving Murray's office, Sundlun wrote a letter to Governor DiPrete reciting the three options the state had been given. Sundlun wrote, "I recommend that you immediately start some sort of process looking toward liquidation." The letter was delivered that night, but Sundlun never heard another word from DiPrete on the issue until December 31, DiPrete's last in office, when the outgoing governor dropped off a two- or three-page plan that didn't solve the problem. Sundlun notified the top leaders of the General Assembly about the impending crisis. He wanted them to know the scope of the crisis in case he needed emergency legislation.[25]

In the ensuing two weeks, other credit unions in the state started to hemorrhage. Public runs were beginning at two of the financial institutions, Heritage and Jefferson. There were questions about whether insiders had heard about the problems and were withdrawing funds. Sundlun decided to pursue the receivership route: liquidate the credit unions and try to recover assets. But he was worried that whatever assets existed would be eaten up in fees. There might be nothing for the 300,000 people in the state, nearly one-third of the state's population, who had credit union deposits. Credit unions were the "poor man's banks" in Rhode Island.[26] In the prosperous 1980s, when the economy was booming and lucrative profits were being made in real estate, many working-class people in the state had put their savings and retirement money in credit unions because the interest rates were percentage points higher than the banks. Even charitable and religious institutions had been sucked in by the extra points of interest. Every legislator had districts full of people with accounts in one of the state's 55 credit unions.

At 6:00 p.m. on December 31, though, Sundlun learned something that called for a drastic change of plans. He and his wife were getting ready to go to a party when another car pulled up. Ed McElroy, the head of the state AFL-CIO, and Joe Walsh, the former mayor of Warwick and a prominent lawyer and lobbyist, got out. McElroy was on the RISDIC board, and Walsh was its lawyer. McElroy handed Sundlun an envelope containing a one-paragraph letter saying the RISDIC Board of Directors had met that afternoon and voted to put themselves into conservatorship due to lack of funds. Sundlun remembered his reaction. "Screw this, now we got to move fast." He went to the party and talked to his legal counsel, Sheldon Whitehouse, a talented young man who later would become U.S. attorney and Rhode Island attorney general. In the preceding weeks, Whitehouse had researched the statutes for ways of handling the banking crisis. He had found an obscure state statue, on the books since the Roosevelt days, which gave the governor the power to seize and close financial institutions experiencing financial crisis. It had never been used before. The governor decided to change his plan. There was no time for liquidation. The next day, New Year's Day and his inaugural day, he would close the credit unions. "Write me a speech saying that," he told Whitehouse. Sundlun also instructed his aide to alert the state police. "I want cops on every one of them from the moment I start talking," he said. It was not that he was concerned about people breaking into the credit unions and stealing money. He was concerned about officials destroying records.[27]

On New Year's Eve, Boyle learned the credit unions were to be closed the next day. He was at the First Night fireworks in Providence when DeAngelis informed him about the problem. There had been rumors of difficulties in the credit unions over the preceding weeks, but no one knew exactly how deep the problem was or that the credit unions were on the verge of total collapse. DeAngelis told Boyle that Sundlun was going to close all the credit unions the next day. Boyle had a strange sinking feeling as soon as he heard the news. "I knew in my mind that things were never going to be the same," he recalled. "No matter what happened, there are things that control one's life and this was going to be one of those factors that would control our political life." He realized, "We didn't create it, but we would have to deal with it."[28]

Caruolo was surprised when the credit unions were closed. "That was a closely held secret. We were stunned," he said. But he wasn't surprised there was a problem. As a practicing attorney, he had heard about questionable loans made by credit unions in the late 1980s. Developers would come in and, with very little collateral, be given million-dollar loans to start new real estate projects. Both Caruolo and Harwood had voted against legislation a few years earlier that would have opened up credit union operations even more. Quietly, Caruolo had advised clients of his that "all of their money should not be kept in the institutions that paid the greatest interest rates, which invariably were credit unions."[29]

With the closing of financial institutions, hundreds of thousands of people around Rhode Island lost access to their money. Personal checks from closed institutions were no longer honored at businesses. People's life savings were tied up, often hundreds of thousands of dollars. Charitable organizations and educational institutions that had accounts in the credit unions lost access to their cash. The financial disaster could not have come at a worse time for the state. The economy already was in free-fall, with unemployment rising and the state budget hemorrhaging fast. The fingers of political blame were being pointed at the insider dealing—long a problem in the state. It's not what you know, but who you know, the common saying went. Just two years earlier, Governor DiPrete had bought a property one day, gotten its zoning classification changed, and sold the improved property right away for $400,000 more than he had purchased it for.

The credit union crisis appeared to confirm what many had long suspected. Something was amiss in Rhode Island government. In 1987, a bill had been proposed to eliminate RISDIC and place state financial institutions under the FDIC. Credit unions rose up in arms over that proposal. Through the intercession of Representative Bob Bianchini, a friend of the leadership, the bill had been killed in committee with very little discussion. In Caruolo's eyes, "The legislature bore significant responsibility for what happened. . . . We saw it as some type of confirmation of the abuses which we had been attempting to point out since the mid-80s."[30] Harwood added, "It cast more suspicion on the General Assembly" and created "a black eye."[31]

Sundlun appointed an outside commission to investigate the origins of the crisis. It was headed by Brown University President Vartan Gregorian, whom Sundlun described as a "tough Armenian from New York." Speaking of the report, he told Gregorian, who had just arrived at Brown in 1989, "It's got to be done by someone who is honest and independent and you're the new boy on the block. I'm assuming you have got the intellectual skill and balls to do it. I know you must be tough enough, otherwise you wouldn't survive in New York as long as you did."[32] In the House, there was emotional debate over how to handle the problem. Sundlun's initial position was to marshal assets, keep overhead low, sell the assets, and pay off the depositors slowly over three or four years. No one would get more than the official $100,000 ceiling on deposits contained in the RISDIC charter. "They made a bad investment decision. They should have been putting their money right in the bank," Sundlun told DeAngelis.[33] The House leadership rejected that approach. Widows, senior citizens, and religious organizations had their savings in credit unions. Don't take a dime of depositor's money, the leadership was told. But DeAngelis could not change Sundlun's mind. The problem was the overall cost of the bailout. The faster you repaid depositors and the more you covered above $100,000, the costlier the solution became. Sundlun was a pragmatic businessman. His goal was to solve the problem, not bankrupt the state for years to come. Sundlun wanted the state's nine banks to help out by "lending $150 million on the note of the state." He would then shove the money out immediately to the smallest depositors to ease the temporary pain. The bankers agreed, but then reneged. After Sundlun saw a headline proclaiming "Banks Decline to Fund Credit Union Crisis," he was forced to go to the public market, which took two months, but the bonds sold out in an hour. "The fucking bankers were just wrong," he later argued.[34]

As leaders fought over the proper response, public opinion turned nasty. Depositors organized to demand full repayment. Anything less would be a betrayal of the public trust, they argued. Every day, angry people crowded into the Rotunda at the Statehouse. The atmosphere was frightening. "People would flock in, they'd fill the Rotunda, they had bull horns to talk to each other. It would reverberate down the corridors. People were locking the doors to their offices. We were afraid there might even be a riot," Cornwell recalled.[35] The crisis dominated the news.

For Kennedy, the turmoil could not have come at a better time. His relationship with DeAngelis had been deteriorating. Kennedy had gone public on December 31 with his press conference criticizing the Speaker on the rules. The crisis was a godsend. "It played into his idea that the House was not being run correctly, that decisions were made behind closed doors, that each individual representative didn't have the correct say in what's going to happen," said his aide Nocera. If Kennedy's reforms had been adopted, the credit union crisis might not have happened. Nocera said, "He was able to use that as a comparison point that all the things that happened wrong in the credit union crisis were because there weren't these reforms that Patrick was pushing."[36]

Kennedy became a crucial communications link in the controversy. Depositors were having difficulty obtaining access to top leaders, as the Speaker constantly was in meetings with the governor. There were hundreds of depositors at the Statehouse every day. "They couldn't get access to the leadership. This is how we got to play a role. . . . We had constituency outreach," said Rickman. Kennedy went to credit union meetings, met with reform groups, talked to the governor, and testified before the Budget Committee. Other than gun control and the rules, it was his most significant leadership on a major issue. On this subject, "Patrick was the leader. He put in the most energy, he called us and took us places. A lot of the ideas were his," recalled Rickman. For Kennedy, the central issue was indebtedness. The biggest problem was depositors over $100,000. The House leadership wanted to pay them all off, regardless of the amount of their deposits. Patrick opposed that. He didn't want to give a blank check to "the high rollers." He did feel there should be an exemption for nonprofits, such as churches, charitable institutions, and scholarship funds, which should get the full amount. Eventually, he settled on a reimbursement plan of no more than $500,000 for individuals. This would cover ordinary people and keep the overall costs of the bailout down to a reasonable level. Not wanting the new state agency, the Depositors Economic Protection Corporation (DEPCO), to take on a life of its own, he proposed the agency would end after 10 years. He also argued the DEPCO bonds should be able to be called in if interest rates went down. Ultimately, Kennedy was not successful on all of his proposals, but it was "the best public discussion ever had in the legislature," said Rickman.[37] After extensive debate, the governor and General Assembly approved a bill establishing DEPCO, which would take over the assets of the closed institutions. Assets would be sold, and depositors reimbursed in full. DEPCO would sell bonds, the proceeds of which would be used to pay back the depositors. The sales tax would be raised three-quarters of a percentage point to finance DEPCO and pay interest on the bonds. The entire cost of the package was estimated at $450 million, and the annual cost to the state would be around $20 million a year.

With discussion about the credit union crisis in full force and public opinion inflamed, opponents of the party leadership raised embarrassing questions. One of the objects of inquiry was Sal Mancini, head of the state Democratic party. Three days before Central Credit Union in North Providence closed, Mancini withdrew nearly $100,000. He was a member of the board of directors but denied having any inside knowledge that Central would be closed on New Year's Day. Most Democrats either defended their party leader or kept quiet. The one exception was Patrick. When asked his opinion, Kennedy replied, "We've got to articulate a policy on this credit union crisis, but how can we articulate it when our chief (Democratic) spokesman is clouded by this?"[38] Kennedy still had not forgotten Mancini's demand in 1988 as Patrick was beginning his General Assembly run to "wait his turn." Now the party chief was on the hot seat for an alleged impropriety.

Information came to light regarding a possible conflict of interest by Speaker DeAngelis. DeAngelis was on the board of directors of one of the closed credit unions and had worked out a deal to get his credit union opened quickly. Rickman discovered that DeAngelis's law firm was being paid to represent one of the insurance companies that covered the credit unions. The firm would earn a couple of hundred thousand dollars for the work. Rickman sent DeAngelis a letter complaining about the conflict. The Speaker should not be on the rostrum during any of the credit union discussions, Rickman argued. It was a blatant conflict and one that should be avoided at all costs. The Speaker called Rickman upstairs, where he faced the entire leadership team—the

Speaker, Lamb, and Boyle. "You are an ass and an idiot," the Speaker said. "You don't know what you are talking about." At that point, Rickman pulled out a copy of the agreement between DeAngelis's law firm and the insurance company and showed it to the Speaker. DeAngelis was stunned. Boyle wanted to know where he had gotten the document. "You probably should be arrested for stealing," he said. "I didn't steal it," Rickman replied. "Someone sent it to me. And if you press me, I'll tell you their name." He looked straight at Tom Lamb. Lamb, of course, hadn't sent the document, but Rickman wanted at least to create some suspicion among the ranks. Rickman told DeAngelis that if he appeared on the Speaker's rostrum the next day for a debate on the credit union, Rickman would file an ethics complaint.[39]

The following day, February 4, 1991, Rickman called a press conference. With him were Harwood, Caruolo, Frank Anzeveno, and Joe DeLorenzo, all bitter foes of the Speaker. Although they were not ideological bedfellows, Harwood and Caruolo had befriended Rickman to further their own war against DeAngelis. The Speaker had major conflicts of interest on the credit unions, Rickman told the assembled reporters. DeAngelis's law firm represented key principals in the dispute, he said. The Speaker should recuse himself from any aspect of legislation relating to the closed credit unions. The group also complained about DeAngelis's autocratic leadership style. "Three or four leadership people make all the decisions in the House," said Caruolo. "That's not how a democratically elected House should operate."[40]

The press conference was interesting as much for who was not there as for who was present. None of Rickman's liberal allies showed up—not Driver or Kushner or Kennedy. "The liberal reformers were chicken," Rickman explained. "Rodney [Driver] respected [the leaders]. . . . He liked the way they threw around their power. He wanted to take it away from them, but he was very impressed."[41] For her part, Kushner didn't attend because she felt Rickman was "off the wall." In her personal journal, she wrote of the press conference, "This is an explosive situation. . . . [They] pointed out that Joe DeAngelis' firm would be representing an insurance company that would be defending the interests of the directors of the credit union. . . . The statement at the press conference went too far. Ray claimed that Joe D. is making a personal profit. . . . This is hogwash." Kushner agreed with Rickman that in Rhode Island, you couldn't "have a person who is a lawyer in a large firm be the Speaker of the House because there is always going to be the appearance of a conflict of interest." But she felt Rickman had "lost control of his anger."[42] As for Kennedy, Rickman had invited him to the press conference, but Patrick hadn't wanted to attend. According to Rickman, Patrick had an aversion to doing things like this with other people. "Patrick, as much as possible, likes to go solo," Rickman explained.[43]

This was more than backbenchers engaged in guerrilla warfare. It was a call to revolution. DeAngelis hired a private detective to investigate Rickman. When the maverick confronted the Speaker on this move, DeAngelis wryly commented that "he was just trying to get to know the members better."[44] The Speaker also called Channel 36, the public television station funded by the General Assembly, to complain about Rickman having a show on the air.[45] For his part, following the conflict-of-interest allegations, DeAngelis was subjected to two hours of grilling by three reporters from the *Providence Journal*. "They had done their research and they knew every single aspect about me and my personal life, my background and whatever assets I had," he said. When it was over, the Speaker felt "they had not laid a glove on me."[46] But Bakst wrote a devastating Sunday column about the press conference and DeAngelis's "perceived conflicts of interest." The Speaker had told the columnist, "I'm not ashamed of anything that I've done in this Assembly." But the clear implication of the story was that DeAngelis had serious ethics problems.[47]

At that point, DeAngelis didn't see Kennedy as one of the rebels. Despite their policy disagreements, Patrick always had been nice to him. The Speaker considered their relationship "friendly" and "respectful."[48] It therefore shocked the Speaker when in late February, two weeks after the Rickman press conference, Patrick publicly called for the Speaker's resignation. Kennedy faulted DeAngelis for "not being more forthcoming about possible conflicts in handling legislation to rescue depositors in closed financial institutions." The Speaker was dishonest, Patrick proclaimed, and should resign his post.[49] A reporter asked DeAngelis about the Kennedy comments. The Speaker said he was sure Kennedy hadn't really meant to call him dishonest. Another reporter called Patrick. Had he meant to label the Speaker dishonest? "Yes, I did," Patrick replied.[50] DeAngelis was beginning to reach the same conclusion Boyle had about Kennedy in the rules fight. "He was being groomed. . . . I was probably viewed as a politician who had been punched around quite a bit the last couple of months. It would be an easy target for him to take on the establishment. I would guess he was advised you have to get a name for yourself as the reformer and this is an opportunity for you."[51]

DeAngelis was weakened but still one of the most powerful political figures in the state. He called on his most loyal troops. "There's a whole class of people up there who all have jobs," he explained. "They're all part of the political system and here was this young guy banging on the leader of the system that provided their jobs for them." The Speaker's staff fed information on Patrick to Boston radio talk show host Howie Carr. The host "loved to pick on [Patrick]," DeAngelis said. "He called poor Patrick 'Patches.' You know the old song, 'Patches, I'm depending on you son.' He gave him the name 'Patches.'" One day on the floor, Kennedy spoke on an amendment having to do with the income tax. The Assembly was considering a surcharge on the wealthy, a position Patrick supported. Scott Nova, a lobbyist for Ocean State Action, a liberal advocacy group that was in favor of the surcharge, was sitting next to him. Rhode Island was one of the few legislatures in the country where lobbyists actually were allowed on the floor during official deliberations. Kennedy made his remarks and sat down, but while the discussion was going on, Patrick forgot to turn off his microphone. He turned to Nova and, in a very clear and distinct voice picked up on the television, said, "What do I say now?"[52]

Statehouse insiders made sure a videotape of the fumbling performance was sent to a reporter who was writing a Kennedy profile for the *Boston Phoenix*, who included the anecdote in his story.[53] Kennedy was not amused. He said, "I just think it's crazy that you've got the speaker's office staff making tapes to try to embarrass me." When asked by a reporter about his reaction to the controversy, DeAngelis advised Kennedy to lighten up. "It's too bad he has to take these things so seriously," DeAngelis said.

General Assembly staffers also circulated rumors that Patrick sent copies of all his legislation to his father's Senate office for approval before submitting the bills. A reporter asked Kennedy about this rumor. "That's absolutely ridiculous," Kennedy replied. "This is why people are so scared to speak up up there. They know that if you do, there's a million and one things they can get you on. . . . They're going to try to discredit me, and I've got to be vigilant not to let them put me in a position where I'm vulnerable."[54]

8 Surviving Palm Beach

With the stress of taking on the Speaker, Kennedy needed a vacation. The General Assembly session had been the most tumultuous in recent memory. He was in a life-or-death struggle with one of the state's most powerful political figures, and it wasn't clear who was going to win. Easter weekend was coming up, and his father had reserved the family compound in Palm Beach, Florida. It would be a time to relax and get his father's advice. Patrick's personal life was in shambles. He had broken up with his girlfriend, Kathleen O'Brien, the previous summer. O'Brien was a graduate of Villanova University whose father was a family court judge in Pennsylvania. She came from a big Irish Catholic family that was strongly Democratic.[1] College roommate Vallee described her as "sweet, genuine, a nice person, and cute," the type of person "you could bring home to Mom."[2] But the relationship had not jelled. "Her schedule was being made around me, and she didn't like that," Kennedy explained.[3]

The upcoming Easter weekend seemed the ideal getaway. The Palm Beach residence at 1095 North Ocean Boulevard had been in the family since 1933, when Patrick's grandfather had purchased the property at the height of the Great Depression for $120,000. The house, known as "La Guerida," had been built for Rodman Wanamaker of Philadelphia in 1923 with a Mediterranean-style design. It had an orange tile roof, a tiled living room, and a 176-foot beach.[4] Owned by the Joseph P. Kennedy Foundation, the residence was jointly controlled by Ted and his sisters. Each weekend, different members of the extended Kennedy family took turns staying at the place. Patrick and Ted would be there this Easter, along with Jean Smith and her four children: Stephen Jr., William, Amanda, and Kym. Patrick did not like Palm Beach. Deep down, he felt the old-line families in that city had never accepted the Kennedys. "The Palm Beach lifestyle is the lifestyle of the idle rich. We could have taken that. But my family has a legacy of public service," he said. The problem with Palm Beach, he felt, was that its wealthy "are more worried about how to get into clubs and golf courses than they are about social justice."[5]

Friday, March 29, was Good Friday. The family had attended St. Edward's Catholic Church in observance of Lent. Dinner had been served in the courtyard to the west of the house, after which the family played charades and a word game. Later, Patrick, Amanda, and William, a 30-year-old Georgetown University medical student, went out dancing at Lulu's, a trendy Palm Beach club. Patrick had drunk half a rum and Coke, a ginger ale, and a sip of champagne, before returning well before midnight. "We were sort of proud of ourselves about getting a decent night's sleep," Patrick said.[6] Ted, however, could not sleep. He had been reminiscing with his sister Jean about his brother-in-law, the late Stephen Smith, who had died from lung cancer. "The conversation was a very emotional conversation, a very difficult one. . . . I was not able to think about sleeping."[7] Around 11:30 p.m., he awakened Patrick and William and asked if they wanted to go out to Au Bar, a popular restaurant and bar in the area. Arriving at the spot, they sat at a table next to a stranger named Anne Mercer. Noticing a sad look on Patrick's face, she joked, "You look like you're having a great time."[8] "Who are you to say anything?" replied Senator Kennedy, defending what he took as a rude comment to his son. He introduced Mercer to his son Patrick, of whom he was very proud. Mercer snapped, "Am I supposed to be impressed?"[9] A brief argument ensued at the table.

Michele Cassone, a 27-year-old waitress at Testa's Restaurant, arrived at the bar around 1:00 a.m. She had gone there with her roommate, Gaynor Gwynne, the daughter of *Munsters* TV star Fred Gwynne. A young man she didn't know asked her to dance with him, but she turned him down. The same young man, Patrick Kennedy, approached her at the end of the night and asked, "Well, if you won't dance with me, will you stay and have a drink and talk with me?"[10] They started talking, and Patrick invited Cassone back to the estate. She got into her gold Toyota Corolla around 3:15 a.m. and followed Kennedy's rental car back to the estate. While Patrick's date unfolded, William Smith stayed at the bar, where he had met a 29-year-old woman from Jupiter, Florida, Patricia Bowman. They danced and she went back with William to the family compound. The next morning, Smith told Patrick, with whom William was sharing a room, that he had sex with the young woman out on the lawn. Did you wear a condom? Patrick inquired. No, his cousin responded. "But thank God I pulled out."[11] There was a scrumptious breakfast, with Patrick consuming three scrambled eggs, half a pound of bacon, and three English muffins. It amazed the cook because, as thin as Patrick was, "you'd think he never ate a meal in his life."[12]

At 2:00 p.m. on Saturday, March 30, Bowman reported to Palm Beach police she had been sexually assaulted at the Kennedy compound around 4:00 a.m. She was escorted to the rape treatment center at Humana Hospital Palm Beach. She told police William Smith had tackled her near the swimming pool and forcibly assaulted her. Smith shortly would be charged with sexual battery, Florida's equivalent of rape. If convicted, he faced a maximum penalty of 15 years in prison. The media feeding frenzy began right away. On Monday, Nocera's brother called him and said, "There's something with the Kennedys at Palm Beach." Sure, Nocera responded. It was April Fool's Day, and he thought his brother was kidding. Five minutes later, he received a call from *A Current Affair*, one of the new tabloid shows that specialized in gossip, but

Nocera still thought it was a joke. "Who would call me from *A Current Affair?*" he thought to himself.[13]

Nocera went over to Patrick's house around 5:30 p.m. Patrick was there, along with Tony Marcella, one of Patrick's friends from Massachusetts. Patrick had arrived from Palm Beach on a noon flight. Nocera told Patrick about the call and asked what had happened. "There was some incident, but it was nothing major," Patrick reported. The state representative didn't volunteer any further details, and as a loyal assistant, Nocera didn't ask. Patrick and Tony left to go see the popular movie, *Teenage Mutant Ninja Turtles.* Kennedy didn't want to be around the house that evening. Nocera talked with the senator's staff and received some advice from Ben Zwinger, Ted's political director. Zwinger advised, "Don't answer any press calls, this is going to blow over in three days." This prediction turned out to be well off the mark. The phone calls cascaded quickly, enveloping Patrick in a tidal wave. The district office had an answering service staffed by Nocera and his wife. *Providence Journal* reporter Bakst called Nocera, leaving messages the staffer took to be threatening. "If you don't talk to me, it's going to be worse," Bakst warned in one message.[14] Ted's office put out a brief statement on Monday through his press secretary saying, "Senator Kennedy was visiting Palm Beach this weekend. He had absolutely no involvement in the alleged incident." The next day, Patrick conducted a short interview with the *Providence Journal.* He said he knew nothing about the incident, except to say he was not involved. He claimed to have been asleep at the time of the incident and did not know the woman involved. "The girl is not someone I know. She was not a guest of mine. I assume she was a guest of one of my cousins," he said. Patrick refused to say which cousins were at the compound over the weekend and said he had just found out about the incident from a Florida newspaper account on Monday. He described the weekend as a "traditional family Easter."[15]

On Wednesday, April 3, the *New York Post* and *Daily News* ran stories reporting the Kennedys picked up two women at a bar. "Disco music was pulsating through the small, intimate nightclub when the three Kennedys walked in," an article claimed.[16] The day the story came out, Patrick attended a session of the General Assembly, and it was a complete circus. Ted's office had advised Nocera to "just get him in and get him on the floor. Then he won't have to talk to the press."[17] But that was impossible. Unlike the U.S. Capitol, where an underground trolley takes members to the Senate floor, in Rhode Island legislators enter the Assembly through the front door of the Statehouse and up a long marble staircase to the House floor. Reporters wanted to know what happened at the family's Palm Beach estate. Was it true he, his father, and cousin William had partied until 3:00 a.m. at a posh nightclub? What about the two women who went home with the men? Patrick refused to answer any questions. His office issued a statement, "As I have already said, I have nothing to do with the alleged incident. The local authorities in Palm Beach are conducting an investigation to determine what happened. I do not intend to make any further statement at this time." The only substantive comment he made was to lash out against tabloid journalism for its sensationalistic coverage. "It's disturbing to be accused of things you're not responsible for," Patrick said.[18]

Kennedy's enemies in the General Assembly basked in this turn of events. Six weeks earlier, he had condemned the Speaker for bringing dishonor to the legislature.

Now the national spotlight was on Patrick, and the tabloid glare was bright. DeAngelis was careful not to make any public comment. "I don't think I ever banged him. My recollection is that I was asked by reporters numerous times to give a reaction and I just never did," he said.[19] But the Speaker's allies were not so generous. Boyle felt it proved Patrick was a hypocrite. "He was quick to come to judgment about the integrity of others, yet he lashed out at the press when he felt his integrity and honesty were being questioned," the House Democratic whip said. "He was calling for the Speaker to resign because he was hurting the House's reputation and because of a perceived conflict and perceived dishonesty. That could easily be turned on him."[20] As new disclosures came to light, the case became the Kennedy Rape Trial, not the William Smith incident. When Cassone reported that Ted had come into Patrick's bedroom the night of the event to say good night, the senator was wearing just a long shirt and no pants. The *New York Post* called it "Teddy's Sexy Romp." Cassone also drew attention when she told reporters that while walking out to the car the morning of March 30, she asked Patrick if he was embarrassed by his father. According to her, Patrick replied, "Yeah, sometimes he embarrasses me."[21] When asked about the statement, Patrick angrily defended his Dad. "I'm proud of my father. He's the reason I went into politics. . . . Some people might think he's not the father that I should have, or that he was away a lot when I was young. But it's none of their business. He's my father, and I'm proud of him. I'm not ashamed of my father."[22]

In mid-May, Patrick's 182-page deposition, the longest of any witness in the case, was released to the public. It detailed his recollection of events Easter weekend. In elaborate detail, he described how the family had spent the weekend, what people did for entertainment, and, most important from the standpoint of the criminal case, his early morning conversations with cousin William. After talking with his cousin, Patrick sensed the woman was a "Fatal Attraction" type, referring to the Glenn Close movie about a jilted woman who stalked her lover.[23] By the end of May, the distinction between the tabloid and mainstream press had virtually disappeared. All the Kennedys involved were being villified based on scant evidence. Mike Barnicle, a popular columnist for the *Boston Globe*, called the event "the end of Edward Kennedy's life in politics."[24] Patrick feared the worst for his family and complained bitterly about tabloidization. "Good journalistic newspapers are finding themselves sucked into the tabloid mentality of gossiping and innuendo. . . . You hear about things that happened long ago that have no bearing on this case but simply feed the frenzy of gossip and innuendo. I just think that that's irresponsible," he proclaimed.[25]

In a classroom visit to Brown University that year, Patrick joked with the students following his introduction, "If all you know about me is what you have heard on *A Current Affair*, I'm in big trouble." But the problem was not just the tabloid press. Taking advantage of the hundreds of reporters and celebrity-gawkers in the area, local entrepreneurs sold a variety of colorful souvenirs. One T-shirt carried the inscription, "The Kennedys: Palm Beach Tour, Easter 1991." Underneath were the names of six local bars visited by the Kennedys that weekend. Another T-shirt crudely warned: "Kennedy Compound: Trespassers will be violated."[26]

For Patrick, the whole episode was a sobering moment. It was the first time he had been linked to his family in a negative way. He worried about his own personal judgment in meeting Cassone at a bar. Even though he was not dating anyone at the time, he understood it did not look good for him to be picking up women in bars. Explaining how the situation had come about, he said "I'm 24 years old. I met this woman. Maybe my judgment was a little off there. . . . But it's important to realize I never forced myself on the girl. I'm not married. . . . It's embarrassing and so forth, by it's not like I'm doing things in government to sell the people down the river."[27] The negative press about Patrick continued, with reporters emphasizing "like father, like son." Patrick was angered that the tabloid press was characterizing him as a drunken lecher based on popular stereotypes about male Kennedy family members. This portrayal was ironic because Patrick really wasn't like most of the Kennedy men. He was shy and sensitive, and, after his high school substance abuse problem, he rarely drank much. Indeed, during that visit to Au Bar, he had been drinking ginger ale. Public interest in the event, though, taught him an important lesson. "He learned that casual conversations that are unimportant can later become public discussion," Tannenbaum said. If someone he met casually in a bar could sell her story to the tabloids and be on national television, how could he develop meaningful relationships? At a deeper level, he began to question whom he could trust. The whole case made it "hard for Patrick to find good people he can confide in," noted Tannenbaum.[28]

The incident wreaked havoc inside his family. The migration of cousins all over the country meant the next generation was not as close as the family myth advertised. Just as the country debated who was at fault in this "date rape" case, so did the Kennedy cousins. There were rumors in the family that this was not the first such offense for William. Privately, some of the relatives believed that William "needs some help."[29] In the first few days after Easter, before the police named William Smith as the alleged perpetrator, there were questions about who was involved. Newspaper reports erroneously indicated John Kennedy Jr. had been at the house. Patrick's April 2 interview with the *Providence Journal*, in which he indicated that the girl "was a guest of one of my cousins," angered some family friends when it became known William was in residence that weekend. To a few, Patrick appeared to be fingering his cousin to save his own reputation. Referring to that interview, one longtime Kennedy friend said, "Patrick hung Willie out to dry." Continuing, the person explained, "It's the same problem that happened at Chappaquiddick. The longer it goes on without being resolved clearly, the more mysterious it becomes."[30] The pressure was unrelenting. The fear was that "by not saying more in favor of your cousin, are you turning against the family?" a close friend of Patrick's noted.[31] The headlines dragged on for months. The family hired a private investigator named Patrick McKenna to look into the background of the woman involved.[32] He uncovered information that later was used to impeach her credibility. Eventually, he would be hired by famed lawyer Johnnie Cochran to work on the O.J. Simpson case and, in the course of the investigation, would uncover the Mark Fuhrman tapes proving that police officer's deeply rooted bigotry.

The Smith case was traumatic for Patrick personally, but it was devastating for his fund-raising. His aide Nocera explained, "It just completely threw everything we were doing offtrack. We could no longer fund-raise. We were trying to keep the office open through fund-raising. We were completely dependent on his fund-raising." Patrick had a major trip scheduled for California, where he was going to raise some money. According to Nocera, "He was supposed to raise about $20,000 on this trip. He was going to be in California for a week. He was going to be at four or five fund-raisers. In the end, most of them were canceled. Two were still on, they were both busts. We ended up losing money by going out there."[33] But Patrick's public support in Rhode Island remained strong. Due to his solid reputation in the state, voters saw him as an honest and caring individual. His efforts to reform state government had created a bedrock of support that served him well. A November 1991 survey found that 73 percent felt Kennedy had handled himself well concerning the rape trial, 15 percent believed he did not, and 12 percent were unsure.[34]

Eventually, the trial began under case number 91-5482, the *State of Florida v. William Kennedy Smith*. On December 6, 1991, Patrick was called as a witness. In anticipation, he had turned to speech coach Tannenbaum for help in preparing his testimony. She coached him about testifying and was paid $2,300 out of his campaign fund. "We talked about remaining calm and telling what he knew. There were lots of pressures on him at that time," explained Tannenbaum. "Most people who didn't know Patrick were going to judge him mostly by how he looked and sounded even more than what he said. That is how people judge other people. I wanted to make sure he felt confident about all that," she said. Along with his lawyer, former Senator John Culver, an old family friend of his father's, they practiced testifying. The group looked at "questions that might come up and questions you try and role-play that come from no where." The questions he worried the most about "were not just questions they would ask about him, but questions they might ask about his Dad and his cousin."[35] The trial was broadcast nationwide on Court TV and CNN, the first big celebrity court case to be televised across the country.

In his 40 minutes of testimony, Patrick explained how he had encountered Smith saying good-bye to Bowman before she drove away the morning of the alleged incident. As the cousins walked toward the house, Smith started to describe what he called a bizarre experience he had just gone through. "He told me he was quite exasperated because the woman was saying all sorts of strange things," Patrick told the court. She referred to him by the wrong name, demanded to see his driver's license, and yelled at him. Two minutes later, after she had driven away, the young men were startled to find the woman back inside the house. Smith went out to talk with her. Returning 45 minutes later, Smith told his cousin the woman was threatening to call the police. Testifying in a voice that wavered at times and showed obvious unease, Patrick provided crucial support for his cousin. Patrick was the closest thing to an eyewitness that a date rape case can have. Other than the two principals, he was the only one who had seen them together right after the alleged incident. He was also the only one in the family who had talked to William that night and the next morning. Patrick contradicted many of the accuser's statements.[36]

By the time the case concluded, the jury had heard 10 days of testimony from 45 witnesses. On December 11, it took the panel just 77 minutes to reach its verdict that

William Smith was not guilty of raping a woman at the family compound. Five hundred reporters from around the world were present for the verdict. Smith's lawyer Roy Black effectively had handled the defense. From the private investigators he had hired to check out Bowman, the dozens of motions he had filed, and his successful effort to get the judge to exclude damaging testimony from three other women who said Smith also had attacked them, his defense was enough to plant seeds of doubt in the minds of the jurors. From Rhode Island, Patrick released a statement. "This has been a very difficult time for my family. I believed in my cousin Willie's innocence all along. The jury's swift verdict will now allow Willie and all of us to get on with our lives."[37] With the verdict, the family had dodged a cannonball. A guilty verdict not only would have sent William Smith to jail, it would have strengthened popular stereotypes that Kennedy men were party animals who were not to be trusted. For the next generation of Kennedy cousins, it was a decision of immeasurable importance. The court sealed documents associated with the case, which meant that anyone seeking copies of depositions would be required to gain permission from Smith's attorney, Roy Black.

The trial ended, but there was one final chapter to unfold. Throughout the summer, the tabloid press had offered thousands of dollars for personal tidbits about the Kennedy family. In Milford, Massachusetts, 22-year-old Rob Remy had been watching the Kennedy saga with keen interest. He knew a secret about the Kennedys. Several years earlier, when Remy had been treated at a rehabilitation center, he had encountered a young man named Patrick Kennedy who was being treated for alcohol and drug abuse. The two had attended the same group therapy sessions. Remy contacted the *National Enquirer*, which agreed to pay him $10,000 for rights to the story. The weekend after Kennedy testified, the tabloid rag publicized the claims that Patrick had spent time in 1986 at a New Hampshire treatment center for substance abuse.[38] Kennedy had heard the drug abuse story was in the works and approached his advisers about how to handle the problem. Should he wait until the *Enquirer* printed the story, or should he get out front with his own version? Tabella advised the state representative to be pro-active and proposed that Kennedy send a letter to everyone in the district confessing that he had endured a substance abuse problem in the past, sought treatment for it, and now was okay. Then Kennedy would invite leading reporters in the state for one-on-one interviews. When Ted's staff found out about this plan, they thought it was a terrible idea. "You don't know what you are doing," they screamed at Tabella. "Well, it's not like you guys are handling things so well either," Tabella shot back.[39] Patrick chose not to send the letter out.

The *National Enquirer* printed the story, and the very media circus Kennedy had feared regarding his hidden skeleton came to pass. Patrick was about to participate in a press conference about pension reform when the drug story hit. Reporters with television cameras went running after him demanding reactions to this new disclosure. What had he been treated for? Was it cocaine, as Remy had told the *Enquirer*? Kennedy refused to respond. He drafted a statement for the press acknowledging his treatment at a drug and alcohol rehabilitation center in 1986. The next day, he mailed letters to all the 2,800 households in his legislative district. "While I believe the problems of my adolescence have no bearing on my public service, the dramatic increase in sensationalized publicity surrounding my family has led to their public disclosure," the mailing stated. "I love my family very much. We have been through a lot together, and we will continue to support each other. If sensational news accounts about me and my family have been the price of public service, then the confidence you [the citizens of the district] have placed in me to serve you has been the reward. Because of you, the reward far outweighs the price."[40] He added that he had not used drugs since the time of his high school treatment. When asked later what he thought of Remy's disclosure, Kennedy replied angrily, "He's got all 10,000 of his reasons," referring to the amount of money paid for the tip.[41]

Being enmeshed in a high publicity rape trial and having his past drug use publicized through the tabloids was not how Patrick thought he would spend his summer and fall following graduation from Providence College in 1991. His plan had been simple. He was looking at three career options: teaching, business, or working with Ira Magaziner, the nationally known strategic consultant. In fact, Magaziner had offered him a job, which Patrick turned down, with the Aging 2000 project promoting new policies about aging and health care.[42] Teaching was another possibility. Patrick had called the graduate director in political science at Brown University about enrolling in its master's program. The program had strength in domestic politics and public policy, and Patrick believed it would give him a credential he could use to become a schoolteacher.[43] Tabella liked this plan. It would take care of critics who said Patrick never had a real job and couldn't empathize with working Americans.[44] But Patrick never submitted an application to the program.

Patrick's choice of what to do with his life eventually came down to something one of his staffers called the "Kennedy myth over money." Nocera explained, "They think there is this unbelievable amount of money out there" for someone with their famous name.[45] At this point in time, between May and November 1991, Kennedy was disillusioned with politics. He had graduated from college, but not yet heard the favorable verdict in his cousin's trial. Privately, he was not sure that the court would exonerate his cousin. It was a tough time for the young legislator. He was not doing much other than flying down to see his D.C. lawyer. His political staff did not see him often during this period. The Assembly wasn't much fun. Ever since he had called on the Speaker to resign, he had been ostracized. The leadership had a firm policy on dissidents: stifle and intimidate them publicly; make fun of them privately. It was a recipe that had worked in previous cases.

The rape trial had soured Patrick on public service. He had seen the downside of being a Kennedy. He personally had done no wrong at Palm Beach. He never had been charged with anything. The worst that could be said of him was that he had picked up a young lady at a bar. For a young single male with no girlfriend, that hardly was a serious offense. But the tabloidization of the mass media thoroughly infuriated him. He challenged one television interviewer who tried to besmirch his reputation, "You're dragging my father and me through the mud, and we weren't even suspects. I find it disgusting."[46] The biggest result of the Palm Beach legal proceedings was that Patrick had been drained financially. Even though he personally was not on trial, he had been forced to hire Culver and Tannenbaum to prepare him for testifying.[47] For months, because of the scandal, Patrick's fund-raising was on hold. According to Nocera, "Palm Beach had drained him personally on legal fees. They drained him politically because he couldn't raise any money."[48]

Two family friends pushed Kennedy to start a business career. Communism was falling, and new markets were opening up. He should get into international trading, they advised, establishing a company to trade with the Soviet Union and Yugoslavia. They had the business experience and Patrick had the political ability to open doors. These men, Robert Foley and Michael Saegh, were Massachusetts businessmen. Foley, who had grown up in Springfield, Massachusetts, and graduated from Providence College, had met Kennedy through Massachusetts politics. The 38-year-old businessman had been involved in political campaigns both for Ted and Joe. He was energetic, outgoing, and optimistic, a born salesman. Saegh was the president of Maystar Corporation in Foxboro, Massachusetts. Foley saw the changes taking place around the world as a once-in-a-lifetime opportunity. They could make a ton of money. The business could open a headquarters in a plush downtown office building. There would be a nice office, car phones, and computers. It would be easy money. Foley pitched the idea to Patrick, and the young man was intrigued and eventually sold on the concept. Foley was 14 years older than Patrick, and very persuasive in formulating ideas. "With the East Block breaking up at that time, [Patrick] felt there might be a point there, that it might be something he might want to do as opposed to going into politics," Foley explained.[49]

Kennedy decided to take the plunge into the business world. He stated, "That was a business that I was excited about the prospects for because I felt in Rhode Island we could benefit a lot from the international marketplace. . . . I could bring different people together who had expertise in an area and make something of it."[50] At that point, a staffer explained, "It was more important to try and make some money than go work for somebody else."[51] The company was Rhode Island International Trade Corporation. Months went into planning the business, and the original articles of incorporation were signed November 21, 1991, and filed with the Secretary of State Corporations Division on November 27. It was less than a month before Patrick's testimony and the not-guilty verdict handed down at Palm Beach. According to the papers filed, the purpose of the company was "to promote and engage in trade, including the publication of a trade catalog and the promotion of trade through trade missions and trade shows, and to do all things connected therewith and allied thereto."[52] The officers of the company were Patrick Kennedy (president), Michael Saegh (vice-president), William T. Hogan III (secretary), and Robert Foley (treasurer). Hogan was a lawyer from Boston who handled the legal work. Patrick put all the money up for the new enterprise and owned it 100 percent. By February 1992, the company had a luxurious office in Suite 840 of the Hospital Trust Tower at 15 Westminster Street in downtown Providence.[53]

Kennedy's previous political staff was dumped unceremoniously. Tannenbaum had been the voice coach. She had coached Patrick in 1988 through the door-to-door visits, the press interviews, and the television shows. She had provided consulting help for his Palm Beach testimony. It was the last job she did for him. She had been more than a consultant to him, almost a surrogate mother. He had called her in the middle of the night, told her about girlfriend troubles, and even raised his substance abuse past with her long before it had become public. Kennedy never explained to her why she was dropped. He simply stopped calling. Perhaps, Tannenbaum guessed, "it may be a reminder of a time when he was less comfortable." Or maybe, "he needed a sense of moving on."[54] Tabella's last stand had been the drug story. He had fought with Ted's staff when they objected to his plan to get out front on the *National Enquirer* disclosure. The senator's advisers, who thought Tabella was charging too much for his consulting services, told him he was an idiot, and in a rash moment, he had told them they weren't any smarter. The last payment to him was May 27, 1992.[55] Nocera was dropped in mid-February 1992, following Foley's review of the day-to-day operations of the political staff. "There was disorganization. The office needed to be better systematized," Foley said. "The data base was screwed up. The whole way the office was administered needed to be brought up to a higher level."[56] Foley set up a lunch with Nocera at Smith's Restaurant, a popular Italian restaurant in Providence, for the two of them. Foley asked, "What do you do all day?"[57] A week later, on February 11, Patrick went to Nocera's house along with Foley. The businessman did all the talking. Foley said, "We need to change the structure of the office because we can't afford the office the way it is. We need to think of different ways to cut back." "We need to get rid of the receptionist," Foley proposed.[58]

Nocera said, "Whatever you want to do. Let's find a smaller office. We can't afford this office," referring to the district office on Smith Street. "Maybe we need to cut the staff back." The latter was a major concession on Nocera's side because the only other paid staffer was his wife, Erin. He said, "Let's work on restructuring the thing." Perhaps they could fill in with more volunteers. Throughout the conversation, Patrick said nothing. He listened as Foley and Nocera talked. Every idea that Nocera proposed to save money was not adequate. Finally, Nocera figured out that it was he who was the object of the cutback. As Nocera got up to leave, Foley said, "We're going to help you find a job." He also volunteered to keep Erin on the payroll until she found a job. Within two weeks, Nocera had a job with Patrick's radio talk show nemesis, Buddy Cianci.[59] The transition was complete. Everyone who had played a major role in Patrick's earlier political career was gone.

Tony Marcella was brought officially onto the staff. The Everett, Massachusetts, native had started out as Senator Kennedy's driver and moved into advance work. When Ted was in Massachusetts, Marcella handled the scheduling and made sure things ran well. He had worked full-time for Senator Kennedy in 1988 before switching to part-time so he could help Patrick in his initial race for Dukakis delegate and the run for state legislature. He joined Patrick Kennedy's team full-time in March 1992, a few weeks after Nocera was dropped. Marcella had met Patrick in 1986 at an annual breakfast that Speaker George Kevarian held in the Bay State. Patrick sat at Marcella's table, and based on that meeting, Marcella concluded that the young man never would go into politics. "He wasn't outgoing or really what you would expect of a politician," Marcella explained. Patrick needed an alter ego. He wanted someone to go out to eat with every night. Marcella was single and could do that.[60] "When you go to work for the Kennedys," Tabella noted, "it is like entering the priesthood. You take a vow of complete devotion. You have to be available all the time, including evenings and weekends. It is really a full-time job."[61]

With his new staff in place, Kennedy eagerly pursued a business career. According to Foley, Patrick "was really trying to decide as any young man does at that age what track they want to follow." He wanted to make his own mark in life.[62] The goal of the new company was to help U.S. firms export to different foreign countries and foreign countries to import their goods into the United States. The company would assist with trade missions and trade shows, especially in new markets that were opening up in the Soviet Union and Yugoslavia. These were the hot new areas in 1991. "Communism had just ended. Democracy was in so they were trying to become free market economies. We thought that might be a good market to be involved with," explained Foley.[63] Patrick visited Russia and several East Bloc nations to check things out and ran into the very same problems that had plagued other entrepreneurs. "It was very difficult to do business in that part of the world. When you go from a communistic state to a capitalistic state, the system itself has to change and that takes several years," Foley said. Patrick found a couple of companies that wanted to get involved in the East Bloc, including a company in southern Massachusetts that dealt with hydroelectric power. But neither deal proved successful. Even with the last name of Kennedy, Patrick discovered that "there was not a systematized way that we could hook up those manufacturing operations in Russia in a successful way."[64] The company would not become the equivalent of cousin Joe Kennedy's successful Citizen's Energy enterprise. In the end, Patrick lost a bundle of money on his shortlived business career. But it didn't matter. Other opportunities had appeared on the horizon.

9 Beating the Speaker

*S*peaker DeAngelis knew his leadership was on the line as he started the 1992 General Assembly session. The banking crisis had left a third of the state's population without access to their accounts. Critics had accused him of a conflict of interest. A crippling recession had raised the state's misery index to record levels. Two local columnists had dubbed him "the Prince of Darkness." Patrick Kennedy had called for his resignation. DeAngelis didn't quite understand why people were so angry with him. In the last two decades, there certainly had been public corruption in Rhode Island with the conviction of mayors and judges. But there never had been an allegation of public corruption in the General Assembly, no bribery, extortion, or vote selling.[1] Yet confidence in the state's legislature was at an all-time low. As Speaker, DeAngelis was the target of much public hostility. On January 7, 1992, he addressed the members of the House, saying there was "discontent, anger, cynicism and suspicion. . . . 1991 was not a year our state ever wishes to repeat." It was time to put former controversies behind. "If we have made mistakes," he implored, "let us correct them and move ahead. And let us remember that the passion of the moment—no matter what the grounds—can never be an excuse to undermine the institutions of government."[2]

The passage of a year, however, did not cool the enmities. The investigations into the causes of the banking crisis had unearthed further damaging information. The Gregorian Commission created by Governor Sundlun had released a critical report on the collapse of RISDIC enumerating several reasons behind the financial collapse. Many RISDIC institutions had strayed from the original credit union concept. Others lacked adequate sources of liquidity to cover unexpected withdrawals. There was weak oversight by the board of directors. Underlying all these problems, though, was a state political culture that indulged RISDIC, treating bills introduced by the organization with favor and those it opposed with disfavor. There was lax regulation of credit unions by the executive branch. Key state politicians did not follow through on early warning signals. A team mentality throughout the political system undermined any type of check and balance.[3]

The General Assembly set up its own investigation into the scandal. Headed by Representative Jeffrey Teitz, it found even more incriminating evidence of a political system in bed with private developers. Insiders did favors for one another. Shortly thereafter, a Brown University poll in February 1992 found that just 9 percent rated DeAngelis's performance as Speaker of the House excellent or good, 21 percent said it was fair, 38 percent felt it was poor, and 32 percent were unsure.[4] Opposition was coalescing in the House, but Patrick's call for the Speaker's resignation represented a major turning point.[5] According to Cornwell, Kennedy's unique contribution was that "he could command the attendance of reporters every time he held a press conference."[6] The leadership was losing power. On the floor, the debate was harder to manage. A few years earlier, in 1987, the state had authorized the creation of an authority to build a new Convention Center in downtown Providence. Developers saw it as a vehicle to revitalize decaying urban areas. The Coopers and Lybrandt consulting firm had done a detailed report, predicting such a facility would be a financial success, but the numbers were coming in below estimates. In 1991, the Convention Center Authority requested bonding authority to build a hotel and office buildings adjacent to the Convention Center in order to attract big conventions. Many of the state's strongest political interests were behind the request. Boyle shepherded it through the Assembly because DeAngelis had recused himself based on still another potential conflict of interest with his law firm. "The *Providence Journal* was in favor of the legislation. . . . The unions want it, the Chamber wants it, everyone was lined up," recalled Boyle. Even Governor Sundlun had made a personal appearance before the Finance Committee to argue on behalf of the bonding.[7]

Debate in the Assembly was furious. Critics questioned the accuracy of the consulting report. Others objected to the state subsidizing a private hotel. Linda Kushner led the opposition against the hotel bonding. Between the $20 million annual cost of the credit union bailout and the $30 million annual expenditure to cover the operating deficit for the Convention Center, Rhode Island was near the top of the country in public debt. She proposed that the Convention Center could have one hotel, either the existing Biltmore Hotel or a new one, but not both, as the authority wanted. The vote on this matter was held up for two hours while Sundlun personally lobbied members one on one. Sundlun and the House leadership ended up winning the key vote, but the margin was very close.[8] Kennedy voted against the new bonding authority for the Convention Center hotel. The leadership won the battle on the project, but lost the war of public opinion. The Convention Center would not show a profit until the year 2023, when its bonds were paid off. In Boyle's mind, the entire controversy illustrated how "politics changed dramatically after the banking crisis. If I told them it was sunny outside, they would look outside the window."[9]

Boyle had started his leadership position with high hopes of changing the General Assembly. Like DeAngelis, he wanted to bring the legislature into the modern era. "I was very interested in computers and how we could revolutionize that place with computers." Boyle was never able to move forward on that agenda, though, because "the banking crisis stalled it."[10] From a public opinion perspective, it became better to be an "outsider" railing against the system than a leadership "insider."

Political insiders cut deals for private benefit while outsiders were forward looking and reform minded. The popularity of the reform position turned most of the House mavericks, such as Rickman, Kushner, and Driver, into statewide candidates, although none except Kennedy were able to advance to higher office. In Boyle's mind, "Patrick was the perfect example of the new politics." As he saw it, by undermining the Speaker and weakening the trust that undergirded the system, Patrick savaged his political opponents. Never mind that the Speaker presented an inviting target because of all the conflicts of interest with law firm clients. "Newt Gingrich did to Jim Wright what Patrick did to Joe DeAngelis," Boyle believed.[11] At the end of the 1992 session, the leadership threw in the towel in a bloodless coup by retirement. DeAngelis announced he would not run for reelection to the House. His decision was followed in short succession by similar announcements from Majority Leader Lamb and Whip Boyle. Kennedy had pulled off the political equivalent of a grand slam. After being underestimated by all his opponents, he had beaten a sitting Speaker of the House and his entire leadership team. "If you define a politician in terms of winning an election, he was successful. He pushed the right buttons in Rhode Island," Boyle conceded.[12]

The retirement of the DeAngelis team meant a succession battle for the most powerful legislative office. The two contenders were John Harwood, who had been on the outs with the leadership team, and Russell Bramley, a man who had served a behind-the-scenes role in the DeAngelis regime. Bramley was more liberal than Harwood and was known for his keen interest in human services, especially substance abuse and early childhood development. Harwood was "a sports guy and all smiles," a former all-star hockey player in high school and college who wasn't known for his issue stances.[13] Harwood and his ally George Caruolo had fought Smith and DeAngelis since 1985, when the two had been removed from the leadership team over their Quonset Point incinerator dissent. Over the years, they had complained about undemocratic rules. They have voted against key amendments to the generous bailout bill on the banking crisis. They opposed the Convention Center. Although neither was liberal, Driver saw Harwood and Caruolo as "the cleanest break with the past. Bramley, nice guy that he is and competent that he is, had been one of DeAngelis's allies. That was really what made the decision for me, guilt by association."[14] Supporters, however, defended Bramley for his social conscience. Lieutenant Governor Robert Weygand, one of Bramley's strongest supporters, argued that "Russ could have been very effective at changing educational systems in Rhode Island. The issues of early childhood development and education are something he feels very strongly about."[15] Harwood was committed to opening up the General Assembly, taking the stance that it was time to bring Rhode Island into the 20th century. Dissidents had a right to get votes on their motions. Leadership should be less rigid and hierarchical. The state needed to have more people involved in deciding key issues.[16] Caruolo was the brains behind Harwood. One of the brightest men in the General Assembly, he was a shrewd political tactician. Caruolo had a strong sense of how institutions worked.

In the week before the final vote in the Democratic caucus, and by his own count, Harwood had a lead of 46 to 39. But the power of incumbency was weighing in on the side of Bramley.[17] Promises were being made and threats delivered.

Disinformation was rampant. Lieutenant Governor Weygand had a meeting with the East Providence representatives in an attempt to move votes away from Harwood and Caruolo. By the night of the Democratic caucus, enough votes shifted that in the contest for majority leader the Bramley forces had triumphed 43 to 42, the narrowest possible margin. To Kennedy, it was a shock that Harwood had lost. The young legislator had cast his lot with Harwood and Caruolo early in the battle. In July 1992, right after DeAngelis had chosen not to seek reelection, Patrick had held a press conference outside the House chamber and announced his support for Harwood. Kennedy personally lobbied representatives on Harwood's behalf. When Harwood and Caruolo were under attack, he defended them vigorously. Because of his efforts, "He was able to convince many people what we stood for and that the direction that we were going was the direction they should be going," said Harwood.[18] But in early January 1993, it looked like all of Kennedy's efforts were for naught. Not only was the loss a deadly blow to Harwood and Caruolo, it was crushing to Kennedy's aspirations as well.

It was time to activate the "insurance policy." In 1986, when Harwood had run for Speaker against Smith, he had started with a considerable number of votes but seen his final vote drop to 18 after Smith and Governor DiPrete formed an alliance and beat back the challenge. This time, Harwood and Caruolo had a secret plan to win the Speakership if they did not prevail in the Democratic caucus. They would go across the aisle and appeal to the 15 Republicans for support.[19] It would be an unholy alliance, one that would have been unthinkable when political parties were stronger. Such alliances were now becoming more common across the country, however. Democrats in Connecticut and North Carolina had struck bargains with Republicans to gain legislative leadership. The same thing had happened in the Rhode Island Senate a few years earlier.[20] The fall-back plan became Option A for Harwood and Caruolo. There was a quirk in the House rules that limited voting for majority leader to the ruling party. The post, after all, was a party position. When that vote had been held, Harwood's candidate Caruolo had lost by a single vote. But the Speaker represented everyone in the chamber. It was a constitutional position, not just a party slot. Therefore, by legal mandate, that vote was of the entire chamber, both Democrats and Republicans.

Harwood and Caruolo had sought to avoid this very dilemma. Unbeknown to most of their fellow legislators that spring, when it became clear Bramley was being groomed as the next Speaker they had offered him the number three spot on their leadership team. He could become their whip, the job currently held by Boyle.[21] Their ticket would have been the unity team, and it undoubtedly would have won the election overwhelmingly. But thinking he had a great shot at the top of the ticket, Bramley rejected the offer. Harwood and Caruolo decided to make entreaties to Republicans. Their plum incentive was rules liberalization. There would be more open discussion and greater opportunities to make amendments and get bills out of committee. To a minority party used to being quashed by Democrats, this offer was attractive. If Bramley really was a remnant of the old leadership team, Republicans weren't very optimistic. They had not fared very well under DeAngelis, so they opted to go with Harwood. The former hockey star put together just enough votes from Republicans and newly elected legislators to win. In the full House, Harwood was elected Speaker on January 7, 1993, by 60 to 39, with one member absent. Among the newcomers, "He is a far better, more outgoing, more affable person than Russ Bramley. [Harwood] ran a campaign among the new people that he was going to change the system."[22] But it was the Republicans who put him over the top. According to Caruolo, "We always viewed Republicans as our insurance policy. . . . We did end up using the policy."[23] It was a startling turnabout in the succession war. From Weygand's standpoint, the move showed "how willing the other side was to do whatever it took to get in control."[24]

The new Speaker's very first appointment was naming Kennedy chair of the Rules Committee. It was an issue that Patrick long had felt was crucial to the proper functioning of the Assembly. When he looked at the dismal past failures of the legislature — the banking crisis, the budget, and the Convention Center — he could see how debate had been stifled and the final decision been corrupted by the lack of open discussion. His new aide Marcella was experienced in reform as an avenue to leadership. Marcella had started his political career with George Kevarian, then majority leader of the Massachusetts House. In 1985, Kevarian decided to challenge the sitting Speaker, Tom McGee. But Kevarian lost, and he was banished from the leadership, thrown out of his majority leader's position, and had his staff cut from 15 down to 3. Marcella was one of the remaining three aides. With Tony's assistance, Kevarian eventually had won the top job of Speaker. When the Speaker's battle was brewing in Rhode Island, Patrick and Marcella arranged for Kevarian to advise Harwood and Caruolo. Kevarian came down to Rhode Island and talked with them on the phone. "He explained to them how he waged his battle in getting early commitments, making some public, and trying to box people in," said Marcella.[25] The big issue in the Massachusetts war had been rules reform. So with Kennedy in charge of reform, he called on Kevarian for advice and set about democratizing the legislature.

Even before Harwood had been elected Speaker, there had been lengthy meetings involving Harwood, Caruolo, Patrick, and Dick Kearns, a legal counsel at the Assembly, with the conversations focusing on how legislatures should operate. Caruolo joked, "It was more like they were in Philadelphia doing the Constitution."[26] There were arguments over philosophy and debates over how to handle reform. Now that Harwood was Speaker and Kennedy in charge of rules reform, the Rules Committee set about turning philosophy into actual procedures. It had been a common tactic to kill things in committee the leadership did not want approved, so Kennedy created an easier discharge procedure. When a bill did not receive a majority in the committee, it still could be sent to the floor with no recommendation if a few people signed a discharge petition. He also made it easier to offer amendments on the floor and harder to make tabling motions that prevented floor debate.

Some of the rules liberalizations did not please the new leadership. Despite their reform rhetoric, Harwood and Caruolo were eager to maintain the powers of leadership their predecessors had held. After all, they now were in charge. They needed to be able to help their friends and disarm their critics. Decentralization was risky because it weakened their control over the process. But reform had been their central promise, and Patrick had been one of their chief kingmakers. "They felt they had to cater to him. . . . Some of [the reforms] were acceptable to them, but they weren't happy about it," explained Cornwell, who was working with the new leadership team.[27] Even Caruolo acknowledged that beyond the early discussions, the Rules Committee had made "some additions in terms of philosophy and specific rules."[28] Soon after Kennedy left the chamber to move up the political ladder to Congress, the new leaders suspended the new budget rules. Just like the old days, the budget was rushed through in one day. House leaders also began to use the "rule of germaneness" to stop debate on things outside the scope of what they were considering. But for Kennedy, the political tide already had turned. His cousin had been exonerated of rape. The House leadership was on his side. Many of the big name contributors who had supported his opponent in 1988 now gave to him. Even Jim Skeffington, a leading bond attorney and brother of Jack Skeffington, was contributing to Kennedy. As his former aide Nocera put it, Patrick had successfully gone from being the "biggest outsider to the biggest insider."[29] It was time to move to the national stage.

10 Running for Congress

*T*he first sign that Kennedy was running for Congress came in 1993, when a short news item announced that he was buying a new house.[1] Although the residence was close to the old, it offered the young man one key advantage. It was located in the First District represented by Republican Congressman Ron Machtley.[2] The GOP legislator was a new face with an impeccable reputation for honesty and integrity. Machtley fit right into the moderate Republican model of fiscal conservatism and social liberalism. Public opinion polls showed that large numbers of voters thought he was doing a good job.[3] Machtley's strong support notwithstanding, Kennedy sensed an electoral opportunity. He had taken on an incumbent state representative in 1988 and won. But Skeffington had been a weak legislator who had fallen out of touch with his district's voters. Machtley was no Skeffington. The congressman was well liked, well respected, and had no personal baggage. Even for a Kennedy, a race against Machtley would be daunting. Most House incumbents who sought reelection won. However, there was an opening in this race that others were neglecting. As one of the few prominent Republicans in elective office in the state, Machtley was being pressured to run for governor in 1994 against Sundlun. Governor Sundlun's popularity had dropped significantly since his 1990 election. Bad news stuck to him like flypaper. The governor had a habit of making intemperate remarks, like the time he said of his 1992 female challenger who was trailing him in the polls, "I've spent my whole life chasing blondes. It's nice to have a blond chasing me."[4]

Kennedy's plan was to squeeze the 44-year-old Machtley out of the congressional race into the gubernatorial contest. The young man started planning right after Harwood had been elected Speaker. "Everyone saw it as a liability to get out against a popular Republican like Machtley. It was the biggest advantage. I had clear sailing for awhile. I was able to establish my own strategy and race. I wasn't getting caught in the backdraft of a bunch of other candidates," Patrick explained. Being the only candidate helped him, he reasoned. "You're the one people are reacting to. I just remember taking it one step at a time."[5] Through his early actions, Patrick set the tone of the whole race. Complaining in early March that Machtley was a member of the minority party in Washington because Clinton controlled the White House and Democrats ruled Congress, Kennedy said, "You have to ask yourself, is he going to be able to do as much to help Rhode Island as a member of the majority party?"[6] A few months later, in July, after it was becoming apparent Machtley was seriously considering a run for governor, Kennedy bragged to a fund-raising crowd, "I really pushed Congressman Machtley into . . . I don't know where I pushed him. Maybe into Narragansett Bay. He's thinking twice" about running for reelection.[7] Two weeks later, Vic Fazio, chair of the Democratic Congressional Campaign Committee, sent out a press release accusing Machtley of "hypocrisy" for opposing an amendment to a midwestern flood-relief bill after having approved a Kuwait cleanup bill to deal with Gulf War damage. It mattered little that the criticism was blatantly misleading. Machtley had actually voted in favor of the midwestern flood-relief bill but had voted against a procedural motion to permit votes on nonflood legislation to be tacked onto the bill.[8]

In September, Machtley announced he was running for governor, a move that took Kennedy's strongest opponent out of the race. He could run for an open seat with no incumbent on the ballot. Patrick set about a coordinated effort to clear the field of Democratic rivals and create an aura of inevitability based on leadership endorsements, early fund-raising, and a strong organization. Kennedy secured endorsements from Senate Majority Leader Paul Kelly, Governor Sundlun, Speaker Harwood, and House Majority Leader Caruolo. Caruolo explained, "We were in on the ground floor of attempting to fulfill his political aspirations. . . . We were working for his congressional bid long before endorsing him in 1994."[9] From Harwood's standpoint, Kennedy would be the most influential House freshman if elected. "He had immediate access to the Speaker of the House at that time, Speaker Foley and [Majority] Leader Gephardt. He had absolute access to the president of the United States. They are on a very friendly basis. And he obviously had an ally in the United States Senate with his Dad and his cousin [Joe in the House]."[10]

These endorsements were a major boon to Kennedy and a crucial turning point in his political career. In 1988, virtually the entire state's political leadership had opposed his initial bid for the General Assembly. In 1991 and 1992, he had fought a bitter battle against Speaker DeAngelis, one Kennedy easily could have lost. In 1993, his favored candidate for House Speaker had barely triumphed, winning at the last minute through an unholy alliance with Republicans. To Kennedy, his newfound leadership support was a firm sign his fortunes had changed. "The fact that I had the Rhode Island leadership support had a quiet sort of power to it. It signified among the establishment that I was established," he said.[11] Not only were the endorsements impressive in and of themselves; they gave Patrick valuable currency in Washington, D.C., and with his family. "Looking back on it, more than any kind of money they could have raised for me, . . . there was a respect people had for leadership in any Chamber. I remember what really got my Dad excited about things was when he found out the Speaker and majority leader were supporting my campaign. He had this institutional respect for leadership."[12]

The same held true for Richard Gephardt. The U.S. House majority leader was an early national supporter of Kennedy. Gephardt sponsored and organized a July 1993 fund-raiser for Kennedy that netted $50,000 from nearly 200 donors in Washington, D.C.[13] Ironically, Gephardt had been one of the presidential candidates Kennedy had opposed in 1988 when he won a convention delegate seat representing Dukakis. While in Washington, Patrick met with presidential advisers George Stephanopoulos and James Carville, Vice-President Al Gore, and Vic Fazio of the Democratic Congressional Campaign Committee, and he paid courtesy stops to the Teamsters and the Communications Workers of America.

The only remaining obstacle was a possible Democratic primary. Scott Wolf had been a congressional candidate in 1988 and indeed was one of the reasons Democratic incumbent Ferdinand St. Germain had lost that general election to Machtley. Wolf had spent the last few years working in a policy job for Governor Sundlun. As he considered his congressional prospects, one of the things Wolf did was undertake a poll in fall 1993 of likely Democratic primary voters. The news was not encouraging. Kennedy had a tremendous advantage in terms of name recognition. Whereas 50 percent recognized Wolf, Kennedy had almost 100 percent name recognition. Patrick was well liked. Criticisms that were being offered around the state—that Kennedy was too young, was inexperienced, and hadn't lived long enough in the state—"were falling on deaf ears," according to Wolf.[14] In the head-to-head matchup, Kennedy beat Wolf very substantially. If he ran, Wolf knew he would be outspent by 3 to 1. In the end, Wolf concluded, "it seemed like a fool's errand. I didn't want to be a Don Quixote." Kennedy had one other advantage over Wolf—the luxury of not needing a full-time job. When rumors arose in 1993 about a possible Wolf candidacy, Sundlun told Wolf he "couldn't remain in his administration if he were an active candidate." That was a devastating blow because Wolf was a middle-class person with little personal savings. He couldn't afford to resign his job a year and one-half before the election.[15]

The goal of the early fund-raising and endorsements was to create a "steamroller" effort, according to state Democratic chair Guy Dufault, who worked closely with Kennedy. Opponents who were thinking about a possible run themselves, such as Lieutenant Governor Weygand and Senate Majority Leader Kelly, were frightened by the early fund-raising. "Once they saw the Kennedy machine kick in as early and as fast and with the money they knew he had at his disposal, it was easier to try to jump on board than to stand in the way of it."[16] In Weygand's case, the fact that he had been lieutenant governor only for two years at this point weighed heavily against a run. "I really felt I needed to establish myself as a statewide officer and policy-maker and establish some of the issues on my agenda so I could get my message to people and let people know what I stood for rather than jumping from one office to the next office."[17]

Kennedy made the rounds in Washington, met with both finance and party people and convinced them he was the most electable candidate. Gephardt saw "Patrick as someone with a chance of a pickup" for the party. Early in the race, Dufault got a call from the Democratic National Committee telling him that "the DCCC was behind Patrick from the beginning."[18] In November, Ted held a fund-raiser at his McLean house in honor of his son. At $500 a person, the event attracted the "glitterati" from Washington and raised $100,000. Senator Claiborne Pell was there and spoke to the crowd about his long-term friendship with the Kennedys. Congressman Jack Reed discussed how the working-class tenements of Patrick's home district of Mount Pleasant were "dear to my heart." In fact, the congressman pointed out that the area was the home of "my father's mother, on Wisdom Avenue."[19] Suddenly, the unmistakable voice of Ted interrupted Reed's speech to jab his son. In a sharp reminder of the near-disastrous 1988 talk show appearance at the beginning of his son's first General Assembly race, when Patrick had not been able to identify major streets in the district, Ted gleefully inquired in front of the gathered assembly, "D'ya know where that is, Patrick?" Yes indeed, his son replied. "It's Health, Wealth, and Wisdom Avenues, and they're all perpendic- . . . uh, parallel to each other."[20] By spring 1994, Kennedy had cleared the field of his toughest rivals. Congressman Machtley was running for governor and Kennedy's strongest Democratic primary opponents—Wolf, Weygand, and Kelly—were out of the race. Kennedy would face only a token primary from Norman Jacques, a former state senator who served 18 months in prison in 1986 and 1987 for sexual assault.

The race was managed by Tony Marcella, Kennedy's close friend and alter ego. They were a good team, complementing one another perfectly. Whereas Kennedy was low key and friendly, Marcella was hyper and intense. The two set about developing their own organization. Ted Kennedy was up for reelection in Massachusetts in 1994, but there would be no sharing of consultants. "We didn't want to be the Kennedy machine from Massachusetts that was reaching into Rhode Island," Marcella said. "We never did that. We split the campaign from day one. We got our own media people. We got our own pollster."[21] It was part of Patrick's desire to establish his own identity.

All that was left was Patrick's official announcement. It turned out to be the most expensive campaign announcement in the history of Rhode Island. Despite his General Assembly vote against the building, Kennedy held his announcement at the Convention Center. It was the only place in the state big enough to hold the crowd. Around 2,150 people attended at $25 apiece. A crowd of famous Kennedys was there from Ted and Joan Kennedy to cousins John F. Kennedy Jr. and Joe Kennedy. In his speech, Patrick said he was running to make a difference for Rhode Island. "I love this state. . . . I have never met people with greater warmth than I have since the day I came here to live and go to school," Kennedy said. He indicated that if elected, he would fight for programs for the elderly and to cushion the blow of defense budget cuts that had hurt the state. He concluded by stating, "In the end there is only one issue in this campaign—and that is: Who can do more for Rhode Island?"[22]

The announcement was vintage Kennedy, heavy on money and celebrity, with plenty of Kennedy family members to entertain the crowd. The event cost $100,000, which meant that with the $50,000 raised, Patrick spent a total of $50,000 on the kick-off. As Dufault pointed out, there were "candidates in the Second Congressional District who were talking about raising $100,000 for their whole campaign." Overall, by this point, Patrick's campaign had raised $407,000, with his contributors representing a who's who of American society culled from his father's Rolodex: San Francisco Giants owner Walter H. Shorenstein, MCA/Universal chair Lew Wasserman, QVC chief Barry Diller, professional golfer Amy Alcott, and Motown Records chair Clarence Avant, among others. It sent "a real signal to people," Dufault said. "Money was not going to be an obstacle."[23]

About the time Kennedy was organizing his campaign, Dr. Kevin Vigilante was about to make the most impulsive decision of his life. A Republican emergency room physician who specialized in treating underprivileged HIV patients, he was thinking about running for Congress. He had never sought elective office before, made a campaign contribution, or worked on a campaign. Indeed, of the previous eight elections, he had voted in only two. The unlikely idea of running first crept into his head in September 1993. Most of the professional politicians had bowed out of the race, frightened by Kennedy's name, money, and organization. The pros had been around long enough to respect political muscle when they saw it.

But Vigilante was not a professional politician and not deterred by the Kennedy name. He knew Kennedy was strong from an organizational standpoint, yet Vigilante did not see him as a high-quality candidate personally. Patrick fumbled words and had difficulty developing lines of thought. Vigilante thought once voters saw the personal contrast between the two individuals, it would be a competitive race. At the end of October, he called John Holmes, the chair of the state Republican party. "He didn't know who the hell I was," Vigilante recalled. But Holmes encouraged the doctor to talk to senior people in the party. Vigilante called Senator John Chafee and Congressman Machtley, and each was positive. By December, he decided to run. "I didn't really deliberate about it a whole lot. Some decisions in life you can agonize over forever and others you just make," he said. Running for Congress just seemed to be the right thing to do.[24]

The novice Republican positioned himself as the outsider taking on a career politician. He supported term limits and lower taxes, both of which were popular with ordinary voters. Because of his record helping the underprivileged, his own consultant referred to him as Mother Teresa. The downside was that he had never been through a campaign before. The world of politics was something he had been interested in at a philosophical level, but "the people who populate that world were foreign to me." The only thing he knew for sure was because of the Kennedy factor, it would not be an average race. It disturbed him that someone would vote for a candidate because of the name alone. His number one problem was raising money. The idea that someone would write a $1,000 check to his campaign seemed like "an absurdity." Vigilante made up a list of 200 people, starting from people he knew in kindergarten. "I called them up and asked them for money," he said. He sent out a mailing in January. One person who was well-connected in local money circles took a liking to him and every week wrote 5 to 10 letters on Vigilante's behalf. Vigilante would meet for an hour with people who had been contacted, telling them what he believed and asking for a thousand dollars. Each individual he met, he asked for the names of five other people he could contact. "The whole fund-raising apparatus is like dropping a pebble in water and watching the ripples go out. You keep working the ripples," he observed. He quickly learned who gives money to candidates. "Lawyers write a lot of checks, people in the business world do. Doctors don't. And academics don't," he said.[25] As he was a medical doctor affiliated with Brown University, that was a problem.

Vigilante's partner in his HIV medical practice held a fund-raiser in New York City. Vigilante did an event in Washington, D.C., organized by his political action committee fund-raiser. His brother, Richard Vigilante, had worked at the conservative think tank, the Manhattan Institute, and now was vice-president of Regnery Publishing, which specialized in books by conservatives. Through him, Vigilante met celebrities like William Bennett and Jack Kemp, who agreed to support his campaign. He bought lists of potential givers and sent them direct mail appeals. He spent anywhere from four to seven hours a day on the phone asking people he had never met for money. Often he couldn't get through to the prospect. When he did get through the secretary, there were lots of nos. His goal was to raise $3,000 to $4,000 a day. When Kennedy held his gala kickoff at the Convention Center, Vigilante had enough money to take out full-page ads in the *Providence Journal* and other papers at a cost of $14,000 using an unflattering picture of Patrick that made him look nervous, young, and foolish. The photo had been taken for *Rhode Island Monthly* magazine in the middle of Kennedy's Palm Beach nightmare. At the state Republican convention in June, Vigilante's campaign manager Paul Moore distributed stickers saying "I work for a living" in order to contrast Vigilante's impressive résumé of helping the needy with Kennedy's status as a political legacy. Even less subtle were the campaign buttons proclaiming, "Say No to Patrick," which cleverly combined an anti-Kennedy message with the antidrug slogan.

Faced with the Vigilante challenge, Patrick felt confident about his prospects. Unlike his initial run, when he wasn't sure if voters would accept him, this time he knew he had a great shot. As far as Vigilante was concerned, Kennedy "just felt head and shoulders above him politically. I just had the sense of where I was and where I was going that I intuitively felt he did not have. . . . He was reacting to me."[26] Kennedy assembled one of the top political consulting teams in the country. His media adviser, David Axelrod, was a former political writer for the *Chicago Tribune* who had gone to work for Senate candidate Paul Simon. Axelrod was a populist who believed in his heart that the Republican party represented economic elites, meaning people who had connections clout, and money.[27] The pollster was Tubby Harrison of Cambridge, Massachusetts, who had worked in dozens of major campaigns, from Michael Dukakis's presidential bid in 1988 and Paul Tsongas's in 1992 to Senate races for Claiborne Pell in Rhode Island and Dale Bumpers and David Pryor in Arkansas. Unlike Axelrod, Harrison was someone who used to consider himself a liberal, but eventually became "less ideological and much more conscious of people's plight and what is moving them." He thought the Democratic party had become out of touch with ordinary suburban voters and needed to pay more attention to their plight. The party shouldn't just be the party of cities, lower-income people, and minorities. The only thing Harrison was predictable on, he said, was "being the bad guy willing to raise the tough questions." The pollster was blunt and impolitic in his presentation of his views. He liked Kennedy because the young man "wasn't stuck on himself."[28]

It was the job of the pollster to determine the respective strengths and weaknesses of the two candidates and the ad man to address those concerns. The first internal poll for the Kennedy campaign was a good news/bad news scenario. The good news was that Kennedy led Vigilante by 51 to 36 percent. But the bad news was that about one-third of the electorate was strongly anti-Kennedy. Vigilante only needed another 15 percent in order to win. There would not be much margin for error. Not surprisingly, given the respective backgrounds of the two candidates, Kennedy had much higher name recognition. Eighty-six percent of the district had heard of Patrick and held an opinion about him, while 72 percent had never heard of Vigilante.[29] Despite its lead, the Kennedy campaign was frankly worried about Vigilante. He was a likable man, the "best first date in politics," said media adviser Axelrod. Vigilante was glib, bright, and articulate. Patrick was shy, reticent, and introspective. Out-of-town reporters who observed the two men up close concluded that "when the lefts and rights were flying, Patrick would crack and Vigilante would thrive."[30] Patrick was seen as someone who could make a difference in Rhode Island through his family connections. His campaign slogan, "He'll Do More for Rhode Island," was a takeoff on Ted's "He Can Do More for Massachusetts" tag line from his first run for the U.S. Senate in 1962.[31]

According to the survey, voters saw Kennedy as having a six-year record of standing up to the gun lobby, rewriting the rules of the General Assembly, and confronting opponents like Speaker DeAngelis. Because of his efforts to save funding for the visiting nurses program, senior citizens adored Patrick. However, voters in the 35- to 55-year-old category were not as keen, resenting the fact that he had never held a job. Vigilante was a stronger candidate than many thought. He was the new kid on the block, not a recycled Rhode Island politician. Untainted by any of the state's scandals, such as the banking crisis, pension abuses, or insider dealings, he could position himself as the noncareer politician who would be an agent of change. Many citizens were concerned that Vigilante's campaign was funded by medical and drug companies. It was one of the reasons Patrick kept referring to Vigilante as "Doctor." He didn't want voters to forget the medical link. Polls showed that citizens worried about the fact that he hadn't voted in a number of recent elections and the way Vigilante equivocated on issues like abortion and gun control. The NRA was a perfect illustration of the problem. Vigilante had solicited its endorsement and made representations that caused the group to give him its highest ratings. When the tie became controversial, Vigilante refused to release his replies to the NRA and made a convoluted distinction between machine guns and assault weapons. In the eyes of Kennedy advisers, this equivocating created a valuable opportunity to paint Vigilante as less scrupulous and more political than Patrick.[32]

In a situation where one candidate (Kennedy) was well known and had substantial negatives and the other was unknown but well liked (Vigilante), the Kennedy strategy was simple. According to Kennedy press secretary Larry Berman, the campaign had to turn Vigilante "into Attila the Hun rather than Mother Teresa. . . . We wanted people to form a negative opinion of him because they had no opinion of him."[33] The Kennedy camp had carefully prepared its political base for a frontal assault on Vigilante by running three positive ads about Kennedy before the primary. The first ad, "Record," was designed to "credential" Patrick. It showed Patrick fighting his way to the legislature, challenging cozy deals, being a strong and courageous voice of the people, fighting taxpayer rip-offs, taking on the gun lobby, and overcoming party bosses. According to Axelrod, the campaign wanted voters to see Patrick as "an agent of change and not an agent of the status quo. The notion of this young guy taking on these powerful forces was impressive to people. In some ways, it reduced their anxiety about his relative youth."[34]

The second ad, "Care," used real people from Rhode Island to discuss Patrick's work saving funding for the Visiting Nurses Association. Axelrod saw real people as "more credible and believable than voice-overs." In an age of massive citizen cynicism, "the more real you can make your work, the more readily people are going to accept it." The third ad, "Target," run before the primary dealt with gun violence. There was no specific mention of the National Rifle Association because polls had found that references to "the gun lobby" were more effective than the "NRA." Unlike 1988, when he had opposed the death penalty, now Kennedy was in favor. The ad showed Patrick shoulder to shoulder with police officers and scenes of confiscated guns on a table. Axelrod had fought with Harrison over this ad. The pollster did not want to run it for fear people would see it as knee-jerk liberalism on Kennedy's part. However, Axelrod won out by arguing that gun control was no longer a liberal issue but a law enforcement issue. Indeed, some of the strongest antigun sentiment in terms of handguns and assault weapons came from conservative, white, ethnic voters. In none of these ads, though, did Patrick speak. The decision was conscious on the part of the campaign. "Patrick is a genuine person. . . . He is not a TV star. It was a comfort thing. [Talking right into the camera] was not his favorite thing," Axelrod said. The positive ads before the primary were crucial to laying the foundation of Kennedy's campaign "without the hindrance of incoming Scuds."[35] Vigilante lacked funds to advertise, so for several weeks Kennedy had the airwaves to himself. The spots helped rebut the idea Patrick was an undeserving candidate and created goodwill for what Kennedy knew would be a tough general election. As Vigilante's campaign manager Moore put it, the ads helped Kennedy paint himself before Vigilante did.[36]

As the race got under way, a self-styled agent promoted Vigilante's cause over the airwaves. Mary Ann Sorrentino was a radio talk show host who detested Kennedy. Years before, in 1986, she had gained fame in Rhode Island as the head of Planned Parenthood and a Catholic who had been ex-communicated by Bishop Gelineau for her pro-choice activities. She now had her own radio talk show devoted to public affairs. In January, Sorrentino had pleaded with Kennedy to appear on her show. Patrick's advisers debated the merits of going on the show, but he did not have good experiences with in-depth radio interviews. There had been the disastrous interview with Buddy Cianci back in 1988 that nearly derailed his first election bid. It was a tough medium for the shy and reticent Kennedy, especially with a voluble host at the microphone. Sorrentino had a reputation among local politicians as a "bushwacking kind of interviewer." More than once, she had invited politicians in the state onto her show only "all of a sudden [to] kick the crap out of you." She had the habit of keeping the guest from responding by talking over the person. Kennedy decided not to go on the show. When informed of the decision, Sorrentino's producer warned Dufault, the chair of the state Democratic party, that she would never let any other Democrat on the show and that if Patrick didn't come on, "she was going to go after him."[37]

For the next 11 months, Sorrentino waged all-out war on Kennedy. Just as Cianci had pilloried him in 1988, Sorrentino took over the tabloid mantle in 1994. She opened her morning show by yelling, "Wake up Patrick! You're supposed to have been out already shaking hands," falsely implying he was still in bed. She constantly belittled his intelligence by playing the songs "If I Only Had a Brain" and "Baby, You're No Good." The day before the Republican primary, she had Vigilante on her show and summarized the race by saying, "This is pitting an intelligent physician who has worked for a living to get where he is, who's a grown man, against a baby who obviously can't put one word in front of another and who's never had a job. He barely got out of school at PC when someone was almost paying them off to put him through. It's not a fair fight."[38] Her constant attacks would become a test of the power of talk radio in a congressional race.

The Kennedy air assault began the day after Vigilante won the Republican primary. An ad called "Fight" asked, "In the race for Congress, who will fight for us? Kevin Vigilante? He's one of dozens of doctors running for Congress this year bankrolled by the medical insurance and drug lobbies to block real health reform [scrolling text listed contributions to Vigilante from medical interests, such as Abbott Labs, American Medical Association, American Supply Association, American Society of Internal Medicine, DuPont Merck, National Emergency Medical, and Orthopedic PAC]. Vigilante's plan is to tax your health benefits. Patrick Kennedy fights for us. He saved the Visiting Nurses program from crippling cuts and he'll stand up to the insurance lobby in Congress. Dr. Vigilante is their man. Patrick Kennedy is ours." Vigilante was stunned when this ad first started to air. He had just won his first primary election, but when he saw the commercial, he thought, "uh-oh. These guys mean business. They're not being nice." As a political novice, the attack was unsettling to him. "This was a whole new thing," he realized. "They were saying nasty things about me." His only prior experience with chaos had been the emergency room. "You walk into an emergency room and you see all hell breaking loose. It's crazy, but you have a feeling in your gut you want to do this first, that second, and something else third." Politics was another matter. Vigilante constantly felt "like we were always playing catch-up or responding rather than controlling the debate and controlling the message."[39]

A week later, Kennedy broadcast another sharp ad called "Who?" It asked, "Who is Kevin Vigilante? Bankrolled by the medical lobby, he's voted only 4 times in 20 years and has no public record. But that hasn't stopped him from distorting Patrick Kennedy's. Kennedy's backed the death penalty, tougher sentencing, and an end to the loophole that lets juvenile felons go free. Kennedy's fought to get guns off our street while Vigilante's won the gun lobby's top rating. He's on their side. Patrick Kennedy is on ours." The aftermath of Clinton's failed fight for health care reform had created public antipathy toward insurance companies and the medical industry. Kennedy tied Vigilante to these unpopular interests. Surprisingly, the Vigilante people never attacked Kennedy as the candidate of labor and trial lawyers, even though these groups were key Kennedy financiers.

Kennedy's attack on Vigilante for not voting was ironic because in 1962, when Ted Kennedy first had run for the Senate, he had been criticized on that very point. At a press conference, to illustrate his concern for Massachusetts, Ted had bragged that he had voted in every primary and general election since the age of 21. But Kennedy's opponent, Edward McCormack, uncovered photocopies of Ted's voting records, which showed Kennedy had cast ballots only in one primary and two elections since becoming eligible to vote. McCormack lambasted Ted for this deceit. In a bitter debate, he pointed out, "You didn't care very much, Ted, when you could have voted between 1953 and 1960, on sixteen occasions, and you only voted three times . . . three out of sixteen . . . and on those three occasions, your brother was a candidate."[40] However, Patrick got by with his criticism because Vigilante never researched Ted's record.

The key battle in the congressional campaign was "who was going to define what the race was about." Because it had accomplished on the positive side what it had wanted to before the primary, the Kennedy camp was in a position to define the electoral choice before Vigilante did. "We consistently got to the next base before he did," recalled Axelrod.[41] Shortly after the primary, with the encouragement of his brother Richard, Kevin Vigilante went to Washington to sign the Republican Contract with America, the brainchild of House Minority Leader Newt Gingrich. The GOP legislator had come up with the idea of bundling Republican positions on cutting taxes, balancing the budget, ending frivolous lawsuits, and weakening regulatory strictures into one package and presenting it as a commitment to voters. In an era of cynicism, Gingrich believed voters would appreciate the covenant represented by the Contract. Vigilante had mixed feelings about the Contract. There were some things in it he believed were "really quite good," such as term limits and the balanced budget, and others that were "flawed" policy ideas.[42] But national Republicans were playing hardball. Party challengers who didn't sign the Contract were denied access to money. Before he signed, Vigilante went to one of the staff organizers and said, "There are things here I just don't agree with." The functionary replied, "That's okay. It's not the point to have everybody agree. Henry Hyde doesn't believe in term limits, but he signed it. The only thing you are agreeing to do is to bring these things to the floor for a debate. You won't lock them up in committee." Vigilante said, "That's fine" and wrote a letter to Gingrich saying he objected to not providing Aid to Families with Dependent Children to women under 18 and the loser-pays clause in tort reform, but then signed the Contract. The campaign money flowed in. Vigilante set up a Gingrich fund-raiser for his campaign, but was forced to cancel it when Sorrentino objected. The radio talk show host said, "Dr. Vigilante, if you bring Newt Gingrich, whom I hate, to the state, I will pull the plug on you."[43]

The day after the Contract signing, Kennedy had lunch with Scott MacKay, a reporter for the *Providence Journal* who covered the congressional race. Kennedy was surprised Vigilante would sign the document. Elsewhere in the country, the national Republican message of downsizing government and restoring accountability to public life was playing well, but New England was more critical about the Republican agenda. But on the other hand, Kennedy figured Vigilante needed the Gingrich money to make a successful run.[44] The only thing he worried about was that "Kevin Vigilante would come up and say, 'Do you have a thirteen-point plan for Rhode Island?'"[45] But Vigilante never made that pitch, and by early October, Kennedy led Vigilante by 52 to 32 percent.

As the campaign moved into the delicate stage of political debates, Patrick told his advisers, "We're going to limit the number of debates. We're in the lead and I'm not going to let Kevin trip me up in any debates."[46] Just two television debates were scheduled, one early in the campaign with the number three station in the market and the other on the public television channel. Patrick did not have much confidence in his debating ability. His campaign manager Marcella noted, "He's not a great speaker. He's not a great debater. . . . He has a low impression of himself when it comes to his speaking ability."[47] Part of Kennedy's doubts came from an unhappy 1988 Young Democrats and Young Republicans' presidential candidate forum at Providence College. At the request of Chris Shaban, leader of the Young Republicans, a debate had been set up with a moderator from the student newspaper, a student panel to ask questions, and an audience of 75 people including representatives from state and local media. Three undergraduates, including Patrick, spoke on behalf of the Democrats, while three others defended the Republicans.[48] Unbeknown to the Democrats, prior to the debate the Republicans had agreed on an aggressive strategy. They knew that expectations were high about how Patrick would come across. "The audience saw him as someone who since the day he was born, they assumed Patrick would be able to grab both sides of a podium and articulate any message about any situation as it relates to government and politics," Shaban recalled. The reality was far different. Describing Patrick's opening moments, Shaban said, "He spoke slowly. There was a sense of nervousness when he spoke for the first time." The student Republicans had a feisty woman on their side who delivered snappy comments. "She would zap in a one-liner," Shaban said, "and we played off of one another. The audience would react." The aggressive GOP attacks caught the Young Democrats off-guard. "One kid up there other than Patrick was very annoyed," Shaban said. "He actually got up from in front of the podium and walked in front. . . . He put down the mike and started talking to the audience." Sensing that the student Republicans' strategy was paying off, Shaban thought the Democrats had lost their cool. He recalled, "I don't think that message came across as well as some of the things we were talking about." By the end, the audience reaction was very positive for Republicans. Shaban said, "I always thought we did better than they did. We were more prepared for it. They were prepared in their notes, but they weren't as prepared as we were for the interaction and the fact that we were going to be aggressive."[49] The coverage in the student newspaper described the debate as a debacle for Democrats. After the Young Democrats challenged the Young Republicans to a debate in 1990, the reporter wryly noted that "The Democrats are trying to gain some respect from the Young Republicans after a poor showing in their debate two years ago."[50]

Against this personal backdrop, Kennedy's first televised congressional debate came on October 7 and pitted Vigilante and Kennedy side by side with questions posed by Charlie Bakst of the *Providence Journal* and Larry Estepa, the Channel 6 anchor. The forum began well for Kennedy. In his opening statement, he pushed his record of "standing up to the party bosses when they wanted to pass a state budget in little or no time, often in the wee hours of the morning." He said he had challenged the boondoggle of the Convention Center and led the fight against the National Rifle Association, which had opposed his seven-day waiting period on gun purchases. It was important, he noted to "stand for something" and be willing to take on "tough challenges." Following several questions dealing with Iraq-Kuwait tensions, Patrick's experience level, campaign negativity, Vigilante's failure to vote, and problems of poverty, Bakst lobbed a surprise entry. The enterprising reporter had found an August 16, 1988, newspaper story where, after radio talk show host Cianci had berated Kennedy into releasing his tax returns, Patrick had announced "politicians should release their income taxes." Now in 1994, Kennedy was refusing to do so, citing concerns over the privacy of his brother and sister. Bakst asked him, "Why didn't you just disclose your income taxes and get this monkey off your back?" Kennedy replied, "I'd love to get this monkey off my back." He pointed out he had filed the required federal disclosure forms and listed his financial holdings. "What the people really want to know, in this disclosure process, is whether you have any stocks or bonds or holding interests that would make your job as an elected Congress person something that could become a conflict of interest." Vigilante pounced instantly. "Talk about flip-flops. Like Flipper. You said to Jack Skeffington in that race, you have an obligation to make your tax returns public. . . . Now you're saying in your case, you're exempt. Why are you special?," he asked. Continuing, he pointed out crucial facts not contained in the federal disclosure form. "Do you pay Social Security tax, do you pay federal income tax, do you pay state income tax, or are these in all tax-free municipal bonds. It would be remarkable, if you paid little or none, and then ask us to send you to Congress. . . . We need to know whether you pay taxes like the rest of us."[51]

The tenor of the debate started to shift. As confident as Kennedy had sounded initially, he now was losing steam. The final blow came shortly thereafter. Bakst quizzed Kennedy, "Sometimes we ask candidates questions not so much for the content of the answer, but just to see how their mind works. Your father raised questions about Mitt Romney's religion. Do you think he was right or wrong in doing it?" Attempting a joke, Kennedy said, "One thing I've learned in my family is never to disagree with any member of my family in public. So . . . (long pause)." Vigilante jumped at the opening. "Does that mean if your father tells you to vote a certain way, you're going to vote in a certain way?" Kennedy: "I'm trying to make light of something that. . . ." Bakst: "I didn't mean to twit you. This is a serious question, so I'll ask it again." Kennedy: "Religion should not be, play a factor in anyone's candidacy." Bakst: "Have you told your father that?" Kennedy: "Charlie, no I haven't. (long pause)."[52]

Right after the debate, reporter MacKay came storming into the Channel 6 newsroom. He had watched the debate on a monitor for a story the next day. He pronounced to Kennedy, "That was horrible. You are really going to feel embarrassed when you see the tape. It was just awful." The *Providence Journal* ran a front-page story headlined, "Vigilante Scores Kennedy on Failure to Disclose Taxes." The article pointed out that Vigilante was the "smoother debater," and that Kennedy occasionally was "searching for answers" and that voters did not know whether Kennedy paid any taxes.[53] Fortunately for Kennedy, when the debate aired two days later, it was at 6:30 p.m. on a Sunday. On another channel, the New England Patriots were in the middle of a dramatic fourth-quarter comeback against the Los Angeles Raiders. Although the Patriots ultimately lost by 21 to 17, the game drained away most of the debate's television audience. Patrick had dodged a bullet. After the taping, Vigilante was giddy. The debate had been fun, he thought. As Kennedy drove by, Vigilante told his girlfriend, referring to Patrick, "I like him. You know, you fight and this and that. He's a nice kid."[54] For his part, Kennedy knew Vigilante had "gotten the best of him," but realized there were other forums to come.[55]

The next week, the two participated in a joint radio forum at WHJJ with no television camera present. Kennedy did much better and with each passing debate, got stronger and stronger in his public presentation. After the radio encounter, Patrick told Berman, "Hey, I can give it back to Vigilante and he doesn't take it that well."[56] As a nonpolitician, Vigilante was not used to public criticism and did not respond well to personal challenges. The morning of the WHJJ debate, Democratic Chair Guy Dufault called up MacKay at the *Providence Journal*. "I'm going to drive these people crazy. I gotta get under Vigilante's skin. He's got a thin skin and here's what I'm going to do," Dufault said.[57] Dufault was the Lee Atwater of Rhode Island politics, a man comfortable with the rough and tumble of party politics. In 1990, he had helped Jack Reed win a congressional seat by feeding negative information about Reed's opponent to the press. Through opposition research, staffers had found out that Reed's opponent, an environmental activist, owned British Petroleum and General Electric, the manufacturer of nuclear power plants. In Dufault's mind, this made her "a hypocrite, a limousine liberal saying that she is fighting for the environment when in fact she had a stock portfolio that had every major polluter in the world." The Kennedy organization had conducted extensive opposition research on Vigilante. What came back was a background marked by "tremendous inconsistencies." Vigilante had bragged about being a successful businessman and even had broadcast an ad about how he had helped his brother start a restaurant in New Haven, Connecticut. According to the research, the restaurant had been in arrears to the Internal Revenue Service for five years and also had a number of Health Department violations. As a matter of general policy, Dufault liked to spread information out around various media outlets depending on the type of story it was. "Sometimes, I would give stuff to [Dyana] Koelsch [of Channel 10], sometimes I would give stuff to Jack White [of Channel 12], sometimes I would give stuff to talk show producers, and sometimes I would give stuff to the *Providence Journal*." The candidate should not personally be involved with this type of negative campaigning, he felt. "It's always the right decision to keep your candidate out of the mud as much as you can. You're better off. My job as chairman was to expose that stuff."[58]

Research had uncovered another damaging fact about Vigilante. A few years earlier, Vigilante's car had been rear-ended, and he had gone to a personal injury lawyer. By the time the insurance company had settled the case, Vigilante had gotten $40,000, a new car, and money for master's coursework at Harvard University. He had suffered severe injury to his back and been in the hospital for six months. The injury was serious enough that he worried whether he would be able to continue his medical career, which was the reason he had recovered funds for the Harvard program. But for someone who had supported tort reform in the Contract with America, there was an apparent contradiction between his own lawsuit and wanting to restrict future lawsuits. According to Axelrod, "The Contract that he signed was heavy, heavy into tort reform language and heavy, heavy heavy into frivolous suits. I know he would to this day contend that his suit was not a frivolous suit and that he was seriously injured. . . . He did ask for a Harvard education, his claim being that because of his back hurting, he couldn't be an emergency room doctor anymore. . . . But to John Q. Public, coming from a guy who was for tort reform, that was an awfully frivolous argument."[59] Axelrod put together a devastating ad for Kennedy pointing out Vigilante's actions. The ad, called "Cure," said, "As the candidate of the insurance lobby, Kevin Vigilante says he wants legal reform, to limit what injured people can collect in the courts. But Vigilante wasn't saying that four years ago when he sued an elderly Providence woman after a traffic accident. Records show that Vigilante demanded not just cash and a new car, but tuition for graduate school at Harvard because he said he was 'severely, permanently, and grievously injured.' [picture of Vigilante at parade leaning over to shake hands and then running up the street]. Maybe he found a miracle cure."

Vigilante heard about the ad while he was at a fund-raiser his barber had put together. After the candidate spoke to the crowd, he got a panicked call from his campaign manager. Vigilante knew right away he was in trouble. With his campaign manager, "Everything was 'we' unless it was negative," Vigilante laughed. Moore told him, "They're attacking you" and described the accident ad. "It was really heinous," Vigilante thought, kind of like "political pornography." Not only was it irrelevant to the political dialogue, Vigilante believed, "most of it was untrue." The campaign was totally unprepared for this assault. "A lot of the things that should have been decided beforehand about what are we going to use, what are we not going to use, how negative are we going to get, how negative are we not going to get, those ended up being 11th hour decisions," Vigilante said. He had delegated much in his campaign because he knew the rap on doctors. "The problem with doctors is they micromanage their campaigns, they are control freaks," he had been told. His advisers convinced him that the ad "was really evil. They sat me down and said this is bad. I wouldn't do this to anybody. It is not nice."[60]

The following day was the next scheduled forum with Kennedy organized by the American Association of Retired Persons. Patrick was talking with reporters when Vigilante came up from behind. Vigilante heard him "blabbing about what an evil guy this Vigilante person is." Kennedy was criticizing Vigilante for "blasting me for not knowing what it was to work my way for my education when he sued his way for his education. . . . He sued for his education. It is up to him to explain how it was that he put in for it." The Republican had not planned on there being a public confrontation over the ad. But he thought to himself, what the hell, "just pretend that you're back in New York in the schoolyard where everyone is equal." As Patrick turned around to his rival, Vigilante just stared at him for the longest period of time. Reporters who were there later recalled they actually were afraid that Vigilante was going to punch Kennedy. Finally, Vigilante exploded, "That ad is unconscionable." Kennedy: "No, what's unconscionable is that you're holding yourself out as being against [tort reform]." Vigilante: "You are misrepresenting." Kennedy: "Then explain yourself." Vigilante: "You are slandering me with things that are not true. It is a terrible commercial. It's terrible. You should pull it. You are questioning my integrity. You say I faked an injury." Kennedy: "I'm not saying you faked an injury." Vigilante: "That's the implication in there." Kennedy: "What's the implication, that you said you were permanently disabled and grievously injured. You called for capping [lawsuits]." Vigilante: "I had my car totaled. I had an MRI that documented a herniated disk at L5, S1. I still do exercises every day, twice a day. And your ad by focusing on this crap has nothing to do with the campaign."[61]

It was the most dramatic confrontation of the campaign. Filmmaker Josh Seftel was there gathering footage for his upcoming PBS documentary, *Taking on the Kennedys*, which would air in 1996. Seftel recalled that as Vigilante skewered Kennedy before the shocked reporters, "Patrick was so stunned. He like shrank, or winced. Really bad." But then, Kennedy recovered and started to counterattack. "If you're the big AIDS doctor, how come I've got the AIDS people's endorsement?" he taunted Vigilante. Seftel felt "it was almost as if Patrick physically grew in size as you watched him counterattack. He was always confident after that."[62]

The next day, Vigilante did something his brother Richard and political advisers had been pushing him to do for weeks as he trailed in the polls. As Richard told campaign manager Moore, "This is now about constantly harming Patrick in every way, shape, or form we can think of."[63] With less than two weeks before the election, Kevin Vigilante opened a frontal assault on Kennedy's fitness for office. At a press conference organized for ironic effect at Kennedy Plaza, a park in downtown Providence, Vigilante challenged Patrick's qualifications for Congress. "In the real world, if I had been a material witness to an alleged sexual assault committed by my cousin, ran from the press, denied any knowledge, only to testify later that I did have knowledge, I could not be a credible candidate for Congress," Vigilante announced. The Republican continued. "In the real world, if I broke the law by using cocaine, I could never have seriously considered running just two years later to become a lawmaker for the state. He concluded, "Not just for the sake of my reputation but for the sake of new people in the future who wonder whether it is worth it to run for office, I can't let him get away with these tactics."[64] From Vigilante's standpoint, "it was self-defense. . . . You have to fight negatives with negatives." At a certain point, you get hit once and don't hit back. But after a few punches, you have to respond. His new view of politics was that "the dirtiest stuff works."[65] Kennedy responded angrily to the attack. "This guy is a fraud, and the people ought to know it. I'm not going to dedicate my whole life to public service to let this guy run me down with a bunch of last-minute negative ads," he said.[66] Marcella was not surprised that these personal issues had come up. "I always thought they would go to that. I never had a doubt that they wouldn't."[67] In his view, people had forgiven Patrick for the substance abuse years earlier. After all, he was "a seventeen-year-old kid. His parents were going through a divorce and he was away at private school and he was experimenting."[68]

Having committed to an attack strategy, Vigilante went all the way. Months earlier, he had received a tip that Kennedy had stiffed an elderly lady on rent for his district office. When Patrick had fired Nocera in 1992 and closed down the office, he broke the lease. Palm Beach legal fees had drained him financially, and he was not in a position to keep the office open since he was opening up his new business office in the pricey Hospital Trust Tower. The woman had accepted a small cash settlement, but was due more. Featuring the aggrieved woman, Vigilante's staff put together an ad that said, "I'm Angelina Rattini. I live on the second floor and Patrick Kennedy rented my first floor. He left before the lease was over. He owed me $3,400. He didn't care if I was hurt or not. I'm 89 years old. I'm not a wealthy widow. And Patrick Kennedy said, 'I don't have the money.' I said, 'You don't have the money?' He's a millionaire. He didn't care about me." The ad helped Vigilante narrow the gap. Harrison informed Dufault that Vigilante "was moving the undecided bloc. So it was a question of how we nipped it in the bud. We felt the best way to do it was to let people know that [Vigilante] was not Dudley Do-Right."[69] President Clinton came to town the weekend before the election and raised a lot of money. The visit cost $70,000 up front to pay for the president's travel and security, but yielded $350,000 in new fund-raising for Democrats.[70] Even with his share of the money, Kennedy was forced to provide still another personal loan to the campaign. In all, he had lent his campaign $133,000. On top of the $100,000 Axelrod had loaned him, this left his total campaign debt at more than a quarter million dollars by the end of the campaign. On the day of the election, a consultant named Tom Lindeman from New Jersey identified people favorable to Kennedy, which helped Patrick turn out the vote.[71] When the final results came in, Kennedy had beaten Vigilante by 86,904 to 73,527 votes, a surprisingly close 54 to 46 percent victory. The good news was that Kennedy was joining his father and cousin in Congress. The bad news was that Republicans had swept the House and Senate, and Gingrich was the new House Speaker.

11 The New Republican Majority

*K*ennedy was upstairs at the Biltmore Hotel watching election returns when he learned that Gingrich had become the new Speaker. "I was dumbfounded," he said. "I couldn't believe that had happened. It was beyond anything I had envisioned happening. It wasn't even in my mind's eye that that could ever be a scenario." During the day, he had gotten worrisome reports. "Everyone is losing big," his campaign manager had reported. Marcella then heard Haley Barbour, chair of the Republican National Committee, announce that Republicans had won a majority of House seats and Gingrich was the new Speaker. It nearly stopped Kennedy's heart. "Oh, my God," he thought to himself. Gingrich was his least favorite national politician, someone who was "a marginal figure, a bomb-thrower, sort of a right-wing nut." He was not a man who had the judgment to run the House.[1]

Kennedy had geared his entire campaign to the idea that as a Democrat working with a Democratic Congress, he could do more to help Rhode Island. The Republican victory meant that for the first time since 1954, Democrats would be the minority party in the House. For Patrick, "it was hard to accept that the House was not going to be dominated by those old party war-horses, like John Dingell and others, that seemed to be fixtures in the Congress." Not only did the Republican Revolution represent a dramatic changing of the political pecking order, the mean-spirited ideology represented by that movement frightened Patrick. It was the exact opposite of everything Kennedy stood for, such as helping less fortunate people. "We are still in the very tenuous political time," he felt. "There is nothing to say that this sociological march towards progressivity, where we have civil rights, suffrage for women, the abolishment of child labor, human rights, all these things that are great accomplishments and achievements have been written into the annals of history and the laws of our country. The fact is they are under constant threat of being eroded and dismantled every single day, especially in this Congress."[2]

The civil war and ethnic cleansing in Yugoslavia also scared Patrick. He had traveled in that region extensively during 1991 and 1992 while attempting to build his export business in Eastern Europe. Now horrible devastation was being inflicted by people who a few years earlier had lived peacefully side by side. "Lord knows, you can't accept the fact that in the modern age, democracy will always be here. All the hell you have to do is say 'How can war happen again and how can you have ethnic cleansing?'. . . . I thought we [were] living in an enlightened time." He feared that the new Republican Revolution in the United States would elevate what he saw as the worst elements in civil society—the National Rifle Association, people opposed to affirmative action, and those who played on popular fears about immigration.[3]

It was a time of personal transition for Kennedy. He would be in Washington, running up the same steps his father and uncles had trod. It was a much better feeling than when he had dropped out of Georgetown, he said, because this time he was there "on my own ticket. Now I am able to enjoy all the great things about being a part of an incredible family and not be overwhelmed or threatened by it. I have managed to carve out my own niche within it without having a bad feeling."[4] Having grown up around politics and seen his father's unsuccessful 1980 presidential campaign, he knew Washington was a tough city. As Marcella bluntly put it, "Washington can be a mean, cruel, closed place. Everyone is out for themselves. There aren't a lot of people who are your real close friends." Yet Patrick's job required that he operate in D.C. to get things done for his district. "The way we look at it is we go down there, we do what we can, he does his legislative work, he does his committee work. He deals with the agencies and the secretary to try and get grants back for this district. Then he comes back [to the state]."[5]

Rhode Island was the place he preferred to be. According to Marcella, Patrick is "actually happier here [in Rhode Island] than he is down there. . . . All his friends are here. This is where he feels at home. Washington is a place that you go to on Tuesday and you leave on Thursday or Friday. . . . The only way he is going to stay successful in Washington is if he stays here [in Rhode Island] and does his stuff. If he starts to stay down in Washington and not come here, if he starts to view Washington as the place where he lives and not Rhode Island, I think that's when you are going to start not being successful."[6] As Kennedy became familiar with Congress, he noticed similarities between it and the Assembly. "You introduce bills as you do here. You cosponsor bills as you do here," he said. "Some of them are going to go and some of them aren't. You know if you are going to get a hearing and get them passed, you need to know the people on the respective committees to which they are referred. You need to have lobbying groups and interest groups that have a stake in the legislation." The biggest difference he saw was that 'there's just more at stake, more people involved, and more zeroes at the end of the ledger."[7]

Kennedy's staff believed there were two ways to succeed in Washington. "You can have a real fast life and go out to the restaurants, go out with different people and really be one of the players, really do wheeling and dealing, or you have to do your own thing and be your own person." Kennedy chose the second course. He went home to Rhode Island every weekend his first year in Congress and by deliberate design chose not to play the Washington social circuit. "He doesn't go out to all these restaurants. He has invitations everyday, this group wants to bring him, that groups wants to bring him. He doesn't do it. He likes to do his work," Marcella said.[8] One Saturday night, Clinton extended a personal invitation to join his table at a dinner commemorating the 50th anniversary of the end of World War II. Patrick said no, so that he could go back to Rhode Island for the weekend. He also was invited to the White House dinner for the president of Mexico. But it was on a Friday night and some of the local leaders from the Rhode Island AFL-CIO were in town for a labor reception. Patrick went to the AFL-CIO event.

His cousin Joe had advised Patrick not to make the mistakes he had made when he first entered Congress. "There are two ways to do this, the right way or the way I did it," Joe had warned.[9] Early in Joe's first year, following the retirement of Congressman Edward Boland, Kennedy had publicly picked a fight with fellow Massachusetts Democrat Chet Atkins over Boland's vacant seat on the powerful Appropriations Committee. Atkins had more seniority, but Joe had announced he "would fight him" for the seat. Joe even had gotten Senator Kennedy to weigh in on his side even though it was an internal House matter. When House Democrats named Atkins to the seat, it was seen inside the Beltway as an open rebuke both of Joe and Ted Kennedy. Another problem had arisen the following year, when during a meeting of Ted, Joe, and Sam Nunn, the respected Democratic senator from Georgia, Joe had lectured the more knowledgeable Georgian on some legislative point. The moment was so embarrassing to Ted that he later bawled out his nephew, saying "Don't you ever, ever talk to Sam Nunn like that!"[10] The family advice was clear. Don't be obnoxious. Pay attention to those in charge. Demonstrate your willingness to work within the institution. Get to know people personally. Patrick took the advice to heart. He spent hours poring over the congressional directory in order to memorize the names and faces of his 434 new colleagues in the House. Representative Martin Meehan of Lowell, Massachusetts, noticed the effort Patrick had made. "It's amazing how quickly he knew every single member he saw. People were impressed by that," he said.[11] The new congressman was terrified about making a big mistake. "I worried that if I missed anything people would say I was not mature enough. I could not afford to start off on the wrong foot," he said.[12]

To signify his local orientation, Patrick took the unusual step of placing his press secretary, Larry Berman, in the district. The congressman instructed his staff to turn down all national media requests. "I have turned down from Jay Leno to David Letterman. I just turned down Paula Zahn. They wanted him on CBS *This Morning.* Paula Zahn called personally to try and talk us into it. I have turned down Peter Jennings doing a piece on new congressmen for *Good Morning America,*" Marcella said. The district press was a different matter. It had virtually unlimited access. If there are calls from "Channel 6, Channel 10, and Channel 12, he'll work with them and we have. The [Providence] *Journal,* the [Woonsocket] *Call,* the [Pawtucket] *Times,* the *Newport Daily News,* the *Bristol Phoenix* have total access all the time. That's our strategy because that's the way we feel. He does not want to look like and he does not want to become this so-called national figure right now."[13]

Patrick's immediate task was winning a favorable committee assignment. Committees were where the major work of the institution got done, such as bill writing and resource allocation. In Patrick's eyes, his committee assignments were "the most critically important political decisions I made." He wanted the Armed Services Committee, now renamed the National Security Committee by the new Republican leaders. In the 1970s and 1980s, on the heels of Vietnam, liberals had opposed military spending on the grounds it took money from needed social programs. The B-1 bomber, big aircraft carriers, and Star Wars defense systems were all seen as unneeded relics of the past. Indeed, Kennedy's father had led the fight against some of these big weapons programs. But Patrick had another view of defense spending. In his mind, it was central to his district's economy. Harrison explained that "defense is not a defense issue, it's a jobs issue."[14] Kennedy saw defense as a way to bring federal money back to the district, especially if, as expected, Republicans slowed spending on domestic programs.

Kennedy had laid the groundwork for his committee assignment during the campaign when Democratic Majority Leader Gephardt had come to Rhode Island. After Marcella learned Gephardt was coming, he asked Kennedy, "What do you want him to do?" Patrick replied, "Okay, it's frivolous, but let's have him go down to Newport. Let's go to NUWC [the Naval Undersea Warfare Center], let's tour that." After taking a tour of the Navy facility, Gephardt told Kennedy, "This was very impressive. This is really something down here." In front of the press, Patrick told the majority leader that the military committee "would be a great committee for me." Reporters then quizzed Gephardt, saying, "This is the candidate's first request for committee assignment. Do you see anything?" Gephardt said, "I see no reason why it's not a good possibility."[15]

That tour had helped Kennedy in the southern area of his district around Newport, which was heavily dependent on defense. The Naval War College was there as well as NUWC. Patrick's emphasis on defense had made a big difference in the campaign. In his mind, "it was the key to getting the *Newport Daily News* endorsement," which counted for a lot because it came just a week before the election when Kennedy's lead was slipping and countermanded some of the negative effect of the *Providence Journal* endorsement of Vigilante. Kennedy's biggest surprise during the campaign was that Vigilante had not mobilized the military community. "To my amazement looking back on it, Kevin just did not register with the military people, the Navy and defense community on that. Naturally as a Republican, he may have had a little more standing at first blush especially next to a candidate with the last name Kennedy, with those people. He just did not put it together. It was the critical difference in our campaigns."[16]

After Kennedy won his legislative seat, he reminded Gephardt of his request, but the leader was in a much weaker position. When Gephardt announced there was a good possibility for Patrick to join Armed Services, he had assumed a continued Democratic majority. With the Republican takeover of the chamber, though, there was a reduced number of Democratic seats on the committee. Kennedy assiduously lobbied nearly all of the 39 members on the Democratic Steering Committee, the group that handled committee assignments. With each representative, he explained how important the committee was to his district and the fact that he had been one of just 10 new Democrats elected during the Republican landslide. After laying this groundwork, he scheduled an early December meeting with Gephardt. "The Republican Age may be a hungry time for most House Democrats chasing the federal dollar," he reasoned. "But the National Security Committee just might become a rare oasis of plenty, given the

GOP taste for a beefy military." A local reporter, John Mulligan of the *Providence Journal*, quizzed him. Did that mean he was looking for a "seat on National Security as a funnel for pork-barrel projects to Rhode Island?" "Absolutely," came the reply from Kennedy. He would serve his district even if it meant disagreeing with his father on big military projects and breaking faith with liberal allies.[17] Kennedy knew he had an advantage because Gephardt had visited his district. "It wasn't something on a piece of paper. It was something in his mind. [Gephardt] had a visual as to how important this was for my district. It made the difference. I remember Tom O'Donnell, his AA said, 'The Leader understands how important this is to you.'"[18] Shortly thereafter, Kennedy was awarded the last seat on the National Security Committee. Joe Moakley, the dean of the New England delegation, attributed the outcome to horse-trading among Democrats. "We pulled it off. We made some deals. We swapped some votes once we saw there was a chance."[19]

Patrick put together his staff. His alter ego and campaign manager Marcella became chief of staff in Washington. Following a brief Caribbean vacation together in November, the two had gotten an apartment together right across the street from the Capitol. Marcella was not a man who courted publicity. "I come from the old school. This is something I learned from the Ted Kennedy organization. The staff is not supposed to be in the press, the candidate or the elected official is supposed to be in the press." One of his jobs was working the family network. "We have a network down there that other congressmen would not have because of the years of the Kennedy family being there," Marcella said. "When we need to talk about an issue in Washington with an expert from Washington, we can pick up the phone and call. We have got this Kennedy network in terms of fund-raising and the brain trust."[20]

Mike Mello was recruited to be the district manager, even though he told Patrick, "I don't know anything about being district manager." With a smile on his face, Patrick replied, "That's okay. I don't know anything about being a congressman."[21] Past congressional district managers told them not to load up the staff with "policy wonks" but rather find individuals who "know how to get answers." If they helped voters find lost Social Security checks or businesses cut through federal red tape, Kennedy would have a loyal friend.[22] If questions came that Patrick's staff could not answer, a call would go out to Ted's staff. "Some rookie legislator, they wouldn't even know how to solve a Social Security problem without calling the Social Security office. Ted Kennedy's office is saying talk to Bill Smith on the 5th floor at 4:10 and he'll get you an answer. . . . The Kennedy staff gives them a breadcrumb to the right path. That is a big giant advantage," party chief Dufault explained.[23]

Much as he had done when he entered the General Assembly, Kennedy found mentors who instructed him in the folkways of his new home. Other than his father, his most important mentor was Jack Reed, the other House member from Rhode Island who in 1996 would win election to the U.S. Senate. Born the son of a school custodian, Reed had been raised in a working-class tenement and had risen to political prominence through hard work and raw intelligence. He had graduated near the top of his class at West Point and was planning a lifetime career in the Army when fate interceded in a most unusual way. Talking with an officer one day, the diminutive 5 feet, 7 inch Reed was told he never would rise to be Army chief of staff. "Why?" a perplexed Reed inquired. "They'll never promote you because you are too short," the officer replied.[24] A few days later, Reed requested an application to Harvard Law School, filled out the form, and was admitted. Because of 40 years of Democratic control, he took party dominance of the House for granted. "You understand that you go to a sub-committee chair or a committee chair, you work with them, you know their relationships, you know the appropriators who are the cardinals of the subcommittee."[25] But in 1994, "The whole world was swept away. It was like when the Habsburgs abdicated or the Romanovs left." Democrats lost control of the policy agenda. Reed went to the floor "expecting to lose every vote." The only thing Democrats could affect was public perceptions about bills, not the final outcome itself.[26]

Because few understood the odd processes of Congress as thoroughly as Reed did, he was the perfect mentor for Kennedy. Reed explained to Patrick "about bills, legislation, things coming to the floor, the Contract items, how much time is the debate."[27] Kennedy respected Reed's knowledge. In his eye, Reed "had a good ear to the ground in terms of Rhode Island, what moves who back here, what kind of feedback he has gotten on various aspects." Unlike the General Assembly, where amendments were seen as threatening by the leadership, in Congress, amendments were the natural order. To deal with these confusing items, Patrick turned to Reed. "Jack's really good at sizing up a lot of the questions and helping me when we talk about it, clarify my own feelings on it."[28]

With new Republican majorities in the House and the Senate, Gingrich set about leading a policy revolution.[29] The representative from Georgia was the acknowledged master of the Republican comeback. After decades in the political wilderness, this extraordinary man hoped to make Republicans the majority party the way FDR had done for Democrats in the 1930s. Republicans would balance the budget, cut taxes, and reduce the regulatory grip of the federal bureaucracy. In the first 100 days of Kennedy's legislative career, the revolution succeeded beyond even the Speaker's wildest dreams. Bill after bill was proposed, pushed through committee, and approved on the House floor. By April 1995, the people's body had, with the exception of term limits, passed the entire Contract with America. Kennedy voted against every item in the Contract except the rule authorizing a presidential line item veto, a bill his father had co-sponsored in 1985. In Patrick's eyes, the revolution represented turning the country's back on every needy constituency. According to his senior legislative assistant Garrett Bliss, the Contract with America "was a cruel, amateurish package of legislation that is a stain on our history that it ever got passed. It just marched through without these people blinking an eye."[30] Kennedy's friend Jack McConnell explained how the Gingrich Revolution devastated Kennedy personally. "Until Patrick found a foothold," he said, "it was hard to get up everyday and do your job."[31] Even though Kennedy thoroughly disagreed with the new Speaker, he respected his adversary's political skills. "He'll do whatever it takes to get what he wants. That's how he had become Speaker. He is so clearly a genius for political organizing and power plays in this political environment," Patrick observed.[32] Gingrich had pushed moderate Republicans out of power in his own party. He added an edge to the rhetoric and a ferocity to the attacks that helped attract media attention to his cause. Better than most opponents, Gingrich understood how "to divide and conquer the Democrats along the fault lines within our party," Kennedy said. "He has effectively divided his opposition, which I think represents the majority. He has successfully advanced a right-wing, extreme viewpoint that I don't think represents the majority viewpoint in this country."[33] In the face of the Republican Revolution, Patrick's basic task, according to Marcella, was to "protect and preserve what the gains we have achieved for the programs he believes in." But at the same time, Patrick realized it might be years before Democrats were back in charge. In that case, he had to "build some kind of coalition in case this thing continues on with Republicans in control. . . . He's going to be in the minority and he's going to be able to get things done," Marcella explained.[34]

Despite his 1989 *Providence Journal* article on "Five Reasons to Feel Unashamed about Being a Liberal," Patrick downplayed his liberal leanings in Washington during the first year. It wasn't clear if the Republican Revolution was a ripple or a tidal wave. On January 18, 1995, Candy Crowley of CNN put together a package for its popular show, *Inside Politics*, entitled "Washington Experiences Scarcity of Liberals." With guests George McGovern and Senators Chris Dodd and Ted Kennedy, the segment dealt with the rise of conservatism and decline of liberalism in the Gingrich era. Patrick was asked to be on the show to represent the youth perspective on liberalism, but Crowley reported that an assistant to the new congressman "explained that Patrick would not give an interview on liberalism because, first of all, he is not a liberal."[35] Instead, Kennedy played the politics of personality and built relations with key Republicans. According to Marcella, the congressman "is very friendly with a lot of Republicans. There are a lot of guys down in Washington who are very bitter that the Republicans are in charge, who are very partisan, who snipe personally. Patrick doesn't do that at all. He is very, very friendly with a lot of conservative Republicans."[36] His goal was to build a coalition in the Republican Congress that would prove helpful to his district.[37] At the same time, Patrick stayed close to Gephardt. The Democratic leader followed a strategy of not surrendering to the new Republican majority and trying to present a contrast to the colorful Gingrich.

Gephardt's first victory came on a defense amendment when Republicans tried to reactivate President Reagan's Star Wars proposal for a space-based defense system. Gephardt was not able to stop the overall bill, but he beat the Star Wars amendment. According to Reed, it was "the first break we had in the steamroller effect" of the Republican Revolution.[38] Democrats felt they could count on Gingrich to be inept at some point. Now that he was Speaker, his every utterance was subjected to intense media scrutiny. Soon, the new leader accommodated Democratic hopes. Despite having brought down Speaker Jim Wright through a suspicious book deal, Gingrich signed a $4 million book deal with Rupert Murdoch's publishing company. Since Murdoch was trying to build a new television network, he had lots of regulatory issues before the federal government. It created the appearance of a conflict of interest for the new Speaker and lots of bad press. Gingrich also made a series of outrageous comments about bringing back orphanages and keeping women out of combat because they couldn't take life in the foxholes. "Is this guy nuts?" Reed remembered thinking to himself after hearing these pronouncements.[39]

The key policy component of the Contract with America was tax cuts. A large tax cut would permanently slow the rate of growth of the federal government and codify the new order in Washington for years to come. To pay for the tax cuts, Republicans proposed to slow the rate of spending on Medicare and Medicaid. The proposal embraced "huge tax cuts at the expense of programs like Medicare and Medicaid that were popular and important to large numbers of Americans. . . . Do you want $245 billion in tax cuts and $270 billion in Medicare cuts and $185 billion in cuts in Medicaid?" Reed asked.[40] Kennedy felt that this was not budget balancing as much as dismantling valuable programs and paying off wealthy Republican constituencies with a huge tax cut. Democrats preferred a plan of targeted tax cuts featuring larger deductions for children, job training, and education costs. Gephardt invited Patrick to sponsor the legislation allowing for the interest deduction on students loans at tax time, which thrilled him. "It is no small thing to introduce a piece of legislation allowing for the interest deduction on students loans on your taxes. That's not a new idea. But to let a freshman introduce the bill with the power that legislation has as a political tool is pretty good," he said.[41] The press conference on the legislation represented Kennedy's official coming out before the national press corps. Prior to that time, he said, he "hadn't had that many opportunities to see how I handled myself in the new national spotlight on Capitol Hill." Public speaking had never been his forte, but this time was different. His remarks at the press conference "really went well. Some days you got it and some days it doesn't come as easy," Patrick remembered. "That day, I had it and it came easy and it came off well. I felt comfortable and confident. I felt credible."[42]

Patrick's relationship with Gephardt blossomed. In the spring, the wife of Democratic Representative Pete Peterson passed away after a long bout with cancer. Peterson was on both of Kennedy's committees, National Security and Small Business, and Patrick thought the Florida congressman was "an amazing guy." Peterson had been a prisoner of war in Vietnam and exuded a great deal of charisma. He later became the country's ambassador to Vietnam. Gephardt put together a delegation to go down to Florida for the funeral Mass, but scheduling conflicts decimated attendance. When Kennedy went to the airport, it turned out Gephardt was the only other member who showed up. The two ended up flying down to Florida and back again. When they got down there, they drove together over to Peterson's district. Despite the various political events the two had attended, this was the first time they had spent much time with one another personally. "It was never where we had personal time to click together, where we got time alone to hit it off," Patrick said.[43]

With Republican budget plans out in the public, Kennedy and Reed held joint hearings in Rhode Island on Medicare and Medicaid during the summer of 1995. Kennedy's perspective was that the Republican budget proposals sounded good until you looked at how they actually worked. "Once people learn about what they are trying to cut and how it's going to affect them in their daily lives, they are a lot more reticent to embrace the cuts. . . . The bottom line is there will be a $1,300 difference in what the dollar will buy in seven years as to what it buys today in a senior's health care," he explained.[44] Through changes in deductibles, co-pays, and additional costs to the recipient's premiums, the elderly would pay higher amounts. Concern about the Medicare issue was particularly strong in Rhode Island. The state ranked fourth in the nation in percentage of people who were 65 or older. When the budget came up for a vote, Patrick voted against the Republican changes.

While fighting Republicans on domestic policy, Kennedy quietly befriended them on military matters. It was not his first alliance with the GOP. Back in 1993, when his friend Harwood was running for Speaker, Kennedy had been forced through political circumstances to develop an alliance with Republicans that put Harwood over the top. Defense was a major pillar of the Rhode Island economy. Each year, the Department of Defense spent about $900 million in Rhode Island, nearly the amount of the entire state government budget. In Newport, there was the Naval Education and Training Center, the Naval War College, and the Naval Undersea Warfare Center. In North Kingston, Rhode Island, and nearby Groton, Connecticut, Electric Boat brought in around $100 million a year on submarine construction, which also provided 1,000 well-paying jobs in an area with too many minimum wage positions. Through the multiplier effect, these dollars generated spin-off business for a number of other industries as well.

The National Security Committee was the prime committee with jurisdiction over military spending. Weapons programs had to be authorized by the committee, as did training money for military personnel. Other than the Appropriations Committee, which determined the actual amount of money spent, National Security was the most powerful committee in this area. Chaired by Floyd Spence of South Carolina, it was one of the least partisan committees in the House. Committees that dealt with education, labor, or the budget generally polarized around ideology. National Security, in contrast, had a reputation for bipartisanship. There was a strong feeling that legislators should not play politics with national defense. From his very first day, Kennedy set about befriending Democrats and Republicans alike. Kennedy's senior legislative assistant Garrett Bliss explained the approach: "He has forged some very good working relationships with some Republicans who really ended up helping him."[45] One such individual was Representative Ben Gilman of New York, who worked with Kennedy on international issues. Bliss once ran into Gilman, who chaired the International Affairs Committee. When the Republican found out he worked for Kennedy, Gilman said, "He is a good guy. You work for a good person." Kennedy invited senior members such as Ike Skelton, Neil Abercrombie, and John Tanner to visit military facilities in Rhode Island. "The parties have different viewpoints as to what constitutes national defense, but when it comes to backing up our soldier in uniform, no one takes a back seat to anyone else in their interests in supporting our troops," Patrick argued.[46]

The key ingredient in a strong military, Kennedy believed, was technology. In the Persian Gulf War, precision bombing and smart rockets had provided the crucial edge for American forces. They had allowed the U.S. military to accomplish its objectives with minimum loss of life. In Patrick's mind, "We need to keep education and training because that's what makes our Army, Navy, and Air Force so leaps and bounds ahead of anybody else."[47] It was where Rhode Island had a significant advantage. Because of the naval facilities in Newport, the Ocean State was one of the nation's leaders in military education, training, and research. Even in a period of military retrenchment, with the Pentagon downsizing, "we need to keep our troops well educated. We do that here in Rhode Island. That's our mission."[48]

To protect Rhode Island's military spending, Kennedy learned about the pet projects of other committee members. If Congressman Sonny Montgomery from Mississippi needed a project, Patrick made sure he voted for it. Or if his colleague Ike Skelton supported the B-2 bomber because it was made in his Missouri district, Kennedy supported it. Marcella explained the philosophy. "One of Patrick's big things being so pro-defense on a lot of these issues is he's doing it because he feels it is going to help him bargain with these people in a better way to help what he needs here with the Navy."[49] Skelton was a hard-line conservative Democrat with a sharp-edged personality. He didn't forgive easily and held grudges if you threatened his interests. Patrick worked hard to build a relationship with Skelton. But early in 1995, the relationship was sorely tested. The B-2 bomber cost $800 million a plane. It was one of the last relics of the U.S.–Soviet Union rivalry. Most military planners had concluded long ago that in an era where speed and dexterity were important, slow and clunky bombers would no longer work. Marcella understood the bomber was obsolete. "Everyone knows the B-2 bomber is not going to work and it won't work," the chief of staff explained.[50] Reed, a West Point man himself, strongly opposed the B-2 bomber. "It's a relic of the Cold War. We don't need a manned, penetrating bomber at those price tags to do what we want to do. We saw the Gulf War in which stealth technology and the F-117 fighter was very effective, but not the B-2 bomber. You just don't need it," he said.[51] Most liberals in the country, including Patrick's father, had been trying for years to kill the program. When the crucial vote on the B-2 bomber came before the National Security Committee, Patrick voted in favor of it. Skelton considered the construction of the B-2 bomber the bread-and-butter industry in his district. Marcella explained Patrick's vote this way. "He knows if he needs Skelton next year to help him push the War Gaming Center down in Newport that we are slated to do for next year, he knows Skelton is going to be there and try to help him."[52] On June 13, with a 17 vote margin, the House decided to spend $553 million to begin building more B-2 bombers.

Kennedy developed the same relationship with Sonny Montgomery. If something were important to Montgomery's district, Patrick supported it. "He knows he can go to Sonny Montgomery, who might not agree with a lot of Patrick's views because he is more liberal socially, but he knows Patrick was there to help him," Marcella noted. It all went back to his father's philosophy on deal making. "I think he has learned that from his father. His father is the ultimate deal maker when it comes to the legislative arena. He is the king in the Senate when it comes to putting coalitions together," said Marcella. According to his chief of staff, Kennedy employed a clear set of criteria in his decision-making. "If he's really dead-set against something and it's bad for his district, he'll vote against it. But if it is something that really doesn't weigh either way on his district and he feels that he can help this guy out and be there for him or not be so antidefense against building this or that, he knows he needs to build things here himself," Marcella said.[53]

Following his vote in support of the B-2, Kennedy came under considerable criticism from liberals, who felt funds should be going for social programs, and military strategists, who believed the B-2 was a complete waste of money. The Union of Concerned Scientists launched a direct mail campaign against Kennedy entitled, "Congress and Its B-2 'Stealth' Attack on Your Wallet." The piece pointed out that the bomber was a relic of the Cold War that was not needed anymore. "Congress has been obsessed with cutting government, yet it refuses to confront government's most obvious excesses." It closed by asking constituents to call their representative and express disappointment regarding the vote. But Kennedy stood by his vote because he knew it was important to Skelton. It was only near the end of the authorization process, with the budget being tight, that there was a clear trade-off between supporting the B-2 bomber and protecting a submarine military contract for his own district. Realizing Skelton would be upset, Kennedy went to the legislator and explained his dilemma. One of the things he had learned the hard way in the General Assembly was the importance of asking permission to vote against a powerful colleague. Kennedy told Skelton he would like to support the B-2 and indeed had voted in favor of it early in the process. But someone had told him that the money for the B-2 bomber threatened his own project in Rhode Island. "What should I do?" Patrick asked the senior legislator. Skelton told Patrick, "Thank you for coming and seeing me. Your district is first. This is your bread and butter. You vote against it. Thank you for helping me early on."[54]

The project Kennedy was working feverishly to protect was the Seawolf attack submarine. Two subs already had been built, and a third one was in the planning stage. No single decision was as important to the Rhode Island economy as the construction of the third Seawolf. The Seawolf brought in $100 million a year to the state and 1,000 well-paying jobs. In March 1995, the third Seawolf for Electric Boat appeared to be secure. Gingrich had expressed support for it, Floyd Spence, the chair of National Security, was in favor of it, and Duncan Hunter, the California chair of the military procurement subcommittee, was behind it. But on April 4, an ominous sign appeared when Spence publicly questioned whether the country needed to keep two shipbuilding operations in business. Electric Boat's only competitor was in Newport News, Virginia. Norm Sisisky, a Democrat, and Herb Bateman, a Republican, were senior members of the committee, and they represented the Newport News area. Owen Pickett of the committee was from Virginia, and he was a strong advocate of Newport News. In the previous session before the 1994 election, there had been a tacit agreement on future construction projects. A new aircraft carrier worth billions of dollars over a number of years would be built at Newport News and the third Seawolf would be built at Electric Boat in Connecticut and Rhode Island. It was an uneasy truce between the regions motivated as much by politics as policy. The New England contingent had had excellent access to Speaker Tom Foley. Sam Gejdenson of the Connecticut area surrounding Groton had been particularly close to the Speaker, having been Foley's campaign manager in his run for Speaker. Foley had been unequivocally in support of the Seawolf's being built in New England. It was good industrial policy, a way to use federal money to buttress the industrial base in that region.

But with the stunning Republican landslide in the 1994 elections, everything changed. Foley was out as Speaker, and Gingrich was in. Spence was the new committee chair. And most important, Hunter became the chair of the subcommittee in charge of military procurement. Hunter was a man full of piss and vinegar, who wanted to make a profound impact on Navy procurement policy. Caught up in Gingrich's revolutionary rhetoric, Hunter developed new ideas on how to build submarines. The old way of thinking had emphasized continuous production. To keep shipyards in operation and skilled craftspeople at work, there had to be multiyear contracts that kept shipbuilding busy. Hunter wanted to change that. Why, he asked, did the country need continuous production? Each year, as needs changed, why not build a different submarine? Continuous production merely drove up the costs and left the nation with subs it didn't need. The facility at Newport News loved this idea. Since it also built surface ships, it did not need continuous production to keep its production line open. It could alternate between building subs and aircraft carriers without risking its business. But for Electric Boat, it was a devastating proposal. As Reed put it, "You can't staff [a production line] and take a recess."[55]

The Navy was livid about this proposal, arguing that submarines could not be fundamentally redefined every year because then there would never be a fleet or a replacement class of subs. A class of submarines was needed to build a fleet. In the past, the Navy had operated 40 to 50 subs at a time and then replaced one fleet with another. Over the course of time, incremental improvements were made to ship design that slowly upgraded the technology of the fleet. Newport News engineered a hearing that called into question Navy plans for Electric Boat. Without any substantiation, planners from the southern facility argued they could save $2 billion on the third Seawolf. In Reed's mind, it was a bald-faced lie, but it created a budget rationale for the new proposal. On May 22, at a markup session on the defense bill, the Virginians and Hunter ambushed the New England contingent on the committee. Without any official warning, Hunter announced his plan to scrap the agreement to build the third Seawolf at Electric Boat, an announcement that enraged Kennedy and Reed. In effect, the leaders of the National Security Committee were reneging on the previous year's deal.

This was a major crisis for Kennedy. If enacted, the decision would strike a dagger through the economy of his home state. Not only would it be devastating for thousands of ordinary workers; it would make a mockery of Kennedy's election promise, "He'll Do More for Rhode Island." The New England Republicans on the panel, Gary Franks and Chris Shays, never had been forced to carry the ball on Seawolf. They were supportive of the third Seawolf for Electric Boat but had not exercised any leadership. Previously, Democratic members had either gone to Ron Dellums, the committee chair, or Speaker Foley, and the matter was resolved in favor of New England. Privately, Gingrich told them not to worry, he was in favor of the third sub at Electric Boat.[56] But the New England Democrats were not reassured by the informal commitment of an erratic man. Kennedy huddled with Representative Rosa DeLauro, who represented the area of New Haven, Connecticut, near the plant. As the time for the committee vote came on May 24, one option was to confront the committee head-on and insist on an up-or-down vote on the third Seawolf. The problem was the New Englanders probably would lose the vote. "To fight and lose in that committee," Reed felt, "would be to fight and lose on the floor. It would reveal not strength but weakness." There was a new crowd of Republican freshmen in the House, none of whom had ever voted on Seawolf. It was a group that was tough on defense, "but they didn't want anything wasted."[57]

That night, Reed called Sam Dalton, the secretary of the navy. Dalton said, "If you think you can win this thing big time, then do it" in the committee. But a victory was not certain, and, in any event, it would expose supporters to a floor amendment to take Seawolf out of the bill. The question was whether supporters could win on the floor, and no one knew the answer. Liberal Democrats were out to gut big defense projects, so they could not necessarily be counted on. Many of them saw Seawolf as a pork-barrel project. Freshmen Republicans couldn't be counted on because they would want to know how committee leaders Spence and Hunter felt. At midnight on May 24, as the issue came to a head, Patrick decided not to call for a committee vote. "You've got to know when to play the hand and when to fold 'em," Patrick reasoned. The thought was, "Why anger the leaders, the Republicans, when you haven't got the votes anyway," he said.[58] Sometimes, not losing is as important as winning. Kennedy's press secretary Berman explained, "The votes weren't there. The lobbyists [for the Navy and Electric Boat] didn't want people to have to go on the record. It is hard to switch votes later."[59]

Rather than risk a committee loss, Kennedy, Reed, and their ally Gejdenson shifted to an appropriations strategy. The National Security Committee was responsible for authorizing the third attack sub, but the Appropriations Committee actually delivered the money. If they could get vague enough language in the National Security Committee, they might be able to win at the appropriations level. The Navy had a good relationship with members of the Appropriations Committee. There had not been nearly as much turnover on that committee. Bob Livingston of Louisiana was the committee chair, and he tended to be less ideological about military matters than Hunter or Spence. The appropriations tactic called for members of that committee to put sufficient money in the bill for the submarine program without any discriminatory language against the third Seawolf. The goal was to make the language general enough so that when the legislation got to the Senate, that chamber could add authorizing language to the tune of $600 million for a new attack submarine. "When they give you the money and there is nothing to prevent you from spending it, guess what, it gets built," Reed explained.[60]

That, ultimately, was how the third Seawolf was financed. It was a long and arduous process. The House Appropriations Committee added enough money to build the third Seawolf. The Senate then authorized the project. When it went to the conference committee between the House and Senate, enough was kept in the bill to finance the project.

The long-shot gamble had paid off. The third Seawolf was saved for Rhode Island. The whole episode was a crucial test for Kennedy and a vivid demonstration of his legislative skills. Just as he had done in the General Assembly, he identified discrete issues that were important to his district and worked hard on them. When he didn't know the answer, he relied on those who did. His service on the National Security Committee demonstrated he knew how to work well within political organizations. As his campaign media consultant Axelrod pointed out, "Patrick is very skilled and very bright and understands the process and how it works and how to affect change. More than virtually all the people who go to Congress, he went there with an idea of how to get things done."[61] Even in a Republican-controlled House of Representatives, Kennedy knew how to work pragmatically to preserve his political future.

12 A State Strategy

*B*arely 18 months into office, Kennedy had a 62 percent job performance rating, one of the highest in the state. He had fought the Republican domestic agenda, brought military grants back to the state, protected the Seawolf, and invited prominent dignitaries to visit Rhode Island. Critics complained that Kennedy was all fluff because he had brought in the president of Italy, the prime minister of Portugal, cabinet members, and the president and vice-president. Yet his press secretary defended the practice as a valuable way to garner media coverage. "Congressman Kennedy is accused of bringing in a lot of special guests and dignitaries," he said. "The reason we do that is we know it is going to capture the attention of the media."[1] Combined with pre-emptive fund-raising, Kennedy avoided challengers in the 1996 election, except for an unknown Republican, Giovanni Cicione. According to Berman, Kennedy "ended up raising over a million dollars in this last two year election cycle. He worked really hard and no serious opposition came forward."[2]

Within the organization, though, life was not so tranquil. Publicly, Kennedy cultivated the image of a well-designed and smoothly functioning political machine. But according to friends, tension reigned between his local district and Washington offices. The local staff complained that Washington chief of staff Tony Marcella kept Kennedy isolated from state people. Dissatisfaction rose to the point where a delegation of district staffers trooped over to one of Kennedy's most trusted friends in 1996. "You have got to intervene with Patrick about Tony," they said. "No one can get to [Patrick]. He is not hearing things. It is destructive. He is keeping him out of the district on purpose. We can't figure out why the fences are being built up." Disturbed by the turmoil, the friend called the congressman with the news. Kennedy was not surprised. "I know, I know, I know," he said when told of the problem. But with all the demands on Kennedy's time, he needed a protector and Marcella served that purpose quite effectively. As the friend noted, "There is a comfort to being in a cocoon and there is a comfort to being an embryo, being the caterpillar who is not yet a butterfly. . . . Tony takes the heat, Tony takes the pressure."[3] Eventually though, Kennedy, who had been sharing an apartment with Marcella, moved to his own place. Two years later, one of the individuals who had made the complaint, district manager Mike Mello, resigned to take a position with the state treasurer.

Around the country in 1996, Democrats were locked in a ferocious battle to regain control of Congress. Gingrich's Revolution had backfired in the fall when Republicans shut down the government.[4] Clinton was reelected, but Democratic congressional candidates were running against incumbents who had higher name identification and greater fund-raising power. With his own reelection secure, Patrick started to campaign for fellow Democrats around the country. He raised enough money to pay off his 1994 loans, including $100,000 to media consultant Axelrod and $133,000 to himself. With Gephardt's encouragement and shared building space, Kennedy established a leadership PAC named the Rhode Island Political Action Committee funded by Kennedy's biggest supporters, such as the Arthur Coia of the Laborers' International Union, and Arthur Goldberg, chair of Bally Entertainment. The committee paid for the congressman's national travels and contributions to 20 other Democratic candidates. Overall, the committee raised $91,246, making it the seventh biggest Democratic leadership PAC. Nearly two-thirds of the donations came from labor unions.[5] Kennedy's finance director James Whitehead pointed out the advantages of the relationship with Gephardt, noting that the Democratic leader has "got some great fund-raising lists."[6]

Kennedy's goal in traveling around the country was "to try and win the House back," Berman said. "He's been down in Washington for two years, he has seen how Newt Gingrich operates. He has seen the Republican extremists. . . . They have introduced an awful lot of legislation that Patrick abhors, things like the Defense of Marriage Act and all sorts of crazy things, like welfare reform that went too far and punished immigrants."[7] The congressman saw the campaigning as extending his own personal influence. "The more friends I make, the more influence I have, the more I'll be able to get done," he reasoned.[8] He told Gephardt, "We don't have much of a race back home. We have a lot of money. Why don't I devote several weeks of the campaign to help Democrats gain back the House?"[9] In all, Kennedy campaigned for 35 Democratic candidates, 22 of whom won.[10] At each event, Patrick would say, "I got up early this morning and I was telling Dick Gephardt I was going to get on a plane and fly three hours, four hours in the air and then drive another hour or so and go into this VFW Hall and meet the greatest bunch of Democrats on the West Coast that you've ever seen, and Gephardt says, 'You must be going to (name of county or town) for (name of candidate).'"[11] In California's First District, Patrick campaigned for Michela Alioto, the 28-year-old granddaughter of the former San Francisco mayor who was locked in a battle against first term Republican Frank Riggs. At the other end of California, Kennedy campaigned for Loretta Sanchez, who was running in Orange County against arch-conservative Bob Dornan, a man Kennedy called the "most strident advocate for right-wing extremism in the country."[12] In an embarrassing mix-up in New Jersey, Paterson Mayor Bill Pascrell asked the early arriving Kennedy, "Young man, where's the Congressman?" Patrick blushed and answered, "Mayor, I am the congressman."[13]

As the campaign drew to a close, the best thing from Kennedy's standpoint was that liberalism had survived as a political philosophy. In the depths of 1995, when

Patrick had been asked to be on a CNN show about liberalism, his aide had denied that Patrick was a liberal. But now, in a 1996 interview, WJAR-TV political reporter Dyana Koelsch had asked Kennedy, "Congressman, you are one of the more traditional Democrats, one of the more liberal Democrats who stuck by some of the Democratic philosophies that are entrenched even in your own family." Patrick had replied, "That's right." Koelsch pointed to Clinton's move to the center and asked whether the time for some liberal policies had passed. Kennedy denied that liberalism was dead. "I think the time for a social safety net, the time for job retraining dollars, and a time for education and a time for health care, which have always been labeled as liberal programs, today is a time for those programs."[14] Even his press secretary acknowledged the shift. In a classroom visit to Brown University, Berman said, "Patrick is one of the more liberal Democrats in the country, he certainly is far to the left of President Clinton. . . . Patrick is like his Dad in many ways. He is to the left and proud of it. . . . Patrick is the first one to say he is proud of his liberal leanings."[15]

Confident on election night that voters would turn out the Republicans, Kennedy chartered a plane to fly to St. Louis for what he expected would be a victory party to celebrate Gephardt's ascension to the Speakership. As the Cessna sped through the night, he told *Providence Journal* reporter Scott MacKay, whom Kennedy had invited on the trip, what he had learned from the campaign. "One thing you find out [is] that it is a big deal to go into someone's district. You can do all the schmoozing you want in D.C. . . . [But] you get a certain cachet when you go to someone's district and help them," he said.[16] Kennedy added, "This is what I am doing for my district. The bottom line is producing for the state and being effective." However, by the time he arrived in St. Louis at 1:00 a.m. to go to the scene of Gephardt's victory party, it was certain that Republicans had kept control of the House. Some of the Republicans against whom Kennedy had campaigned, such as Bill Martini of New Jersey and Bob Dornan of California, had lost. "Thank God," Kennedy proclaimed when he heard news of the New Jersey representative's defeat. "Martini gave me a load of grief for going into his district against him."[17] But other of his targets were reelected, such as Ohio Representative Bob Ney. Seeing Kennedy on the House floor before the election, Ney had chewed him out. Kennedy said of the conversation, "We'd been sort of friendly. I said, 'Listen, it's nothing personal. I like you, but I don't like your politics. If you can commit to me now that you'll vote for Dick Gephardt for Speaker, I won't come in to campaign against you, how about that?' And he just stormed out of the chamber."[18]

Following the election, Berman was sanguine about possible political damage to his boss. "We do fully expect a strong opponent in '98 only for the simple reason that Patrick went around the country and campaigned against Republicans. I am sure he pissed off the Republican party sufficiently enough that they are going to find someone," he said. "The biggest mistake the Republican party made was giving Patrick a free pass here this past two years," Berman said. "That gave him time to go across the country. . . . So now it will be payback time in two years. The Republican National Committee will try to pump in a lot of money to at least keep him here in the state. They know they can't defeat him. But if they find a candidate that is tougher, maybe they can tie him a little bit here."[19]

With the 1996 elections behind him and Republicans still in control of the House and Senate, Patrick paused to consider his future. In 1995, when asked the toughest thing about being in political life, he had named "the time issue with respect to being able to spend time with people and develop solid relationships." He had noted that politicians "just have a catch as catch can schedule that doesn't allow you to devote much time to personal relationships that could give you great personal fulfillment."[20] Because he was at the early stages of his career, he was not able to live life based on a personal schedule. "I am still at the stage where I have to go based on what is on my political schedule because I just have not gotten into the swing of things enough. I am much more organized and established than I ever have been before. But by the same token, it has to be solidified," he said. He had a Washington girlfriend whom he described as "somebody I love tremendously. I feel very comfortable with her."[21] He did not discuss her much publicly because she was Jewish and the daughter of a former Long Island congressman who had been killed. Ever since his cousin John had gotten married in the fall to Carolyn Bessette, Patrick had become one of the country's most eligible bachelors. Kennedy had inadvertently been the one who broke the secret about John's wedding the day of the event. He had been campaigning for Dennis Kucinich in Cleveland when word leaked out. In front of 18 television cameras, Patrick became the first Kennedy officially to confirm the news. When asked about the rumor, Patrick replied, "Yeah, my cousin got married this afternoon." His press secretary Berman got a call from John Kennedy's publicist saying, "This is not supposed to come out, don't say a word, deny it."[22] But it was too late, and Patrick's admission created one of the biggest stories of the year. Ever the good politician, though, Kennedy made sure he was standing in front of a Kucinich banner when he confirmed the Kennedy wedding.

There was one other object of concern in Patrick's life, abortion and the Catholic Church. In spring 1996, a bitter legislative debate had broken out over a late-term procedure known as "partial birth abortion," a controversial technique by which women with life-threatening complications had their fetus extracted. Most Democrats, including President Clinton, believed women should have the choice of using the procedure if their doctor thought it were necessary, while most Republicans wanted to ban the procedure. In a shocking affront to pro-choice organizations around the country, Kennedy became one of the few Democrats to support a ban on partial-birth abortions. The vote was agonizing for Kennedy, putting him between his general pro-choice orientation and what he saw as public opposition toward the procedure. Discussing the matter with one Rhode Island friend, he explained, "I felt I had to do it politically. I couldn't give [opponents] the fodder to put me way out there on an extreme. I didn't feel that I had built up enough yet to be out there. This seemed to be the one vote that would allow me to do that." Yet Kennedy remained troubled by the vote. After Congress passed the ban and Clinton vetoed it, the measure came back to the House for a veto override. During one of their weekly get-togethers, Kennedy said to his father, who had sided with pro-choice forces, "I want to change my vote." Ted instantly objected. "You can't do that. As much as you are wrong, you can't change. You have got to live with it. If you make a mistake, stick with it."[23] Kennedy cast a pro-life vote on the veto override.

That fall, the Catholic Church again reared its head in Kennedy's life. While being interviewed by *Providence Journal* columnist Bakst for a Sunday article, Patrick got into hot water after being goaded into an intemperate comment by a jibe from Congressman Robert Dornan of California. Discussing the Defense of Marriage Act, which Patrick detested and Dornan supported, Dornan had said Kennedy's late grandmother, Rose Kennedy, would have "deep admiration for my voting record" and "intense disgust" for some of Patrick's stances. Patrick reacted strongly to Dornan's use of his grandmother to attack himself. Dornan was "raving mad," Patrick argued. Besides, he pointed out, times change. His grandmother never would have envisioned the Catholic Church having woman priests. In what became an explosive remark, he added, "I hope in the near term the Church crawls out of the Stone Age and lives out what I believe is the message of the Gospel, and that is that everyone is equal."[24]

The statement, which was a small part of the column itself, became controversial throughout the diocese. Catholic officials were outraged. Despite Bishop Gelineau's pious disclaimers about not publicly commenting on the actions of specific public officials, this time the Catholic hierarchy responded full force. In a front-page story headlined "Kennedy Attacks the Church," the *Providence Visitor*, the official weekly newspaper of the Catholic Church, condemned Kennedy in unusually strong and personal language. Citing a number of church authorities, the article said Kennedy had an "unfortunate lack of knowledge" about church teachings. Diocese theologian Father Robert McManus said of Kennedy, "He's drifting apart from politics. One should never converse about something when one doesn't know what one's talking about." Another priest was quoted as saying Kennedy "should take some time off from his congressional duties and go back to Western Civilization class at Providence College to learn that the church did not exist in the 'Stone Age.'" Notwithstanding Kennedy's recent vote on the church side of the partial-birth abortion issue, the story noted Kennedy's general pro-choice position on abortion and "disrespect for human life." McManus claimed those who hold such beliefs "do this at their spiritual peril."[25] It was not clear if the latter statement was a veiled ex-communication threat. But in light of Gelineau's earlier and very public ex-communication of Mary Ann Sorrentino over her abortion views, this thermonuclear blast did not go unnoticed.

Kennedy quickly arranged a private meeting with Bishop Gelineau to make sure this flurry of criticism did not escalate into something far more serious. He had seen others in the state tarred and feathered for being out of line with church doctrine and did not want to become the next casualty. The meeting eased the immediate problem and calmed church rhetoric. Shortly thereafter, when Gelineau announced his retirement, Kennedy issued a statement praising the bishop as "a man of great courage and conviction who has been a strong leader of the Diocese of Providence for 25 years."[26] Gelineau immediately returned the favor. The evening of his announcement, WJAR-TV reporter Jim Taricani interviewed Gelineau and asked him why the church was not more critical of Patrick Kennedy's pro-choice abortion stance. Did the Church have a "hands-off policy" on criticizing the Kennedys? Rather than repeat the harsh personal attacks of the *Providence Visitor*, Gelineau replied with a kindly statement about

Kennedy. "I don't think that Patrick or Senator Reed purport themselves to be pro-abortion," he said. "They both say and many other politicians do say that they don't want to interfere with the right of a mother to have an abortion but they themselves are against abortion and they don't think it is right for legislation to be enacted which will force people to have a birth instead of an abortion." Pouncing on this opening, Taricani jumped on this soft statement about Kennedy. "Isn't that a bit hypocritical? How can you say one thing and do another?" Gelineau replied with a weak criticism, tepid in comparison to the broadside hurled by his own diocesan newspaper against Kennedy a few months earlier. He said: "Well, it is. I'm against what politicians frequently say. They think they can cover it up this way."[27]

Patrick's political career faced new challenges. Following his partisan attacks on Republicans in 1996, House Republicans offered little help on government contracts or legislation. At the same time, Kennedy's political stance was complicated by President Clinton's decision to cut Medicaid and balance the federal budget. In his State of the Union Address and budget message, the president signaled that his second term would play to the middle of the political spectrum, not to old-fashioned Democratic liberalism. Kennedy's press secretary announced, "Patrick thinks that President Clinton has kind of sold out the Democrats on this budget."[28] In the preceding two years, Kennedy successfully had attacked Speaker Gingrich for coldheartedness in downsizing government. Now his own Democratic president was proposing a similar course of action. It undermined the core of Kennedy's strategy for surviving the Republican Revolution.

The first sign of trouble for Patrick was in February 1997 when a Brown University poll showed a sharp drop in Kennedy's job performance ratings. Whereas 62 percent in September 1996 had rated him excellent or good, just 47 percent did in February, a drop of 15 percentage points. Some voters resented Patrick's forays around the country in 1996 and his abrupt departure from the state on election night to fly to St. Louis. Others were upset with Kennedy's position on the Narragansett Indians' proposal to build a casino in Rhode Island. Rather than interpreting his view as pro–Native Americans rights, as he argued, his statements were seen as pro-gambling, which was not very popular in the state. Even *Providence Journal* columnist Bakst, normally sympathetic to Kennedy, had written a scathing column about the young man's gambling position.[29]

In the face of these challenges, Kennedy developed a novel survival plan. Thwarted in Washington by a centrist president and Republican Congress and criticized at home for not devoting enough time to the district, Patrick moved toward a state-based strategy of keeping his name in the public eye. Much like the rest of the country, Rhode Island was going through a health care revolution. Hospitals were merging. Weak units were being closed. Out-of-state companies were taking over local institutions. Managed care was spreading rapidly. The national revolution hit Rhode Island when the Nashville-based Columbia/HCA Healthcare Corporation announced plans to purchase the ailing Roger Williams Medical Center and create the state's first for-profit hospital. Columbia had a reputation around the country as an aggressive cost-cutter that carefully watched its bottom line. Over the years, it had absorbed 300 hospitals, 135 surgery centers, 550 home-health providers, and a growing number of physician practices. The company controlled 7 percent of all the hospital beds in America. As the country's largest for-profit hospital corporation, there were concerns about whether it would continue to provide care to the poor, whether it would merely skim the cream off the health care market, and whether it would serve community interests.

The previous year, Roger Williams had provided care for 6,714 in-patients and 120,000 out-patient, emergency, and home care patients. It had a staff of 1,800. *U.S. News and World Report* cited the medical center as one of the top 100 American hospitals in eight different categories. Almost $5 million in free care was provided to those who could not afford to pay. As part of the takeover, Columbia agreed to pay $1 million a year to the city of Providence in property taxes and spend $10 million to upgrade the facility.[30] Since the purchase had to be approved by the state, Kennedy was not dependent on the Republican Congress for action. Rather, he could work with his Democratic political friends in the General Assembly. As his press secretary Berman bluntly put it regarding the Columbia issue, "We are trying to use that to overcome some of the bad publicity over the Narragansetts issue."[31] Patrick's position on the hospital takeover was unabashedly negative. Interviewed on a WJAR-TV news show, he condemned the Columbia purchase: "It doesn't take a rocket scientist to understand that for-profit is about taking money away from the system. And that's the nature of for-profit. Community-based, not-for-profit is about taking the money and providing for increased quality of care and also expanding health care. For-profit health care will make our worst dreams about Medicare and managed care come true."[32] At forums around the state, Patrick blasted the Columbia buyout plan. It would hurt seniors, devastate free health care to indigents, and dramatically transform the hospital landscape. In one such meeting held March 10, Kennedy brought to the state Congressmen Pete Stark of California, Sam Gejdenson of Connecticut, and James McGovern of Massachusetts to testify against the takeover of Roger Williams Medical Center. As Kennedy's senior legislative assistant Garrett Bliss pointed out, "Stark is the leading congressman on this issue. He comes from the same point of view that Patrick does." Bliss regularly talked to Stark's staff about details of Kennedy's health care proposals: "I'd give Katie a call and I'd say Katie, this is what is going on. This is what we face in Rhode Island. . . . Fax over to me what you have so far. I'll fax over things we would like to add to it or change to it."[33]

Kennedy's local ally, House Majority Leader George Caruolo, introduced legislation limiting for-profit hospital companies to owning only one Rhode Island hospital and imposing tough charitable care and financial disclosure requirements. Patrick immediately sent letters to all 150 members of the General Assembly asking them to support the bill. In the letter, Kennedy wrote, "As a former member of the Rhode Island General Assembly, I am writing to urge you to support the Non-Profit Hospital Sale Act." He warned, "The problem is that Columbia has prided itself on being the Wal-Mart and McDonald's of the industry, treating health care as a commodity to be bought and sold, with profit as its only concern. Health care is not like purchasing a pair of socks or a Big Mac."[34] Shortly thereafter, several federal government agencies announced investigations into questionable business practices at Columbia. Among the charges were that the hospital chain inflated the seriousness of the illnesses being treated so as to qualify for larger Medicare reimbursements, that doctors affiliated with Columbia had financial conflicts of interest, and that the company had broken the law in several takeover battles.[35] Robert Urciuoli, the president at Roger Williams Hospital, himself was accused of conflicts of interest over the hospital's negotiations. How could Urciuoli negotiate in the community's interest with a for-profit company that might turn out to be his boss, critics demanded.[36]

Not all public officials in Rhode Island shared Kennedy's criticisms, however. Republican Senator John Chafee questioned the negative view of for-profit hospitals. Interviewed on a local news show, he said, "My own view is that in other states, they have it. They have for-profit. And I don't see it as such a terrible threat. Obviously, there is some supervisory efforts that go with it."[37] Governor Lincoln Almond complained about the "antibusiness" nature of the legislation. The bill would make hospitals in Rhode Island "noncompetitive and costly," he said.[38] And in Washington, one powerful man, Republican Senator Bill Frist of Tennessee, was upset with Patrick's crusade. The senator was a multi-million-dollar stockholder in Columbia/HCA. Frist's father had established the Hospital Corporation of America in 1968 with the purchase of a Nashville hospital. In 1993, Columbia had bought out HCA. Over the course of the company's development, Frist, his wife, and his son had seen their Columbia stock portfolio grow to somewhere between $5 and $25 million. Early in 1997, Kennedy had a face-to-face meeting with Senator Frist, who told Kennedy he was "not happy" with Kennedy's efforts to restrict Columbia's takeover of Roger Williams. Frist denied that the company was "corrupt" and said in regard to the charges, "They're all allegations" and are "all untruthful."[39] Within a year, though, after a series of indictments against his company, Frist suffered Columbia stock losses of at least $5 million.

As the vote on the hospital conversion bill neared in the Rhode Island Senate, Kennedy aired an unprecedented 30-second television ad, financed by his campaign committee, demanding action on the legislation. Speaking before a backdrop of a bookcase and American flag, Kennedy said, "Out-of-state conglomerates that put profits above people are trying to take over our community hospitals. As our state legislators debate this issue, I urge you to speak out. We must reject those who care more about making profits than making people well."[40] At a press conference the same day his ads started running, Kennedy attacked Columbia for "its unending media campaign" and "high-pressure tactics." Over the course of the spring, Columbia had spent more than $425,000 advertising its own views on the takeover. At a Statehouse hearing on the proposed bill, Urciuoli was asked how if his hospital were taken over, it could make sure Columbia did not spawn negative headlines in Rhode Island given the problems Columbia faced elsewhere around the country. Taking direct aim at Patrick Kennedy, Urciuoli quipped, "When the Kennedy family has problems around the country, you don't look at Patrick Kennedy and say he must be like the rest of them."[41]

A survey, though, showed that Rhode Islanders favored a one-hospital limit on for-profit health care companies. Within hours of the survey's release, Kennedy's office faxed out a press release with the headline, "Poll Results Make It Clear That Restrictions on For-Profit Hospitals Are in the Best Interest of Rhode Islanders." In the release, Kennedy said, "The poll shows that Rhode Islanders are worried about turning over their hospitals to the profit-at-all-cost corporations like Columbia/HCA. Rhode Islanders have been following this issue closely and have spoken out in favor of the position taken by myself." Kennedy condemned Governor Almond's threat to veto the legislation. "For him to threaten a veto of this legislation would be a careless disregard of Rhode Islanders who clearly want strong limitations placed on these for-profit hospital corporations," Kennedy warned.[42] But after the legislature passed the bill, Governor Almond vetoed it as negative for business. He said, "Right now no state in the country has a requirement of this kind. Becoming the first in the nation to erect enormous barriers to for-profit hospitals and unduly restrict hospitals currently operating in Rhode Island is not what I want this state to be known for."[43] Kennedy immediately blasted the veto, complaining, "I say to Governor Almond and Senator Chafee, shame on you for becoming the mouthpieces for Columbia/HCA. Columbia, the bully of the health-care industry, doesn't want to play by Rhode Island's rules."[44] Almond's veto was to no avail, though. With overwhelming Democratic majorities in both chambers, the Rhode Island House and Senate gathered the 60 percent vote necessary to override the veto and imposed the toughest rules in the country on for-profit hospital takeovers.

For Kennedy, the legislation was a clear victory. He had taken on a controversial corporation and rallied the General Assembly and general public to his side. But the triumph came at the price of rising negatives. From February to June 1997, his negative job performance ratings had risen and were twice those of fellow Democrats Senator Reed and Congressman Weygand.[45] The problem was that the hospital legislation was not the only time Kennedy had weighed in on state issues in a strident manner. Following passage of the national welfare reform bill, states across the country announced plans in 1997 to cut off public assistance to legal immigrants, a move required by the new federal law. In Rhode Island, this meant that 12,000 Rhode Islanders who received food stamps and Supplemental Security Income would lose around $22 million in benefits. Governor Almond, a Republican, announced a plan to aid legal immigrants with state money, up to a limit of $5.2 million, and lobbied members of Congress to repeal the ban on aid to legal immigrants. Yet Kennedy sharply criticized Almond in a press interview for a "complete lack of respect" on the issue. "He is not offering leadership when the state desperately needs leadership," Kennedy pronounced. The governor should mobilize support from the state's businesses, labor, religious, and charitable organizations.[46]

The criticism attracted press attention because it ran contrary to the typical collegiality of relations among politicians. Public officials rarely criticized one another in such personal terms and members of the federal delegation generally did not intervene in state issues. When asked about the comment, Kennedy acknowledged that the reason he was getting involved with state matters was his difficulty of pushing things in Washington as a member of the minority party. "Sometimes . . . the only place where I think I have any say in public policy debates is back in Rhode Island, where I have friends in the legislature," he said. Almond press secretary Eric Cote condemned Kennedy's comments, saying the congressman prefers to "lob political grenades" rather than coming up with solutions. Senator Chafee had been through the same barrages over the Narragansett Indian casino issue, with the congressman repeatedly vilifying Senator Chafee's attempts to require a voter referendum on a casino. To a reporter,

Chafee aide Keith Lang claimed Kennedy was "the only member of the state delegation in the last 20 years who is not collegial" with his fellow representatives. Later, Lang explained, "This delegation has always worked together. . . . We always have stood together on what is best for Rhode Island and joined in taking the credit when there was credit to be had. . . . As far as I am concerned, Patrick goes on his own. He wants the credit. He wants to be out-front. He's number one and everyone else is a distant number two."[47] Despite the criticism, Kennedy was not repentant. "It is safer to not upset anyone and do nothing. I think people would rather know where a leader stands, even if they don't agree with him."[48]

As Rhode Island debated its policy options, the political feud continued between Kennedy and U.S. Senator John Chafee. The 74-year-old man had spent weeks in 1996 campaigning on behalf of fellow Republicans. After traveling coast to coast, he was hoarse, had lost 10 pounds, and was diagnosed with pneumonia. "I have never been through anything like it," Chafee admitted.[49] It wasn't just the illness that was disturbing him, though. For months, fellow U.S. Senator Ted Kennedy had been telling everyone in Washington that his son, Congressman Patrick Kennedy, was running for Chafee's seat when it came up in the year 2000. Every time Chafee heard the story, it infuriated him.[50] It was ironic that Ted was pushing his son against Chafee. Once on a plane flying from Washington to Rhode Island, Senator Kennedy had been seated with a friend when Chafee had boarded the jet, walked past the men, and sat several rows back. After the Rhode Island senator had passed, Kennedy had leaned over to his traveling partner and said, "You know, John Chafee is one of the best people in the Senate because his word is his word. You can trust him."[51]

Chafee had been in government for three decades, first as a member of the Rhode Island General Assembly, then as the state's governor, the secretary of the navy, and U.S. senator. Although a Republican in a heavily Democratic state, he was trusted at home and respected in Washington. Chafee was a Rockefeller Republican, conservative on fiscal matters and moderate on social issues. As a testament to this fact, Chafee had won a landslide reelection in 1994, getting 65 percent of the vote. Ted's behavior struck Chafee as uncommonly rude. The Rhode Island senator was an old-fashioned Yankee whose forebears had been one of the influential "five families" that ruled the Ocean State. He wasn't used to being treated this way.

Years ago, Senator Chafee had feared the arrival of this moment. His staff kept a file with information on current and future political rivals. When Patrick Kennedy first had run for the General Assembly in 1988 as a 21-year-old college student, his name had been added to the file as a potential rival. Six years later, Kennedy won a seat in Congress and was nipping at Chafee's heels. From that initial election, Chafee had been keeping his eye on young Kennedy. Chafee was so interested in Kennedy's 1988 race against Jack Skeffington that Chafee's office had secretly arranged for Alpha Research, a local polling firm, to conduct an exit poll on primary day. People in Chafee's office had supplied the volunteers who conducted the poll. According to an individual familiar with the study, Chafee's staffers "were very interested in this race. They saw Patrick Kennedy as a long-term threat to Chafee, and they wanted to understand what happened in 1988."[52] The exit poll results had been publicized after the primary, but no one realized Chafee's office secretly had made the survey possible. It would have been embarrassing for it to become known that a U.S. senator was so seriously worried about the campaign of a 21-year-old college student. The news that a Republican senator was involved in a Democratic primary for the state representative's race in the Ninth District would be political dynamite.

Now there was so much speculation about a possible Kennedy-Chafee matchup in 2000 that local television stations were conducting public polls on the contest. According to Channel 12, it was a dead heat. Forty percent supported Kennedy, 39 percent Chafee, and 21 percent were undecided.[53] Channel 10 put the race at 43 percent for Kennedy, 41 percent for Chafee, and 16 percent undecided.[54] Kennedy was taking potshots at Chafee in a clear effort to squeeze the senator out of the race, just as he had done with Congressman Machtley in 1994. Elections always were easier when there was no incumbent on the ballot. The first barrage of criticism had come in the summer of 1995 when Kennedy and Representative Jack Reed held joint hearings and denounced Republican Medicare cuts as cold and heartless.

At a breakfast meeting in August 1996 with Rhode Island delegates to the Republican National Convention in San Diego, Chafee returned the fire. Speaking of the Democratically controlled General Assembly, Chafee told the delegates that the legislature was "antijobs," and the "No. 1 villain" in the state's economic decline. Pointedly, he included both Kennedy and Reed in the criticism, noting that they had come out of the Assembly. Referring to Democrats in the Assembly, Chafee said, "They're doing tremendous harm to the state of Rhode Island, and I don't think good men should be silent. People should speak out and say, 'Don't let these clowns get away with this.'"[55] It was strong language for the normally even-tempered Chafee. Two weeks later, Kennedy attacked Chafee's vote in support of the Defense of Marriage Act. The legislation had passed Congress and been signed into law by President Clinton. Among other provisions, it reaffirmed unions between a man and a woman as the only acceptable form of marriage. The bill was strongly opposed by gay rights activists for its obvious slap at homosexuals and lesbians. Kennedy said he was "disgusted" by Chafee's vote in favor of the act.[56]

Then there was the open war between Kennedy and Chafee over the Narragansett Indians, a 2,000-member tribe that lived in southern Rhode Island. The Narragansetts had a 39 percent unemployment rate and per capita earnings of $9,000. Long envious of the nation's biggest and most profitable casino operated by the Mashantucket Pequots at their Foxwoods Casino in Ledyard, Connecticut, the Narragansetts had been trying to find a way to build a casino in the Ocean State. In a clear move to ward off construction of a casino on Rhode Island tribal lands, Chafee had persuaded his friend, Republican Senator Slade Gorton of Washington, to attach an amendment in 1996 to the appropriations bill that required the Narragansetts to submit to a statewide referendum before they could build a high-stakes gaming facility in Charlestown. Senator Gorton's ancestors had come from Rhode Island, and he was a major opponent of Indian rights. Two decades earlier, as his state attorney general, he had outraged Native Americans by limiting their salmon fishing. He also had challenged Indian sovereignty rights as chair of the Senate Interior Appropriations Subcommittee. Gorton had a niece at Brown University who was an outstanding hockey player, which Chafee used to maintain a personal link with Gorton. According to Chafee, "We'd chat about that. I get the Brown athletic bulletin that has pictures of women hockey players and when I would run across one of his niece, I would be sure to give it to him."[57]

Due to his position as chair of the relevant appropriations subcommittee, Gorton was in a crucial position to insist on this amendment. According to Chafee's state office director Keith Lang, "Gorton was very concerned about casinos in Washington. So he was sympathetic to us. If he had cut it off at the subcommittee, it would have made it difficult. But he indicated early on he was supportive."[58] In the final hours before passage of the appropriations bill, the Clinton administration let the amendment go through. "Unless the administration who has the power of the veto feels deeply about a provision in the law, the tendency is to sign it," Chafee pointed out. "There is no reason for them not to have signed this particular one based on that issue. I explained to the Secretary of Interior [Bruce Babbitt] and sent him the documents showing him it was just as I had indicated it was."[59] Although the president's chief of staff Leon Panetta later claimed to have opposed it, the reality according to Chafee's office was that Panetta "let it stay in the bill."[60]

Much of the state's political establishment—Reed, Senator Pell, Governor Almond, and Democratic allies in the General Assembly—applauded Chafee's efforts. There was a consensus that given Rhode Island's history of corruption, gambling should not be expanded. But one politician in Rhode Island did not share that view. Kennedy attacked Chafee's bill as discriminatory against Native Americans. In his view, the Narragansetts were being singled out for disadvantageous treatment. Referring to his own position, Kennedy explained, "If people spend any time learning about the history of this country's terrible legacy in regards to the treatment of Native Americans, they will understand."[61] Chafee did not sympathize with this view. He ridiculed Kennedy's criticisms, saying "I don't believe he understands the background of the situation."[62] Later, he added, "The clear line here is the gambling. [Kennedy] apparently supports gambling. . . . You can't have it both ways. That's trying to ride the horse in two different directions."[63] Kennedy did not back down. He attended rallies with the Narragansetts, pressed the line of attack in press interviews, organized a congressional hearing on the subject, and publicly defended his stance not as pro-gambling, but pro–Native American rights. "I've been following my family's fight on behalf of Native Americans," he said. "It would be uncharacteristic of me not to carry on the fight that my family has fought."[64] It was consistent with his family's past leadership on behalf of the disadvantaged. Besides, the congressman argued, Chafee was crossing the line by questioning his knowledge of the federal code. "[Chafee] insults me by talking about how I don't know" the law on Indian gambling, Kennedy claimed.[65]

The relationship between the two was becoming dysfunctional in a very public way. When questioned about the unusually vitriolic nature of the disagreements with Chafee, Kennedy said, "I won't hesitate to point out where I think that as moderate a Republican as John Chafee may be in Rhode Island's mind, his voting on behalf of the state runs contrary to its best interest."[66] Chafee's biggest problem, according to Kennedy, was the conservative Republican agenda in Washington. Speaking of

Chafee, Kennedy said, "He might be moderate, but he's having to toe their line. I'd much rather toe the Democratic line these days than have to be John Chafee toeing their extremist agenda." The senator was puzzled by this open warfare between him and the young Kennedy. On the surface, he always had gotten along well with Kennedy. "Any relationship I've ever had with him seems to be rather pleasant," Chafee noted. In a pointed reminder to Kennedy, Chafee explained how inappropriate the congressman's behavior was. "Usually in relationships down here you don't start off attacking a colleague. You discuss an issue rather than a personality," he said.[67] As far as Kennedy's attacks on him, Chafee said, "I've chosen to ignore them."[68] From the flurry of press releases, interviews, and counterreleases, you would have thought the U.S. Senate race between the two was in its final leg. Sensing an interesting story, Charlie Bakst devoted an entire Sunday column to the race with the provocative headline of "Chafee vs. Kennedy: A Race You'd Love to See." In the story, state Republican party chair John Holmes downplayed Kennedy's qualifications for the U.S. Senate. "It's not even a race. It's like talking about the minor league versus the most respected, the most admired. It's like such a joke, it borders on being pathetic. . . . This young man hasn't learned what John Chafee's forgotten about issues like the environment and national defense."[69]

It was another case of the political establishment downplaying Kennedy's prospects. In 1988, Democratic chief Salvatore Mancini had warned Patrick to "wait his turn" because he was too young and inexperienced. In 1994, Republicans said Patrick was unqualified for Congress because he had never held a job and didn't understand the concerns of ordinary people. Both times, Kennedy had won. Now Republicans were trumpeting the line that Patrick was a pathetic minor leaguer who did not deserve admission to the most exclusive club in America, the U.S. Senate. They were ignoring the strengths Patrick brought to the race and the clear personal growth he had demonstrated over the past decade. Even Providence Mayor Buddy Cianci, no big fan of Kennedys since a face-off on talk radio in 1988, admitted of the looming U.S. Senate race that "Kennedy would be a formidable opponent" and that "he's getting to be a better speaker, getting around more."[70] The young man had done better than the pros had expected.

As Chafee's staff considered various options, one individual consulted was Tony Pesaturo, a local pollster and political adviser. Pesaturo knew Kennedy well, having been Skeffington's 1988 campaign manager. From this perspective, the manager gave Chafee's people some frank advice. He said, "If they were serious about running, they had to start early. They have to raise money early and they have to get Chafee defined in the public mind. If he just lets things drift over the next couple of years, he'll be seen as irrelevant." From Pesaturo's standpoint, Chafee was in trouble. Kennedy was defining the issues. He was out talking about Medicare, the budget, the Narragansett Indians, and the Gingrich Revolution. The issues were his topics, and he was defining the matters very clearly. "Republicans have to find an aggressive challenger who will criticize Patrick and point out the flaws. They can't give Patrick a free ride" as they had done previously when there was almost no public criticism of Kennedy. Pesaturo understood how tough high-profile campaigns were. He had just lost a congressional race as a campaign manager. One day, after his opponent had lost the party endorsement, Pesaturo had been quoted in the newspaper saying the man had suffered a "body blow" in failing to get the endorsement. His boss had criticized him saying that it was important "to be nice to the opponent." Shortly after that, Pesaturo had gotten a call from Kennedy's chief of staff Tony Marcella. The campaign manager had complained to the chief of staff about the criticism he was getting for his newspaper comment. Marcella had replied, "You can either be nice or you can win." The Kennedys, Pesaturo said admiringly, understood how to win.[71]

Chafee's general problem was that he was becoming an endangered species in his own party. At a time when both the Senate and Republican party nationally had moved firmly to the right, the senator was a moderate. Even his own staff acknowledged the change. "There are people in the Republican Senate who are real ideologues who view the world from that standpoint. Anyone who does not subscribe to their agenda is somehow not a member of the team," said Keith Lang.[72] Most of Chafee's close friends in the Senate were gone. "What's happened," he explained "is that moderates now are just down to those from New England, and that doesn't include the two senators from New Hampshire. There aren't that many from New England." The result of all these departures was that "it's narrowed my group, the people I normally would be associated with."[73]

For Kennedy, the change was more nefarious. The national political realignment was affecting how Chafee voted. In his mind, Chafee was no longer voting as moderately as the man liked to let on. "Senator Chafee is in a position of straddling the hobbyhorse of the Republican right. He's got to make good with them if he wants to maintain his position in the Senate."[74] Chafee's position of chair of the Senate Committee on the Environment and Public Works put the senator in a powerful position to affect public policy but left him dependent on his fellow senators. Following the 1994 Republican takeover of the Senate, some conservative members had talked of ousting Chafee from his position along with Senator Jim Jeffords, a moderate who chaired the Labor Committee.

The Rhode Island senator pointed out to his colleagues that altering the rules on committee chair selection "was a very dangerous path to go down. It was dangerous for everybody." Such a shift would create "a litmus test for somebody to be chairman." To make sure no one missed his point, Chafee made a veiled threat to leave his party and take other moderates with him. Noting that Republicans held the Senate by only 55 to 45 seats, he argued, "You get five or six Republicans upset by this and they could say the heck with this, we are walking out of here."[75] To keep his chair position, though, Chafee made subtle changes in how he ran the committee. According to Lang, "He indicated to people there was no question where he stood on the issues and that wasn't going to change. But he was willing to work with people and listen to people and not dictate his position to them, but would try to work toward the consensus he talked about."[76] It was a sign of how treacherous the footing had become for a moderate Republican in the national GOP.

13 The Risks of Fame

As the feud with Chafee unfolded, the big story in Washington was the investigation into Democratic fund-raising. Two weeks before the 1996 election, a party operative named John Huang was alleged to have funneled illegal money from foreign nationals to the Democratic National Committee. The problem, though, was that not all of the money was legitimate. Individuals with working-class jobs gave hundreds of thousands of dollars to the DNC even though they had no obvious financial means of doing so. One embarrassing example came when Vice-President Gore raised large amounts of money from Buddhist priests who lived on subsistence wages. Even more troubling, it was revealed the Lippo Corporation had spent $400,000 hiring disgraced Clinton friend, Webster Hubbell, right after he had resigned his government position for fraudulently billing his Arkansas law firm. Was it hush money, the stories inquired, to keep Hubbell from talking about Whitewater? In short order, other new allegations followed. Individuals who contributed at least $50,000 to the Democratic party were allowed to sleep over in the White House Lincoln bedroom. In return for large contributions, rich donors were invited to attend informal coffees with the president at the White House.

The charges could not have come at a worse time for Democrats. With Republicans still in charge of the investigatory apparatus in Congress, both the House and Senate launched in-depth probes into the accusations.[1] As the investigations got under way, the charges moved beyond President Clinton to other leading Democrats. House Democratic Leader Gephardt had to return thousands of dollars to Asian American contributors who were associates of Lippo. So did other top Democrats, such as Ted, Patrick, and Joe Kennedy. Then, on March 17, 1997, the *Wall Street Journal* broke a story about a controversial Democratic donor named Roger Tamraz. Tamraz was a wealthy Lebanese oil financier who was trying to build a multi-billion-dollar, 930-mile oil pipeline from the Caspian Sea to the Mediterranean, right through the turbulent territories of Armenia and Azerbaijan, countries that were bitter enemies. Tamraz sought a meeting with President Clinton to plead his case even though the investor had a checkered past. He was wanted for questioning in Lebanon regarding $200 million in missing cash from Bank al-Mashrek, Lebanon's second largest bank. He was a middle-man on controversial oil deals involving a disgraced former chief of Saudi intelligence and had played a role in the multi-billion-dollar swindle known as the Bank of Credit and Commerce International case. With the help of the State Department and Harry Gilmore, the U.S. ambassador to Armenia, Tamraz arranged a June 2, 1995, meeting with Sheila Heslin, the National Security Council's expert on Central Asia, but Heslin offered no help. "I was very clear with him that the NSC, the White House, the U.S. could not endorse his project," she said. Heslin "recommended [to the NSC] that Tamraz have no further meetings because there was no compelling foreign-policy reason for such meetings."[2]

An Energy Department specialist on oil in the Caspian Sea begged Heslin to change her mind. Noting that Tamraz was promising hundreds of thousands in contributions in exchange for a meeting with President Clinton, he pleaded, "Don't be such a Girl Scout."[3] Though Heslin did not budge, the Lebanese oil mogul wouldn't take no for an answer. "I thought, you know, through the DNC I could make a policy heard," he said. In 1995 and 1996, Tamraz and his oil company Tamoil, Inc. made $177,000 in contributions to the Democratic party, attended an October 1995 fund-raiser at Senator Kennedy's house, and sought a meeting with the president to plead his case. Tamraz considered the contributions to be "a small amount, which I considered peanuts, to be sitting down with the most powerful man in the world."[4]

In December 1995, two months after a $100,000 contribution to the Virginia Democratic party, Democratic National Committee chair Donald Fowler called Heslin to ask the young staffer to overturn her recommendation that Tamraz be denied access to White House meetings. Shortly thereafter, and over the objections of NSC staffer Heslin, Tamraz was cleared for high-level functions. He attended four White House events with President Clinton, including an April 1, 1996, coffee klatch and a June 22, 1996, reception, dinner, and premiere of the movie, *Independence Day*. Also attending the April 1 coffee were Marvin Rosen, the Democratic National Committee finance chair, and Eric Hotung, a wealthy Hong Kong businessman who later would purchase Ted Kennedy's Virginia estate for $6 million, one million more than the asking price.

The Tamraz charge went beyond previous accusations. While Democrats had been criticized for coffee hours with the president and sleep-overs at the Lincoln bedroom, this case suggested that Democrats, for partisan fund-raising reasons, had overturned Clinton's national security advisers and used top-secret Central Intelligence Agency reports without any security clearances. The story immediately derailed Anthony Lake's nomination to become CIA director because he had been in charge of the NSC during this time. But Lake was not the only casualty of this affair. The Tamraz disclosure sent shock waves through the Kennedy family. The Lebanese tycoon had a number of involvements with the Kennedys. He had contributed $2,000 to the 1996 campaign of Patrick Kennedy, given $5,000 to Ted, raised $25,000 in campaign funds for Ted Kennedy, and met privately with him on December 7, 1995, to discuss the oil pipeline deal. Even worse, Kennedy's new wife, Victoria Reggie Kennedy, who was of Lebanese descent, had served as Tamraz's lawyer in 1996. The links unleashed a major congressional investigation into possible conflicts of interest in Kennedy's dealings with Tamraz.

The Lebanese tycoon was a big fan of the Kennedys. He had hired Mrs. Kennedy in March 1996 to recover assets in Lebanon. "I happen to like the Kennedys; they like me. I wanted to be helpful to them. What is the big deal?" he asked as the inquiry attracted press attention.[5] The new Mrs. Kennedy had been introduced to Ted by her parents in 1991, two months after the Palm Beach incident involving William Kennedy Smith. The tall, attractive woman was 37 years old and recently divorced. The two immediately had hit it off and had gotten married July 3, 1992, at Kennedy's home.[6] Patrick inadvertently had missed the ceremony when his flight from Providence was canceled at the last minute. A lawyer by training, Vicky Kennedy had gone to work in the prestigious law firm of Marvin Rosen, the DNC finance chair and a Kennedy fundraiser. When the Tamraz charge first surfaced, a *Boston Globe* reporter had inquired of the senator's office whether she had represented Tamraz. The spokesperson said Mrs. Kennedy's client list was "confidential" and could not be discussed. However, after it became clear Mrs. Kennedy had represented Tamraz on legal matters, Kennedy's press spokesperson Jim Manley switched tacks and admitted Tamraz was a client. But he claimed, "There was no conflict of interest, no mingling of the two." Mrs. Kennedy generally didn't discuss her clients with Senator Kennedy, Manley said.[7]

As the controversy unfolded, Rosen became a central figure in the fund-raising scandal. The man was DNC finance chair during the 1996 campaign and long had been a major fund-raiser for Senator Kennedy. During the course of its investigations into Clinton, the firm had become an object of attention in its own right. The charge was that Rosen had used his DNC fund-raising contacts to get clients for his law firm. There were many unanswered questions, both for him and for Mrs. Kennedy. It wasn't clear who in December 1995 had pushed DNC chair Fowler to call NSC staffer Heslin on behalf of Tamraz. The one thing that was odd was that in late February 1997, right before the Tamraz charges hit the press, Mrs. Kennedy had resigned her position at the Rosen law firm. When Tamraz testified on September 18, 1997, before the Senate Government Affairs Committee, the oil mogul minced no words about his reason for giving $130,000 to the Democratic National Committee and $170,000 to various state party committees and individual candidates. The gifts were to pry open the doors of access. "It's the only reason," he said, "to get access." Did he think he had gotten his money's worth, Senator Joseph Lieberman of Connecticut inquired. "Yes," he said, and "next time I'll give $600,000."[8]

The Tamraz issue was not the only one that was generating bad press for the Kennedys. Patrick's ties to gambling interests were starting to attract unfavorable notice. He was raising a lot of money from executives at the Bally Entertainment who ran casinos, Native Americans interested in building casinos, and GTech, a Rhode Island gaming company that ran lotteries around the world. Between 1994 and 1996 alone, Kennedy had raised $36,500 from GTech officials and its lobbyists. This included $9,000 from the company's chairs, Guy Snowden and Victor Markowicz, and their wives, $5,500 from GTech's Florida lobbyists, and $6,500 from the corporation's Texas consultants George Shipley, Ben Barnes, and Ricky Knox. The *Houston Chronicle* had printed a lengthy investigative article on Kennedy's GTech connection. The piece explored GTech's penchant for hiring politically connected lobbyists and making large campaign contributions to members of Congress. The key legislator cited in the article was Patrick Kennedy. The story alleged that Kennedy, alone among Rhode Island politicians and in contrast to his previous position opposing the expansion of gambling, backed the Narragansetts in order to curry favor with gambling interests.[9] As a state legislator in 1991, Kennedy had voted against a bill allowing simulcast gambling at Newport Jai Alai and Lincoln Greyhound. What the story did not say was that Kennedy also had been taking trips on GTech's private jet.[10]

In 1997, two Oklahoma oil executives, Nora Lum and Gene Lum, pleaded guilty to charges of funneling illegal contributions to Senator Kennedy in his 1994 reelection campaign. According to court papers, the Lums "arranged for numerous conduit or 'straw' contributions to give money to the Kennedy [campaign]" and reimbursed the straw contributors.[11] These contributions caused Kennedy "to file reports with the Federal Election Commission which falsely reported the names of the . . . straw contributors . . . and concealed the actual source of the funds." Although the senator was not aware the donations were illegal, the revelations forced him to return $19,000 in campaign contributions. Patrick Kennedy announced he was returning $3,000 in contributions from the Lums and $2,000 from Tamraz.[12] In regard to Tamraz, Kennedy's chief of staff Tony Marcella explained, "Patrick never met him, never talked to him, never knew him."[13]

It was not the only time Patrick had to return a tainted campaign contribution. The Hsi Lai Buddhist temple outside of Los Angeles that landed Vice-President Al Gore in political hot water also trapped Patrick. After Gore's temple ties were probed in the Senate hearing, it was disclosed by the temple treasurer, a Buddhist nun named Man Ho, that Kennedy had received $5,000 in campaign contributions following an October 5, 1996, temple visit. Kennedy returned the money after discovering that the five individuals making the contributions were illegally reimbursed by the religious group for the campaign gifts. In 1998, as part of the investigation into illegal fund-raising at the temple, Maria Hsia was indicted for causing Kennedy to file false campaign statements. (She was later convicted.) In a telephone interview with the *Providence Journal*, Kennedy explained his temple visits were "a gesture of deference and respect" that led Asian Americans supportive of his position on immigration issues to contribute to his campaign. No money exchanged hands inside the temple, he argued. But returning the money was the right thing to do, Kennedy said, because "today you had the head of the temple who's in charge of their money saying under oath, with immunity, that she reimbursed those who were involved with the fundraisers for me or who organized my trip with money."[14] That made the gifts a case of money laundering, which was illegal under federal campaign laws.

As the campaign finance controversies swirled around the Kennedys, a much more personal scandal reared its head. Joe Kennedy's former wife, Sheila Rauch Kennedy, wrote a devastating book entitled *Shattered Faith*, which detailed Joe's effort to have his first marriage annulled.[15] The two had been married in 1979 and were the parents of twin boys born in 1980. Two years after their divorce in 1991, Joe petitioned the Boston Archdiocese for an annulment, and over her objections, the annulment was granted. The book detailed Joe's acerbic temper and verbal abuse of his wife. According to the book, he repeatedly referred to his wife during their marriage as "a nobody." When she protested the annulment petition, he mocked the Catholic Church. Referring to church doctrines on marriage, he said "I don't believe this stuff. Nobody actually believes it. It's just Catholic gobbledygook."[16]

Shortly after the book appeared, an even worse bombshell detonated. The *Boston Globe* reported that Joe's brother Michael, the 39-year-old head of Citizen's Energy and a husband for 16 years to Victoria Gifford Kennedy, had over a five-year period been having an affair with the family's teenage babysitter. According to unnamed sources, the affair had started when the babysitter was 14 years old. If true, the charge would make Michael Kennedy the object of a statutory rape charge. The two families owned nearby homes, took camping vacations together, had dinner together once a week, and shared carpool responsibilities. In January 1995, Victoria Kennedy discovered Michael and the babysitter together in bed. Kennedy attributed the affair to a drinking problem and entered a treatment program for sex addiction and alcohol abuse. However, after completing that program, he continued to see the young woman. Neighbors saw the two together and informed the babysitter's father, businessman Paul Verrochi. After he confronted his daughter, she admitted the relationship and the family informed Victoria Kennedy, who separated from her husband.[17]

Reminiscent of the Palm Beach rape accusations against William Kennedy Smith, the media went wild. "Kennedy Babysitter's Sex Diary," proclaimed the headline of supermarket tabloid *The Globe*. Even the *Boston Globe's* Pulitzer Prize–winning columnist Eileen McNamara joined in the attacks on the Kennedy family. In a scathing column about Kennedy men, she wrote that "for Kennedy men to objectify the girls they seduce as playthings and to dismiss the women they marry as nobodies is to do so at their political peril."[18] The fallout from the negative news stories was immediate. Joe Kennedy's favorable standing with Massachusetts voters plummeted. According to a Boston Globe/WBZ statewide survey conducted April 28 and 29, Kennedy's earlier big lead over opponents for the 1998 Massachusetts gubernatorial contest evaporated and his own favorability ratings dropped. Whereas in January, 60 percent had viewed him favorably and 24 percent saw him unfavorably, in April after the annulment and babysitter disclosures had come out, 43 percent rated him favorably and 39 percent gave him unfavorable marks. Twenty-eight percent said stories about the annulment and brother Michael's alleged affair with the babysitter made them less likely to support Kennedy for governor. Forty-eight percent believed that members of the Kennedy family did not treat women fairly.[19]

As the controversy unfolded, press speculation centered on whether Joe Kennedy was telling the truth when he claimed he knew nothing about his brother's babysitting scandal. A *Boston Herald* poll in June found that 48 percent of voters did not believe Joe Kennedy was being truthful, 19 percent felt he was telling the truth, and 33 percent were unsure.[20] A besieged Joe Kennedy was forced to apologize both for his own treatment of his former wife and the scandal involving his brother. Speaking to the Massachusetts Democratic Convention, Kennedy explained, "I had a marriage that didn't work out. I can't tell you, and I can't put into words, how sorry I am about that. I said things that I wish I'd never said, and I did things I wish I had never done."[21] In regard to Michael's problems, Kennedy said, "On the matter of my brother, I am so very sorry, so very sorry, for what has happened to the Verrochi family. I extend to them the deepest apology that I can say." Senator Ted Kennedy echoed these comments. He said, "Joe was right to make the statement he did; I know he thought about it. It's a very sincere statement. I think he spoke for all the members of the family."[22] But a *Boston Globe* survey revealed that 60 percent of state voters felt Kennedy's apology was political and only 17 percent thought it was sincere. The public was evenly split in its favorable/unfavorable ratings of the congressman.[23] It was not until July that District Attorney Jeffrey Locke called off the investigation on the grounds that without the cooperation of the family babysitter about a possible underage relationship, it was impossible to prosecute Michael Kennedy.

Just as the controversy was simmering down, John Kennedy Jr. publicly criticized Joe and Michael Kennedy as "poster boys for bad behavior." Writing in a *George* magazine commentary, John noted in regard to his cousins, "Two members of my family chased an idealized alternative to their life. One left behind an embittered wife, and another, in what looked to be a hedge against mortality, fell in love with youth and surrendered his judgment in the process."[24] A back-lit picture of a nude John Kennedy Jr. accompanied the essay. The personal column became front page news in newspapers and on television across the country. As one talk radio host jokingly asked, "Is it Kennedy bashing when the bashing is done by a Kennedy?"[25] Reporters grilled Joe as to his impressions of his cousin's criticisms. Paraphrasing the inspirational speech of President John Kennedy, Joe described his reaction as "Ask not what you can do for your cousin, but what you can do for his magazine."[26]

Within a few days of the comments, Joe Kennedy announced he was withdrawing from the Massachusetts gubernatorial election. Citing the undue media attention to personal and family matters, and the difficulty of getting anyone to pay attention to the substantive issues he cared about, Kennedy said, "I have decided not to be a candidate for governor in 1998." Continuing, he pointed out, "You have to be realistic about the fact that people are very angry at members of my family and me in particular, and I accept responsibility for that." Behind the scenes, his aides recited the toll taken on their candidate by the months of bad publicity: his ex-wife's book, Michael's escapades, unfavorable stories, and bad polling numbers. "There was just this circus atmosphere, this incredible frenzy," one Kennedy source revealed. "He would be chased down the hallway by reporters."[27]

The family controversy was not how Patrick Kennedy wanted to be seen nationally. The Kennedys had always done well in politics for two reasons. Voters liked them personally and felt they couldn't be bought. The reputation for trustfulness and personal integrity had served them well over a long period of time. Given the state's colorful history of corruption, Patrick always had ranked high in terms of personal honesty. During his first campaign in 1988, when he was under personal attack, and in the dark days in the General Assembly, when he was locked in a bitter fight with Speaker DeAngelis, Patrick's honest reputation had saved his political life. But in this new climate, with charges of unethical fund-raising, substance abuse, mistreatment of women, and sex scandals, this family image was in serious danger of being eroded. Christopher Kennedy noted that at least eight or nine members of the 28 people in his Kennedy generation attended Alcoholics Anonymous meetings.[28] Even cousin John Kennedy Jr. acknowledged the problem. Interviewed by syndicated radio talk show host Don Imus, Kennedy said, "Kennedys sells magazines or newspapers. . . . So when Michael's difficulties, or Joe's, or my uncle's or me or my cousin—all those things tend to attract people's attention. That's why people keep putting it on. Regrettably, maybe we keep providing them material."[29]

Comedian Argus Hamilton joked that "Joseph and Michael Kennedy are in all kinds of trouble over women. It's starting to tarnish the family name. Their cousin's campaign slogan in Rhode Island is 'Patrick Kennedy—No Relation.'"[30] And an editorial in the *Boston Globe* gamely predicted a new television sit-com entitled "Kennedys Behaving Badly."[31] But the scandal was no joking matter in terms of political damage. Rhode Island Republicans openly discussed the possible spillover effect on Patrick. Chafee office manager Keith Lang said, "Clearly, he trades on that name. If that name has been so sufficiently tarnished that a Kennedy would lose an election [in Massachusetts] or be in a very close election that otherwise would have been a larger victory, it tells you something. There's a lot been said about the Kennedys for many years that people have not heard or have chosen to ignore. More information is getting out to support the fact there is an underside to Camelot."[32]

Even local reporters, normally kind toward Kennedy, attacked Patrick. On *A Lively Experiment*, a widely watched local PBS show, WJAR-TV reporter Jim Taricani blasted Kennedy's unwillingness to submit to on-air questioning: "He continues to refuse to do one-on-one interviews on panel shows like *10 News Conference* or *A Lively Experiment*. It is getting a little tired, that whole routine about making excuses because he's afraid to face tough questions."[33] Patrick compounded the problem right after Joe's pullout by refusing to talk to the state's most prominent political columnist, *Providence Journal* reporter M. Charles Bakst. Instead, Patrick trotted out his chief of staff, Tony Marcella, to explain his refusal to talk. "He has his agenda and the rest of his family has their agenda," Marcella explained. But as Bakst pointed out in a Sunday column entitled, "Joe Kennedy's Campaign Should Be a Warning to Patrick," the Rhode Island congressman incessantly brought in celebrity relatives to campaign for him and used the family name when it benefited him. Refusing to talk to the press, Bakst wrote, demonstrated Patrick's greatest vulnerability—"an occasional unwillingness or inability to confront awkward situations."[34]

Asked about that column in a classroom visit to Brown University, Kennedy district office manager Mike Mello explained: "Sometimes, questions are difficult and we'd rather not answer them. We all have been in situations like that in our personal lives. . . . So you want, if you can, take a step back and try to analyze what your position is and come up with the best response that you can, given the situation." Pragmatically, Mello pointed out that Kennedy was in an enviable position with the press. In terms of not talking to the press, he said, "you might think that there would be some kind of repercussion. . . . But there isn't. Every day is another day. [Journalists] need to report the news and we need to talk about issues that are important. We haven't noticed any retaliation." Voters never complained that Kennedy wasn't "on Channel 10 enough," Mello said. "[Rather,] people say when I call Kennedy's office, does he help me or does he not. . . . The more people that we can help, the more people will speak highly of us and help us get elected."[35]

Regarding Kennedy's campaign finance scandals, Mello noted that money scandals simply were not a major concern for ordinary voters. "They want to know are their taxes going up, how much are you going to pay for interest on your student loans, are student loans available to you, that's what you care about. . . . I don't know that campaign finance is a huge issue for people." Citing campaign finance reform proposals, Mello said, "There are other issues we think are more important, that we would fight for, that he believes in more strongly and he wants to spend more time focusing on."[36]

Despite these hopes on Kennedy's part, the Bakst column proved prophetic. Three weeks after Bakst's column, a Brown University survey revealed a further slide in Kennedy's job performance numbers. Whereas in September 1996, 62 percent of registered voters thought Kennedy was doing an excellent or good job, in September, 1997 after months of bad publicity for him and his family, just 44 percent felt that way, a drop of 18 percentage points.[37] The news sent Bakst back to Kennedy to get his reaction to the numbers. In a move that violated the most cardinal rule of press relations, Kennedy for the second time in a month refused to talk to Bakst. Instead, Kennedy's office issued a written statement proclaiming, "In an era when pollsters and consultants dominate the political landscape and make decisions for candidates, I have refused to follow the model of many of my contemporaries. I have chosen to stand up and be counted when controversial issues come before me. . . . I have decided to fight for issues that I believe in, and not follow polls that tell me where to go. In the long term, the people of Rhode Island will come to respect my opinions and the fact that I am candid." After interviewing several state political figures who made very critical comments about Kennedy, Bakst closed his column, "Dropping in Polls, Kennedy Needs to Rethink His Message," with the comment that "It's too bad Mr. Candid Stand Up Guy seems so uptight about talking to me about an adverse poll."[38]

Shortly thereafter, Kennedy held his annual holiday party at his house for local reporters. Bakst debated whether he should attend. "What do I need this for," he asked himself. But hoping to smooth things over, he decided to go. Seeing Kennedy in the dining room, Bakst approached the congressman and said, "We are going to have a better year this year." By the tone of his voice, he hoped to communicate "when I want to talk to you, you are going to talk to me." Kennedy replied tersely, "I told you there are two things I don't talk about, polls and my family." Neither statement, in fact, was true. During the heat of the Rhode Island hospital conversion act controversy, Kennedy's office had sent out a press release praising a Brown University survey that showed the public on the representative's side. And he shamelessly invoked his family whenever it suited his political needs. Almost as if on cue, Kennedy's chief of staff Tony Marcella immediately stepped between the two men and defused the situation by saying to the columnist, "Come on, let me show you around."[39]

The next year did not start out any better for Patrick Kennedy. On New Year's Eve, cousin Michael Kennedy died in a tragic skiing accident. Out with a group of family members and friends in Aspen, someone had tossed Michael a Nurf football while he was going downhill on a ski slope. Turning around to catch the ball, the 39-year-old man slammed into a tree and snapped his spinal cord. The death generated weeks of news stories about a curse on the Kennedys. Not only was the clan having to deal with the tragedy of the untimely death, some in the media had the temerity to blame the family itself for Michael's death.[40] Columns pointedly speculated whether the family's tendency to take risks inadvertently exposed it to dangerous situations. These interpretations unkindly communicated the idea that the Kennedys were to blame for their tragedies.

Within a couple of months, Joe Kennedy announced he was leaving politics and not running for House reelection. The events of the last year had deeply affected him. Michael's death, in particular, had hit him hard. Speaking of his reasons for returning to Citizen's Energy, Joe said, "The last year has brought me a new recognition of our own individual vulnerabilities and the vagaries of life. Because of my brother's death, I have a new responsibility for Citizen's Energy."[41] Patrick, for one, was not surprised. According to his chief of staff, Tony Marcella, "It has been coming for a long time. A lot of things took their toll on him." Joe's retirement would broaden the spotlight on Patrick as the most senior elected official of the next Kennedy generation. Marcella pointed out, "It will draw more attention to Patrick. It will help us politically around the country and in terms of his standing in the House. But we'll miss him. We did a lot of strategizing with Joe."[42] When asked if he was ready for the national spotlight, Patrick said, "I am ready for the pressures. I have been in public life now from the Statehouse here in Rhode Island to now serving three years in Congress. I'm feeling more like I am coming into my own." But in a reminder of the importance of staying focused, Patrick noted, "We always need to keep our feet on the ground and focused on the work at hand." Ever cognizant of the need to appeal to Rhode Island voters, he added in regard to Joe's leaving that, "if it allows me to gain more attention because I'm the only one, I hope it will help Rhode Island because that's what I am there to do."[43] His chief of staff predicted that as "the only Kennedy in the House," Patrick would have more demands on his time. "Now instead of 100 people looking for him to go to their district and state Democratic party committees asking him to give the keynote Jefferson/Jackson dinner speech or the King/Kennedy speech, we'll have double the amount of people coming."[44]

As if these difficulties weren't enough, trouble was brewing on the political front for Patrick. State Republicans were actively recruiting challengers to run against him in 1998. His poll numbers were down, and local press coverage was increasingly critical. Nationally, the GOP wanted to find a way to keep him tied down, so that he could not spend as much time raising money for other candidates. The most serious electoral threat was a 48-year-old woman named Nancy Mayer, Rhode Island's general treasurer. Elected in 1992, she was very popular. Although she held a low-visibility office, Mayer had made a big name for herself by cleaning up the state's scandal-plagued pension system and acting as a watchdog for the general public. She had little respect for

Kennedy's intelligence and deeply resented the congressman's attacks on Senator Chafee. "I have a great deal of admiration for the kind of senator he is," she said of Chafee. "He has the utmost integrity. He is a politician for all the right reasons."[45]

For her, Kennedy represented all that had gone wrong in American politics: the triumph of image, the rise of celebrityhood, and media domination of politics. "The kind of politics he represents is a caricature because it is knee-jerk and it's not thoughtful. You press a button and something comes out." Increasingly, she believed, thoughtful people were being discouraged from running for office. In her experience, she had found that "issues that are very important to the future of this country are not issues that you can easily get across in a campaign. They are issues that can readily be distorted. . . . Journalists want yeses and nos." Yet at the same time, she realized that many opponents had seriously underestimated Kennedy. "He is turning out to be an extremely adroit politician," she said. In recognition of his success at cultivating support from those of Irish, Italian, or Portuguese ancestry, she noted, "He plays ethnic politics as well as anyone I ever have seen play them."[46]

There was something, though, that she didn't understood about Kennedy. In fall of 1996, she had shared a stage with him at the Rhode Island Mall on a beautiful fall day. The air inside was stale, and the two were trapped at a public event for what seemed like hours. Trying to engage Kennedy in personal conversation, she had blurted out a playful question that hit far closer to home than she had intended. "Patrick," she asked, "what are you doing here. You're too young for this. You should be outside at a football game having fun with your friends." His reaction stunned her. Flushing deeply, he was speechless. Kennedy brushed off the question and never really responded. Mayer clearly had touched a raw nerve in the young politician. The conclusion she drew from his reaction was that he felt inner turmoil at the competing tugs of career versus having a satisfying personal life.[47]

With the open encouragement of the GOP establishment, Mayer considered whether she should run for Congress against Kennedy in 1998. Even with the political damage Kennedy had suffered in 1997, he was a Kennedy in a Democratic state in New England, the home base of the family dynasty. Mayer had run for the U.S. Senate in 1996 against Jack Reed and been thoroughly beaten, 62 to 38 percent. Kennedy, however, had some weaknesses. The young man had injured himself in 1997 with his bitter attacks on Senator Chafee. All of that year's tumultuous news about the Kennedys had been devastating—Michael Kennedy's babysitter affair, Joe Kennedy's decision not to run for Massachusetts governor, John Kennedy Jr. posing nude in *George* magazine, and Seymour Hersh's book attacking President John F. Kennedy entitled *The Dark Side of Camelot*. The voting public in Rhode Island saw Patrick Kennedy as a polarizing political force who no longer was spending much time in the state.[48] In fall 1997, Kennedy inadvertently created problems for himself by telling a Dubuque, Iowa, reporter that in 1998, he intended to campaign for 50 Democrats around the country.[49] He was in Iowa stumping for Chet Culver, the son of former Senator John Culver and the attorney who had acted as Patrick's lawyer during the Palm Beach trial of cousin William Smith. Kennedy's casual remark sent shudders throughout Rhode Island political circles because of its clear signal that the young man intended to be away from Rhode Island for the 1998 campaign. His 1994 slogan, "He'll Do More for Rhode Island," was starting to sound hollow.

In late 1997, Mayer made her move. Appearing on the local public affairs show *A Lively Experiment*, Mayer was quizzed by *Providence Journal* columnist Bakst about her congressional intentions. The treasurer conceded prominent Republicans around the state were attempting to get her to run against Kennedy. She said the door was "slightly ajar." Then with a taunt that bore right to the heart of Kennedy's weakness, she warned, "if I do run this race, I don't think Patrick Kennedy will spend Election Night in St. Louis."[50] Unbeknown to Bakst, Mayer had some provocative polling information about a possible run against Kennedy. Everyone in the state considered Kennedy unbeatable. But a fall poll commissioned by state Republicans had included a single question pitting Mayer against Kennedy in the First District. The Democrat was ahead, but only by 7 percentage points.[51] Cheering her on was Senator John Chafee, who by now was entirely fed up with Kennedy. "I was hoping very much she would run for Congress," he said.[52] Early in 1998 on *A Lively Experiment*, Bakst had asked Chafee about the possible Mayer candidacy. His response was direct and to the point. "I have encouraged her. I don't think you can find a finer public servant in the state of Rhode Island than Nancy Mayer." Pressed as to how she could win given her poor showing in 1996, Chafee praised her as a "very constructive individual" who was always "carefully prepared," both obvious jibes at Kennedy. Chafee pointed out several vulnerabilities in Kennedy. Alluding to the Narragansett gambling casino, the senator pointed out that if Mayer were elected, "you wouldn't find her favoring the extension of gambling in Rhode Island."[53]

In late February, Chafee financed a private, First Congressional District survey through Alpha Research Associates. In addition to overall favorability and job performance ratings, the survey asked about possible head-to-head matchups between Chafee and Kennedy for senate as well as Mayer and Kennedy for Congress. The poll probed whether Chafee or Kennedy best represented the survey respondent's position on 10 different issues: Social Security and Medicare, federal government spending, environment, national defense, education, campaign finance, Narragansett Indians' gambling, improving the Rhode Island economy, bringing federal dollars to Rhode Island, and constituency service. It also measured a variety of perceptions about the two men. For Kennedy, the poll examined whether he did a good job representing Rhode Island, spent too much time politicking, cared about constituents, was out for himself, had good connections, brought home the bacon, used questionable fund-raising tactics, and was an up-and-coming leader in Congress. With Chafee, the poll asked if his seniority was a plus, if he was getting too old for the job, cared about constituents, was out for himself, and was seen as working hard. The overall results were encouraging for Chafee. In Kennedy's home district, which obviously was the toughest ground for the senator, Chafee led Kennedy 55 to 33 percent. Chafee's press secretary Nicholas Graham said the senator's staff was "very pleased" with the results. "We were extremely competitive with him if not slightly ahead in those tough areas [in the northern part of the district]. We really kicked some rear end the further south we went," he said.[54] In Graham's mind, these numbers confirmed the sense that things were going well for Chafee. The senator, he said, was "seen as a bridge-builder and in that sense we have done very well. And I think the poll reflected that. No need to change course, we just saw a need to continue batting away at the same style of pitches that have been thrown at him."[55]

But events conspired to torpedo Chafee's grand plan to have Mayer run against Kennedy. In late January, a scandal involving President Clinton exploded on the national scene, and dramatically altered the political landscape. A 24-year-old White House intern named Monica Lewinsky was accused of having a sexual relationship with the president. For months, the controversy dominated the press. Commentators openly spoke about a Clinton impeachment or a resignation. For Democrats around the country, the burning question was how Clinton's fortunes might affect them. On the grounds that the best defense is a good offense, supporters of the president attacked the independent prosecutor Kenneth Starr as a partisan man engaging in a witch-hunt fueled by rumors and innuendo. Locally, Patrick Kennedy opened up on Starr. Interviewed on *10 News Conference*, the representative said, "Kenneth Starr seems hellbent on playing politics rather than practicing justice." The prosecutor was leaking major details of the grand jury to the press, which the congressman described as "entirely illegal."[56] At the same time, Kennedy blasted the press for its obsession with private lives. Asked to explain press interest in scandal, Kennedy said, "You need to look at the ratings that these shows like Jerry Springer and others garner to see why the media focus so much on this stuff. It is what sells."[57]

Nationally, as in Rhode Island, the counteroffensive worked. President Clinton's job performance ratings skyrocketed to 67 percent. Voters saw Starr as a partisan prosecutor who was out of control. Along with the strong economy, Clinton's resurgent popularity boosted Democratic incumbents, including Kennedy. The first Brown University poll of 1998 revealed that Kennedy's job ratings had climbed back to 58 percent believing he was doing an excellent or good job. Between the sympathy engendered by Michael Kennedy's death and the pro-Clinton spike in national sentiment, Patrick had regained almost all of the positive evaluations he had lost in 1997. Even more impressive, a head-to-head matchup with Nancy Mayer showed him leading her decisively by 51 to 30 percent among district voters.[58]

Chafee's February poll found the same result. Even though Chafee had a big margin over Kennedy, the Democratic congressman led Mayer. In the head-to-head matchup, Kennedy "was substantially ahead of me, enough that you would sit up and take notice," Mayer conceded.[59] After a nightmarish year, in which anything that could go wrong did, Kennedy had become the comeback kid of Rhode Island politics. Although there were reasons other than the poll that persuaded her, Mayer decided to run for attorney general, where there was an open-seat election. In the end, Republicans were left with the same position they had been in during 1996—a no-name, poorly funded challenger, Ron Santa, who did not represent a serious threat to Kennedy. For Mayer, the whole episode demonstrated the weakness of the Republican party. "There is no party support in terms of people, money, or organization. Everybody is cut loose ＼ do his or her own thing."[60]

Freed of a major competitor, Kennedy continued his travels around the country ˡf of Democratic candidates. As his press secretary Berman put it, "When they put on an event in California or Iowa, it is a big deal when the Democrat brings in a Kennedy. . . . It automatically means press, TV coverage, and you are going to raise a lot of money."[61] At one rally for a New Mexico congressional special election early in 1998, Kennedy shared the platform with First Lady Hillary Clinton and House Democratic Leader Dick Gephardt. The campaign spokesperson for the local Republican candidate quipped: "I can't think of a better way to make sure Republicans show up at the polls than to have [Democrat] Phil Maloof standing side by side with a Clinton, a Gephardt and a Kennedy."[62] Kennedy's continuing travels on behalf of the Democratic party earned him major chits for advancement within the House. Party leaders pushed him for a coveted seat on the Appropriations Committee following the 1998 elections, the powerful committee that approved all House spending bills. He also was a finalist to head the Democratic Congressional Campaign Committee, the major fund-raising arm for House Democrats.

For his own part, Kennedy downplayed the new career possibilities. "I don't want a lot of ill will. I don't want people to say, 'Hey, you're getting it because you are a Kennedy.' I have several years to go before thinking about leadership."[63] Yet behind the scenes, his staff was salivating at the House leadership possibilities. Speaking of the DCCC, Marcella said, "If he gets it, he would become the fifth-ranking Democrat in the House and be in the leadership ranks. It would be a major platform from which to speak out." Noting the longer-term possibilities, he added, "He could stay in the House and rise rapidly into the Democratic leadership. People aren't sticking around very long in the House."[64] The new "staying in the House" strategy of Kennedy's represented a recognition that the old approach of running for the Senate by forcing Chafee out of the race was not working. Chafee press secretary Graham pointed out Kennedy's problem: [the Kennedy staff] "did not see advancing the idea that he might run for the Senate working to his advantage either legislatively or in political terms in Rhode Island any longer." Continuing, he explained, "My feeling was that it was clouding their image too much. . . . The more they talked about the 2000 Senate race, the less positively people viewed him as working toward senior issues on health care and all those kinds of things." In addition, the shift was dictated by all of the negative campaign fund-raising stories involving Kennedy. "Anytime the Senate race 2000 issue was raised, the whole issue of money came back into focus," Graham said. "Last year and this year was so dominated by campaign finance reform. Those two messages coming together, Kennedy being the money hound and Congress working toward campaign finance reform resolution were not clicking. One of them had to be withdrawn. What was withdrawn from the equation was the constant chatter about money and Senate 2000."[65]

Despite past fund-raising controversies, the money hunt was going well for Kennedy. In finance reports, Patrick ranked ninth of the 435 people in the entire House in campaign monies raised—despite the fact that he was running against an opponent no one had heard of. Around 80 percent of the money was coming from out of state. Substantial chunks of the cash raised went for travel around the country. In 1996, for example, 12 percent ($78,000) of Kennedy's overall expenses went for travel, the highest among the New England congressional delegation.[66] And he was gaining recognition around the country. In May, Kennedy was the recipient of an honorary doctors of laws degree from Muhlenberg College in Pennsylvania and delivered the main commencement address.[67]

At his 1998 reelection announcement, Kennedy put together a major rally attended by his father and mother, along with Democratic Leader Dick Gephardt. Gephardt defended the young man. "A lot of people in public life understandably take care of their own situation and don't find much time for their colleagues or their compatriots in politics. That's not Patrick. We are trying to win the House back. . . . He knows that without a majority, we don't get to bring up legislation."[68] Patrick meanwhile touted his interest in health care. Reminding the audience of his battle against the for-profit company, Columbia/HCA, he ad-libbed, "I won't forget Governor Almond saying it is going to be bad for business in this state. Look at what happened. Columbia/HCA has gone down the tubes."[69] Interviewed after the rally, Joan Kennedy said she was thrilled about Patrick's success. "That is what he wanted to do. And he is very good at it. I'm just happy for him because he is doing what he wants to do." Then, in recognition of all the personal baggage he had overcome in his life, she added, "This has been wonderful for Patrick."[70] When asked by a reporter what was the difference between campaigning for Patrick and Ted, Joan pointedly noted that, unlike her former husband, "Patrick says thank you."[71] Reflecting on the turmoil of the previous year, chief of staff Marcella explained the relieved feeling within the Kennedy camp. "When there are times that are not so good, you just go forward. You put your head down and you just go through it. You do the best you can. You stay your course, stay strong to what you believe in, and work your base."[72] Kennedy's travels around the country had not harmed him an iota. He was back in charge of his political destiny.

14 The Fight for a Democratic Majority

*W*ith his rapid comeback following the nightmarish 1997, Kennedy turned his attention toward the national stage. Assisting him as he had been doing for several years was his congressional mentor, Dick Gephardt, the House Democratic leader. In many respects, the two men were the political odd couple. Gephardt was the son of a midwestern milkman whose disclosure form listed his net worth at negative $45,000, Patrick the millionaire heir to a celebrated New England family. A staunch union man and defender of the working class, the Missouri representative had a reputation for being cold and aloof in his dealings with people. In his fictionalized, political tell-all novel *Primary Colors*, Joe Klein unfavorably described Majority Leader William Larkin, a man modeled on Gephardt, as "good instincts, . . . but too cool. . . . I've never seen him blink. He's got that steady gaze."[1] In what the novelist considered a telling political fault, Larkin was a man who always ordered mineral water, even when alcohol would help him seal a political deal.

Kennedy had two qualities that were of interest to Gephardt: a celebrity name and an ability to raise money. Despite press charges about the "dark side of Camelot" and anger at the new generation of Kennedys, a large number of people around the country still idolized the family.[2] The magic was not limited to the previous generation of Jack, Robert, and Ted. At one reception in St. Louis, a participant admitted, "The name Kennedy is magic." Another noted, "I've always had a place in my heart for the Kennedys." Even Patrick could see the pull of his famous last name. "Many people come to meet me for my family name, to tell me what my uncles meant to them."[3] Aside from their financial alliance, Gephardt had become Patrick's most important mentor other than his father.[4] Their relationship was so close that in Gephardt's hometown, Kennedy jabbed his ally in a good-natured manner. Dressed in casual attire—a rumpled white polo shirt and wrinkled khaki pants—at a reception preceding the annual dinner of the St. Louis Labor Council, Kennedy confessed, "Gephardt told me to dress casually, and then he's out here wearing a shirt and tie." The young man joked that he should have ignored the clothing instructions because with his young age, "I need as much help looking like a congressman as I can get."[5]

But it was not just short-term politics that drew the two together. Gephardt was worrying about the long-term vision of his party. After several years of Republican rule, many party loyalists were starved for a traditional Democrat who would reassert progressive values. What was the virtue of holding the presidency if it meant an agenda dictated by Republican principles on crime, welfare reform, and a balanced budget? As this debate unfolded—within the party and in the country as a whole—Gephardt understood the crucial position held by the Kennedys. In his very first race for the presidency in 1992, Clinton had made a point of playing up to Ted Kennedy, emphasizing how his 1963 White House meeting with John Kennedy during a Boys Nation convention had drawn him into public service.[6] A flattered Ted Kennedy had endorsed Clinton and worked hard for his election. In the White House, Clinton raised money for the Kennedy Library and consulted often with Ted during the effort to pass universal health care. Following that debacle and the 1994 Republican takeover of Congress, Clinton kept in touch with Kennedy even as the president drifted to the right. It was a relationship both men needed, Clinton to protect his liberal flank, and Kennedy to maintain his best presidential access in three decades.

Keeping silent about the party's future direction, though, was another matter. Throughout Clinton's second term, Senator Kennedy was feeling less and less easy about the president's program. Clinton had signed the welfare reform bill, about which Kennedy had reservations, right before the 1996 election. In 1997, Clinton had agreed to balance the budget by the 2002. Reluctantly, Ted had voted for the bill because it included money for the Kennedy-Kassebaum child health initiative. Patrick and Joe Kennedy voted against the balanced budget agreement. Even though the bill would balance the budget, establish a $24 billion child health program, and provide $84 billion in tax cuts, Patrick Kennedy opposed the bill on the grounds that spending cuts posed a danger to Medicare beneficiaries. "One thing I do know," Kennedy said, is that the amount being spent on tax cuts would go a long way toward ensuring Medicare's long-term solvency.[7] Patrick was not necessarily opposed to a balanced budget. But according to his chief of staff Marcella, "There was no need to rush it through for political gain. People wanted to say we voted for a balanced budget. That is fine, but let's be responsible, let's look at what is being done, let's make sure it is being done the right way." The budget could be balanced over a longer period of time, such as 10 years.[8]

The budget vote attracted attention because of the split between the Kennedy generations. Ted not only voted for the agreement, he joined cheering legislators on the south lawn of the White House when President Clinton signed the bill. After the ceremony, the senior Kennedy said, "Today we celebrate an unprecedented achievement for America's working families and their children."[9] Ever careful not to alienate his father, Patrick told the *Providence Journal* regarding his no vote, "I talked to my father about that. He said I was doing the right thing for what I was fighting for."[10] In one stark irony as the House vote was taking place, Patrick found himself right next to House Majority Leader Richard Armey of Texas, a big supporter of the agreement. After Kennedy had voted against the agreement, he turned to Armey and said, "I want to thank you for voting yes. You just helped my father receive $300,000 in tax benefits." Recalling the story at a press conference, Armey said he replied, "Patrick, I love your daddy more than you do, because you voted no."[11]

The next week, Patrick wrote a letter to the editor of the *Wall Street Journal* defending Democrats who opposed the legislation. Entitled "America Needs 'True' Democrats," Kennedy attacked a column written by Al From, president of the Democratic Leadership Council (DLC) and a leading advocate of New Democratic centrism. From had criticized Kennedy's House mentor, Gephardt, for opposing the balanced budget and tax cut agreement. Defending Gephardt as well as other liberals within the party, Kennedy wrote, "For working- and middle-class families, the notion of a New Democrat only weakens the true core of Democratic values."[12] Kennedy's response was ironic because in 1994 as he was gearing up for his first run for Congress, he had considered forming a Rhode Island version of the DLC and campaigning as a New Democrat. At a meeting at his residence, a group of supporters had debated the merits of such a move. Those present argued that it was exactly what Patrick should do and that running as a centrist would be the best way to guarantee victory. By the end of the meeting, the general consensus was that Kennedy should run as a New Democrat. However, one late-arriving adviser, Robert Walsh, felt it was a terrible idea. The DLC guys didn't have the same values as Kennedy, and DLC sponsors included groups, such as the National Rifle Association, which were anathema to Kennedy. Besides, Walsh argued, if Patrick did this, "the headline would not be 'Kennedy Follows Clinton Lead'; it would be 'Patrick Kennedy Breaks with His Father Politically.'" Soon thereafter, Patrick dropped his brief DLC flirtation.[13]

In 1997, Gephardt gave a speech at Harvard University that called for a "new progressivism for a new century" and criticized the futility of the politics of "small ideas." With a sharp jab at Clinton and Gore for their centrist drift, the 12-term Missouri representative spoke in populist and class-conscious terms about how many Americans were being left behind by corporate America. "Despite the profits and promise of this new economy, our old problems are enduring," he said. "The current recovery has not narrowed but indeed widened the gap between the wealthy and the working class. . . . We need a Democratic party that is a movement for change, and not a money machine."[14] The speech was written by media consultant Robert Shrum, an adviser and good friend to Senator Ted Kennedy.[15]

The reaction from the Clinton White House came instantly. Senior presidential adviser Rahm Emanuel fumed over the speech, saying "for Congressman Gephardt to attack President Clinton while the President is trying hard to unite this party for the '98 elections can only harm our party and prospects. It sounds like politics over principle, especially given his flip-flops on multiple issues."[16] The latter was an allusion to the fact that since winning election to the House in 1976, Gephardt had changed his position on issues such as abortion. At various points in his career, Gephardt had been known either as a New Democrat, an Old Democrat, or an Atari Democrat concerned about trade issues. The Missouri representative had been one of the original founders of the DLC and had tried to steer the party away from old-fashioned liberalism. Now he was criticizing Clinton and Gore for that very same repositioning. Reacting to the

White House criticism, Gephardt explained, "Anybody who has any sense understands that as circumstances change, as facts change, you have to change your strategies for what you're trying to do, but your values, what you believe, what you care about doesn't change."[17]

To make its point clear, the White House put the squeeze on Gephardt's Rhode Island protégé. Right before a crucial House vote on "fast track" authority for the president to negotiate trade agreements, a bill Patrick opposed and Clinton favored, signals were sent regarding a possible threat to funding a Rhode Island project of interest to Patrick, money for the Blackstone Valley National Heritage Corridor. Kennedy had gotten a phone call from a Blackstone official stating that the $500,000 funding might be excised by Clinton. A Kennedy aide felt the timing was suspicious. "All of a sudden, a day before the (fast-track) vote, one of the most important projects in our district gets looked at. It seems weird."[18] Kennedy press secretary Berman offered a more pointed interpretation. "Patrick was one of the first people to support Gephardt. It pissed off Al Gore. We have a terrible relationship with him. They did petty things."[19]

If that threat weren't enough, Gore had made a show in 1998 of coming to Rhode Island to appear at a Social Security forum with Senator Chafee and attend a fund-raiser for Representative Robert Weygand, both rivals of Kennedy. Congressman Weygand was a moderate New Democrat who had gained fame and then the lieutenant governor's seat in Rhode Island by wearing an FBI wire into the office of the mayor of Pawtucket after the man demanded a bribe for a landscaping contract. Weygand's political views were a clear antithesis to Kennedy's liberalism. Not only was Weygand pro-life on the abortion issue; he believed that the best way to help American workers was "to promote and help business and the economy and jobs." Weygand felt that "through proper incentives, [you could] promote businesses that promote workers and labor."[20]

Kennedy and Weygand had tangled over several issues. Kennedy was pushing a bill in the General Assembly to restore sovereign rights to the Narragansetts and was supporting federal legislation guaranteeing the tribe's right to open a reservation gambling hall without voter approval, positions Weygand strongly opposed.[21] The clinker for Representative Weygand was that the Narragansett tribe lived in his district, not Kennedy's. Speaking of the gambling hall legislation, Weygand complained, "This is being proposed by Patrick, who doesn't represent the district, while the person who represents it is vehemently opposed to it. I'm just disappointed that Patrick has decided [to support the bill]."[22] From his standpoint, Kennedy was "absolutely wrong on this issue, the voters of Rhode Island have told him he is wrong, and he is doing things in a different district that is not his to represent. He is wrong on every single ground and he has absolutely no support or valid reason for what he is doing."[23] Making sure Kennedy did not miss the point, Weygand added a veiled threat. If Kennedy continued pushing the legislation, "I am not going to stand by and allow that type of thing to happen."[24] To show how serious he was, Weygand enlisted the help of Rules Committee Chair Gerald Solomon, the powerful New York Republican leader who publicly had fought with Kennedy over assault gun legislation. The bitter floor confrontation between Solomon and Kennedy had been the lead story on the national television news shows that night. At the time, Patrick was particularly steamed about gun violence because his girlfriend's Jewish father, a Long Island congressman, had been assassinated by Palestinians years before. Ted Kennedy praised his son's outspokenness, saying "All his career, even when he decided to run for president in 1980, he wasn't the first story on all three networks."[25] Meeting with Weygand on the gambling issue, Solomon promised, "There is no way" the federal bill would be voted on by the full House.[26]

The Rhode Island Social Security forum produced another confrontation when Kennedy was refused a speaking role and kept off the platform with Gore. Complaining to *Providence Journal* columnist Bakst, Kennedy pointed out that ordinary voters "don't understand . . . bickering and pettiness that goes on between politicians."[27] To another outlet, he would add, "Perhaps the Gore political staff is running a political race a year before they should. Perhaps they are trying to send me a signal because of my closeness and support for Gephardt."[28] Before the event, Kennedy's chief of staff Marcella had called the vice-president's office to register a protest, but to no avail. The speaking list was firm. Kennedy said, "My office contacted all of the organizations involved in putting this forum together. They were told . . . that the final decision on who would be allowed to address the forum was with the Vice President's office."[29] However, when asked about Kennedy's exclusion, Gore explained that politics was not the reason for Kennedy's failure to have a speaking role. "We do not pick who comes," Gore said. "I had zero say."[30] AARP spokesperson, John Rother, one of the organizations co-sponsoring the event and the man who had invited the speakers, noted a benign reason for Weygand's involvement over Kennedy. The latter "wanted very much to participate, but there wasn't room. We have Representative Weygand introducing him because the event is in his district."[31] Yet others doubted this explanation, especially after it became known that the AARP's first choice for the event had been Brown University, which happened to lie in Kennedy's congressional district. The open fight between the two Democrats led former Republican party chair John Holmes to conclude, "You have these two young men by the names of Weygand and Kennedy that clearly don't want to be in the same room, let alone the same state. It gives Rhode Island a black eye." Then pausing for poetic effect, Holmes asked the $64,000 question, "Do the people of Rhode Island suffer?" as a result of the conflict.[32]

Soon, the answer was a loud and clear no! Surprising all the political experts, the Democrats did unusually well in the 1998 national elections. Typically, the party controlling the presidency loses House seats in midterm contests. That had been the case for every midterm in this century, with the exception of 1934, when the country was in the throes of the Great Depression and Democrats made unprecedented gains. With the Clinton presidency under siege due to the Monica Lewinsky scandal, many observers expected Republicans to pick up seats. After having denied engaging in "sexual relations with that woman" in January, Clinton's admission in late summer 1998 that he had engaged in an affair with Lewinsky thoroughly infuriated Republicans. They launched a formal investigation that eventually would lead to a House vote impeaching the president and a Senate trial. The charges pitted fellow Democrats Weygand and Kennedy against one another as the House debated impeachment. Weygand was more openly critical of Clinton's behavior, pointing out, "It is a big obstacle along that road to finalizing the things he wants as a legacy for his presidency."[33] At first, Kennedy was more cautious, noting that "with the president's admission, things have changed quite dramatically from where things started with the president's initial denial."[34] Privately, his fear was that an enterprising reporter would make a connection between Clinton's affair and Ted Kennedy's previous womanizing. "We were afraid that people were going to say when you were a little boy, wasn't your father involved with other women? We didn't want to get into that," his press secretary explained.[35] But following a trip to Puerto Rico with First Lady Hillary Clinton, Kennedy came out swinging, saying Clinton's affair "is better left to God and family than the Congress and the media to judge."[36] When Weygand announced he would vote along with the Republican majority to start an inquiry into possible impeachment, Kennedy blasted Weygand for "trying to cover his backside."[37]

In part due to public concerns over GOP handling of impeachment and other domestic policy issues, Democrats came within 11 votes of retaking a majority of the House in the 1998 election. In short succession, Gingrich resigned as Speaker and Gephardt announced he was staying in the House rather than run for president. The potentially calamitous breach between Gore and Gephardt was healed, and the way was cleared for a strong party effort to regain the House. Put in charge of the drive to take majority control of the House was Patrick Kennedy. At the tender age of 31, Kennedy was named chair of the Democratic Congressional Campaign Committee, the major arm of the Democratic House leadership in charge of campaign fund-raising and candidate recruitment for the 2000 elections. He would supervise a staff of 126, be number five in House leadership ranks, and hold a major position to shape party fortunes.

Being chair of the DCCC meant Kennedy could not run for Chafee's U.S. Senate seat in 2000. But that did not bother Patrick. He felt comfortable in the House and was doing well. As one adviser put it, "He really likes the House. He sees himself making a niche for himself in the House. He has moved into the leadership. . . . He likes the hurly burly of the House, the caucuses, and the friendships he is building, and how he goes around the country helping people."[38]

The only person disappointed by Patrick's decision not to run for the Senate seat was his father. Even after Patrick ruled out a Senate bid and Senator Chafee announced his own retirement, Ted continued to urge his son to go for Chafee's seat for nearly a year after the DCCC appointment. As one family friend noted, "If Ted had his decision, he would have rather seen Patrick run for the Senate." That way, they could make history by being the first father and son to serve simultaneously in the senate. When parental pressure failed to move Patrick, Ted and his staff resorted to the extraordinary step of lobbying Patrick through the *Boston Globe*. In an effort to create a groundswell of support for a Senate bid, Ted's staff leaked erroneous reports that Patrick was taking another look at the Senate. But parental pressure went for naught, as Patrick resisted his father's private and public lobbying.[39]

From Gephardt's standpoint, the DCCC slot for Patrick represented recognition of the young man's hard work for the party. The chair was "not the type of appointment that should be based on seniority, but rather on ability, energy, and enthusiasm,"

Gephardt felt.[40] The latter were qualities Kennedy possessed in abundance. In recognition of the young man's new prominence, Vice-President Gore called with congratulations and an offer of a peace lunch. Speaking to *Providence Journal* columnist Bakst, Gore praised Kennedy, saying "Nobody in Congress—House or Senate—can match Patrick's energy and drive for this task. Mark my words. We will regain control of the House of Representatives in the year 2000 and Congressman Patrick Kennedy will get the principal credit."[41] Kennedy also was given a seat on the coveted Appropriations Committee, although his actual holding the spot was deferred until after the 2000 election. Back in Rhode Island for the announcement, Kennedy defended himself against all the criticisms over the past two years about his travels around the country on behalf of the national Democratic party. "When I went around the country, I may not have made the people here too happy who were wondering where I was all the time. But I can tell you this, I was making a lot of my colleagues happy, and it helped me be a more effective representative on behalf of you here in Rhode Island," he said.[42]

As the new head of the Democratic Congressional Campaign Committee, Kennedy had the biggest job of his political career. With Democratic gains of nine seats in 1996 and five in 1998, the party had come tantalizingly close to retaking control of the lower chamber. By any stretch of the imagination, the comeback since the 1994 election was remarkable. Kennedy hoped to take advantage of continuing public disenchantment with the harsh tone of Republican actions on gun control, Medicare, and Social Security to pick up those last few seats necessary for a Democratic majority. Party optimism was high. According to DCCC Political Director Karin Johnson, the biggest difference between 1998 and 2000 was that "people think it is possible to get the House back. In '98, no one thought that was the case. This helps with fundraising and recruiting. After 1994, it was hard to recruit candidates. Possible contenders asked, 'Why run and be in the minority?'"[43] With his new job, Kennedy garnered praise as a rising star of the national Democratic party. Vice-President Gore said, "It is highly unusual for someone who has served only a few terms in Congress to be placed in charge of the national effort to win back the Democratic majority. This happened because Patrick earned the position because his House colleagues know he has the fire, passion, drive, and dedication to make that goal a reality." Congressman John Lewis echoed this sentiment. "Kennedy leap-frogged over several House members who had more seniority," Lewis explained. "People appreciated all the work he has done on behalf of the party. He has raised a lot of money and made a large number of campaign visits on behalf of Democrats. Gephardt supported him very strongly."[44] His chief of staff Tony Marcella could see the difference in how Patrick was treated, compared to 1994, when he first had entered Congress. "He is treated more like an equal. . . . A lot of members respect him for what he has done and how he had done it and his attitude and the way he conducts himself in politics and legislatively."[45] With his leadership position in Congress, Kennedy was way ahead of where most people thought he would be. He was a full 20 years younger than everyone else in the House leadership. Staff members boldly predicted that one day, "Rhode Island could have the Speaker of the House."[46]

Kennedy's task at the DCCC was to find money and issues that would enable his party to regain control of the House. Congressman John Lewis predicted that "Kennedy is going to raise a record amount of money and do it earlier than it ever has been done. We have planned a number of gala occasions all across the country featuring major figures from the party. Both Clinton and Gore have made it a major priority to get the House back."[47] In short order, Kennedy pledged to raise $50 million for the fight to regain House control, a big increase over the $37 million raised by the DCCC in the previous campaign cycle. Fund-raising was helped by a novel Kennedy pledge. Democrats who contributed at least $100,000 would be invited to a September weekend retreat at the Kennedy family compound in Hyannis Port.[48] The campaign key was money plus message. Democrats needed to raise enough money to be competitive, and they would use the cash to talk about issues people cared about, such as education, health care, and jobs. Kennedy sensed a major turn in the political situation. "In '94, we were sort of on the defensive . . . on guns, on abortion, on taxes, on welfare. . . . The environment now is people are concerned about their health care. They don't want HMO bureaucrats and bean counters deciding what their health care is going to be," he noted.[49]

The impeachment issue was a clear undercurrent in Democratic efforts. At the time of the vote, Kennedy had warned House Republicans that "a vote for impeachment could backfire. . . . There will be consequences to this vote. Don't have any illusions at all about it."[50] Speaking the day of the vote to CNN congressional correspondent Bob Franken, Kennedy complained about GOP hypocrisy: "No one wants to see this president impeached over something so partisan as this, especially in light of the Speaker's [Bob Livingston] own admissions of infidelity, and acknowledging the fact that the former Speaker, Newt Gingrich, was caught lying 13 times to the Ethics Committee in Congress. . . . There's such duplicity and there's such hypocrisy in the Congress today."[51] By May, though, Kennedy was backing off the impeachment threat. "I don't believe that I am going to—nor are we in the DCCC going to—make a big to-do about impeachment. I don't think we need to," he explained.[52] The country was more interested in the economy, education, health care, and education. It was a stark confession that impeachment played out in very different ways in various parts of the country.

As a sign of how volatile the public opinion climate was, the country was rocked by a tragic mass murder of students at Columbine High School in Colorado by two gun-wielding teenagers. The drama generated saturation media coverage and agonizing debates over what was wrong with American society. Republicans focused on family values, violent videos, and movies produced by the entertainment industry. Democrats, on the other hand, blamed the easy availability of guns. When the House failed to enact gun control, Democrats complained the GOP was in bed with the National Rifle Association and that the party was out of touch with the American public. Kennedy predicted big gains for Democrats in 2000. "I'm going to hang . . . the guns around their neck on Election Day," he warned.[53]

But in the heat of this congressional debate, Kennedy created problems for himself when he told an interviewer on June 18 that Democrats "have written off the rural areas" in their bid to retake control of the House because those locales were not sympathetic to gun control. The statement was made public when reporter Steve Roberts disclosed Kennedy's comments during the national airing of the PBS show *Washington Week in Review*. Roberts's discussion was followed on Sunday when his wife Cokie Roberts repeated the comment during the ABC show *This Week with Sam Donaldson and Cokie Roberts*. *Providence Journal* writer John Mulligan included the statement in a newspaper story.[54] Gleeful Republicans immediately castigated Kennedy's gaffe. Republican National Committee Chair Jim Nicholson took the unusual step of writing a letter to the editor of the *Providence Journal* condemning Kennedy's statement.[55] Kennedy admitted he made the comment but explained that he recanted the point right after he said it and asked reporters to strike it from the record. During the same interview in which he made the statement, he explained that Democrats were poised to pick up rural seats in several states. Kennedy criticized Republicans for attempting to "make political hay" from his gaffe. "The notion that we're writing off rural districts is ridiculous. It was an emotional response to a very personally important issue to me. It had nothing to do with my politics or my chairmanship of the DCCC," he explained. "What is really being spun out of control is a very emotional response that I gave to a reporter who I think was baiting me for this kind of controversy. My family and I feel very strongly about this issue, and for good reason."[56] Republicans promised to broadcast Kennedy's comments in television commercials targeted on rural districts in 2000. National Republican Congressional Committee Chair Tom Davis said, "Writing off rural areas is a very cynical idea, and I think it's going to come back to haunt many rural Democrats in the next elections. From a blatantly political point of view, I'm glad he said it. But it was way out of line, and we're certainly going to make it known."[57]

DCCC Political Director Johanson called the threat to run ads against Kennedy "a dumb strategy. That's not what voters care about. They care about where candidates stand on health care, education, Social Security, and taxes." From her standpoint, she was continually amazed "that Republicans have a tin-ear on what people care about." They were so used to running against old-line liberals that they didn't realize "how far Democrats have come back on issues we were weak on. It is hard for Republicans to say Democrats are big spending liberals anymore." Having a Kennedy at the head of the campaign committee boosted fund-raising, but his ascension also had one other benefit. "It has made the DCCC more of a high profile organization. He and his family are so well known that we now have sizzle." The only problem she acknowledged was "in more conservative areas, we don't know if he will go campaigning."[58] To a reporter, Kennedy openly admitted, "I'm not the guy who is going to be out there trying to persuade recalcitrant voters from border states."[59]

It was a tacit acknowledgment that Kennedy evoked different reactions across the country. NRCC pollster Glenn Bolger felt that Kennedy's appeal was very strong in the Northeast but much less so in the South and West. In rural areas, Bolger believed having Kennedy at the head of the DCCC put local Democrats on the defensive. "There are [rural] Democrats who can break through, but they can't be Kennedyesque," he said. To the extent that the party leadership leaned to the left, it called into question whether rural, southern Democrats would have clout in Congress.[60] Republican strategists believed that one opportunity for them was that "Patrick Kennedy now is a leader of the Democratic party. What he says carries a lot more weight."[61] NRCC Political Director Terry Nelson pointed out that "Kennedy is not well-known for his bounding intelligence." But, Nelson conceded, in order "to demonize Kennedy, he has to give people ammunition. If he does that, he will be held up to additional attacks."[62]

As Kennedy got organized at the DCCC, his NRCC counterpart was rallying his own troops for the upcoming elections in 2000. Representative Davis was a 50-year-old conservative first elected from Virginia to the House in 1994, the same year as Kennedy. He was pragmatic in nature, and his goal was to keep Republicans in charge of Congress. A consummate political detail man, Davis knew more about the intricacies of congressional districts across the country than anyone else in his party. At a January party retreat, he showed GOP representatives a tape of "Democrats back in charge, with footage of a jubilant Speaker Gephardt and other Democratic leaders." When Kennedy's picture appeared on the screen, audience members roundly booed. Several weeks later, Davis had aides tape to House legislators' chairs "copies of a *Washington Post* article summarizing the AFL-CIO's $46 million spending plan" for 2000. The accompanying message from Davis was "46 million reasons to stick together!"[63]

The 2000 elections were shaping up as the Super Bowl of American politics. Not only were the political stakes high due to the close race for control of Congress; the election would be a grand opportunity for the country to debate its policy direction. The crucial decision for Democrats was whether they should bargain with Republicans in order to pass legislation or stake out clear alternatives that would distinguish them from the GOP and help appeal to voters. House Democrats still were bitter over the president's earlier compromises with Republicans on welfare reform and the balanced budget. They feared Clinton would do the same thing to strengthen his legacy as a centrist. When asked about this dilemma, Kennedy said it was more important to legislate than confront. "We're much better off when our issues are being discussed. These are Democratic programs. Continued success of these programs will only accrue credit to the Democrats."[64] Yet at the same time, he was cognizant of the political potency of Democratic positions on issues such as health maintenance organization reform, gun control, and education. Asked his view of 2000, Kennedy said, "Dick is hanging tough. He's saying: Here's our agenda. If the Republicans want to help us pass it, great. If not, Americans are going to notice in 2000."[65]

The biggest uncertainty was how the presidential campaign would impinge on congressional races. Democrats worried about Gore's early weakness but downplayed the danger to legislators. "Does it help to have strong help at the top of the ticket?" Johanson asked. "Yes. But if not, it won't be disastrous for us."[66] From Kennedy's standpoint, "as long as the 2000 presidential campaign is competitive, our people will come out."[67] Republicans, however, saw the early election popularity of Texas Governor George W. Bush as a godsend. One party official ackowledged that the Republican strategy was "to address issues the American people want, but not end up as we did in '95 and '96 where Congress became the issue in the presidential election. We don't want the president painting us as out of step and too reactionary."[68] In 1996 and 1998, former House Speaker Gingrich had been demonized by Democrats. None of the current GOP leaders, though, such as Dennis Hastert, Dick Armey, or Tom DeLay, had very high visibility. "Newt was a unique figure in being well-known," Bolger pointed out.[69]

From Kennedy's standpoint, the Republican right wing still held great power within the GOP-controlled Congress. House Majority Leader Dick Armey and Senate Majority Leader Trent Lott were "far right and very intolerant of diversity and are the kind of people who do not represent what this country's all about, which is a country that's inclusive of everybody," Kennedy said. Bush understood this problem and was "trying to distance himself as much as he can because he knows the Republicans in Congress are not what he needs to be tied to if he wants to win the White House."[70] Kennedy saw his job as repeating the words "right-wing" and "extremist" as much as possible to remind voters of the true nature of his opponents. This irritated National Republican Congressional Committee chair Tom Davis, who argued, "Patrick thinks that anybody who disagrees with him is an extremist."[71]

Kennedy saw the primary GOP strategy as divide and conquer. "Their efforts to scapegoat are legendary," he said. "They have attacked illegal immigrants, they have attacked gays and lesbians. If they can scare people and use divisive tactics, they will. . . . Their tactic is to say liberal, liberal, liberal because they have nothing else to say. They fall back on the old tax and spend charges."[72]

In addition to their own efforts, Democrats counted on outside groups to play an important role in the election. Increasingly, such groups were running ads in close congressional races and attempting to influence voters over the heads of official candidates.[73] Forces such as the AFL-CIO, Sierra Club, and the National Abortion Rights Action League had tremendous resources and could say things more bluntly than either candidates or parties. As Mark Weiner, DCCC finance director, predicted regarding the 2000 elections, "There will be more independent expenditures than ever before."[74] Democrats hoped to harness the energy and money of these organizations in order to return their party to power in the House of Representatives.

Turnout would be the key element in deciding control of the House. Kennedy understood that Republicans would attack him. "They will use the Kennedy name to try to polarize the election," he said. "It will help galvanize their base, but it also helps galvanize our base. . . . If there is a small turnout, exciting the base is a winning strategy. We don't need to win the middle in order to recapture the House."[75]

15 The Kennedy Phenomenon

*A*fter a decade of public service, Patrick has become the highest-ranking Kennedy of his generation. The only other family members of his cohort holding elective office are Kathleen Kennedy Townsend, the lieutenant governor of Maryland, and Mark Shriver, a state representative in Maryland. As Patrick's press secretary Larry Berman put it, "The kid is a millionaire, he could have just taken his money after Providence College and lounged on the beach and hung out with a part-time job. Instead, he has taken his family's calling of public service."[1] The Kennedy name clearly was a crucial part of his rapid upward mobility in national politics. As one local observer slyly commented, "If his last name wasn't Kennedy, he would be at Thom McAnn helping you to try on these shoes. Do you want the hush puppies or the suede shoes?"[2] Yet Kennedy possessed two qualities that held him in good stead politically: persistence and hard work. Speaking to a Tennessee fund-raising reception in 1998, he said, "It's not always a glamorous and romantic thing to keep the fight going. I certainly have been able to be educated to that, seeing my father struggle all these years trying to keep up the fight of his brothers, and not doing so in a way that was as romanticized and glorified as my uncles' time in public life. And yet, you know what, he's never given up."[3]

These were lessons that Patrick put to use all the time. "Instead of taking a weekend off to go sailing on Cape Cod or spending it relaxing somewhere," his chief of staff said, "he'll go out and help candidates." Kennedy loved giving speeches and meeting people around the country. Comparing the 1990s to the 1960s, Marcella said, "We don't have the great leaders or the great marches or the great rallies that we had in the '60s, but those issues are still here. We still are fighting the same fight that Martin Luther King and Robert Kennedy were fighting."[4] Indeed, Kennedy was gaining public renown as a fighter for the less fortunate. Speaking to a reporter, he noted, "A hallmark of my political life from the beginning was to rattle the cage and get people to see what is really going on in government."[5] He still was not the best public speaker. "When we write speeches for him, he gets all nervous. He is better speaking off the cuff and talking. He is much better with groups he is familiar with or people he likes," press secretary Berman explained.[6] And on some issues, he could be shockingly outspoken. "He is not your average politician who is middle of the road and afraid of polls. He has come out in favor of same-sex marriages," Berman noted. "Tony, his chief of staff, cringes and says how can you do that, some of these things he comes out with. But he believes in them. He says I am who I am."[7]

Observers questioned whether the family's mystique would extend to the next generation of Kennedys. But in July 1999, when a plane piloted by John F. Kennedy Jr. crashed, killing him, his wife, and sister-in-law, the outpouring of public grief demonstrated clearly that public interest in the Kennedys remained strong. For days, Americans were glued to their television sets in hope that the plane would be found with the passengers alive. Millions grieved along with the Kennedy family as the bodies were recovered and buried at sea. For Patrick Kennedy, John had always been a close friend and an inspiration. "He carried his name with such great dignity and I know I share that same name with him." When asked whether he thought John would have entered politics, as had been speculated, Patrick explained the importance of John establishing own identity in terms that also had great meaning for himself: "If and when he decided to get into [politics], it would have been a period when he would have been able to define it on his terms. He would have been talking to an audience that was more familiar with him than with his father." Reflecting on his own situation, Patrick said, "I had a big luxury. I could do it and not have it be a federal case. He couldn't have afforded to make any of the blunders and mistakes that I've made, because they would have stuck with him so heavily and they would have been so over-reported and publicized." If anything, the tragedy illustrated the new media era that had unfolded. Speaking about the rise of 24-hour news stations and saturation coverage of major new stories, Patrick said, "This [media] environment is so out of hand. I don't want to add to the frenzy."[8] With that, he declined to answer any further questions about the death of his cousin.

Thrust into a spotlight he had not chosen by the untimely death of John Kennedy Jr., Patrick responded in the only manner he could, answering a few questions to satisfy the media and then retreating into his personal privacy. It was a cycle *Providence Journal* columnist Bakst had seen before. "When he got to Congress, increasingly, I notice two contradictory postures that he would alternate between being extremely outspoken and being episodically and conspicuously inaccessible," the reporter noted. Following JFK Jr.'s death and publicity concerning this book, Bakst had sought an interview with the congressman. Among other things, he wanted to know Kennedy's reaction and what he remembered about his deceased cousin. "I got nowhere," Bakst reported. Then seeking to negotiate access, he dropped the idea of talking about JFK Jr. and indicated he would ask only about the forthcoming biography, but still was refused. Through his chief of staff, Kennedy indicated that he wouldn't do the interview and that in terms of the biography, he thought "there are probably a lot more interesting people to write books about."[9]

The entire episode reinforced the idea that Patrick still was a Kennedy. His life had alternated between being a Kennedy and pursuing the family legacy on the one hand, and carving out an individual identity on the other. It had not been easy navigating the tug of war between these competing objectives. Growing up, he had witnessed the negative side of public life and the disastrous consequences for his parent's marriage. His first impression of politics had not been positive. But through Joe Kennedy's 1986 congressional campaign, he had learned how to convert the obsessive public interest in his family toward general goals that brought him personal satisfaction. The celebrityhood gave him an opportunity to help others less fortunate and extend his family's legacy of public service. Speaking of a conversation he once had with his Aunt Jackie, Patrick had been thrilled to discover her enthusiasm about his run for Congress. "I was very anxious to see how she felt about me running. . . . I was in a sense in a small way trying to continue [the family legacy]." One of the things he always had admired about her was the manner in which she maintained her common touch by shielding herself from the media. It was a style of coping that Patrick found worthy of emulation.[10]

The demands of living a highly visible life encouraged Patrick to regulate access by outsiders. One friend, Jack McConnell, noted in regard to Kennedy, "He keeps a lot in for whatever reason, maybe it is the guard of having been a Kennedy, maybe it is the constant paparazzi and press. There are very few people he allows in."[11] It was a quality that Bakst also had noticed. Early on, the reporter had observed that Kennedy "is not somebody who often volunteers things." During a 1988 interview with Ted and Patrick, Bakst had told the senator that he had gone to Andover. It was only later when Bakst asked Patrick where he had gone to high school that he learned the young man, too, had attended Andover. The same pattern had occurred when a reporter was covering a Kennedy fund-raiser during his General Assembly days. Hearing that Kennedy was charging $100 for donors, which was considered high for a beginning legislator, a reporter asked Kennedy if the rumor was accurate. Kennedy confirmed that it was, but never indicated that upstairs at the very same restaurant, a heavy-hitters reception was charging $250 to $500 a person. Within the Kennedy family, Bakst felt, the prevailing attitude was "not let the public know too much."[12] It was a way of maintaining some semblance of humanity given the extraordinary interest in all things Kennedy.

Part of what makes Kennedy tick, according to Bakst, is his desire to "validate his own personal individual existence. It is not just that he is a Kennedy or riding in on his father's fame, but that he also has accomplished something on his own." Continuing, Bakst pointed out that "at a subconscious level, I think he is always driven to show his family and world and prove to himself he actually can do something. He was very frail and sickly and regarded early on as a lightweight. I think he wants to get things done and move onward and upward."[13] *Providence Journal* political reporter Scott MacKay, who has covered Kennedy for more than a decade, felt the same way. What motivated Kennedy, MacKay said, was that "he really did want to show his father that he wasn't the wimpy asthmatic kid. He had to live up to a very high family standard."[14] Now in the year 2000, he was coming into his own. He had arrived politically and personally. Since he ranks fifth in the Democratic House leadership and is considerably younger than anyone else in the leadership, it is easy to conceive that one day down the road he could become U.S. House Speaker or a senator.

Either possibility was a long way from 1991 when the 24-year-old Kennedy had committed the ultimate act of political insurrection by calling for the resignation of the Rhode Island House Speaker. That stunning call for DeAngelis's resignation was a defining moment in Kennedy's life and a sign of how much American politics has changed over the past 30 years. In earlier eras, it would have been political suicide for a young state representative to call a press conference to denounce a powerful politician. Politics was hierarchical, leaders controlled the advancement of the rank and file, and loyalty to the party was paramount. But traditional rules have been rewritten all across the country. A new type of political leader has emerged who has transformed American politics: the celebrity politician who is rich, independent minded, and media savvy. Revolutionary in its scope, this development has altered the landscape and had dramatic consequences for the way in which our system operates. Following the success of the Kennedy family, America has witnessed a boom in actors, athletes, astronauts, and entertainers entering public life.[15] It now is common for celebrities and legacy candidates with famous last names to seek elective office.

Many factors account for the rise of celebrity politics in the United States. One is the high cost of modern politics. Unlike elections in the last century, which featured minimal campaigning by candidates, races in the contemporary period are costly affairs. It takes either personal wealth or access to people with money to broadcast television ads, conduct polls, and appeal to diverse sets of voters. Historically, political parties were a major route for upward mobility by those born without social or economic advantage. Individuals of modest means could count on party organizations for voter mobilization and persuasion. However, weak parties in the modern period force candidates to build their own campaign organizations. Celebrities also are advantaged by the media-dominated nature of the current process. Reporters look for good stories, and no one makes better copy than celebrities. In an era of citizen cynicism about traditional politicians who have worked their way up through the ranks, candidates who are rich and famous and have not spent a lifetime cutting political deals are more likely to be trusted by the electorate. New faces from outside politics and those who are viewed as being too rich to be bought bring enormous credibility to the process.

Obviously, not all celebrities bring the same advantages or skills to public life. The children and grandchildren of Franklin Roosevelt, for example, were never successful in building political lives for themselves. Some famous people such as Ralph Nader and Oliver North have sought and been defeated for elective office. Within Kennedy's own family, cousin Kathleen Kennedy Townsend lost her first try for Congress. In looking at the Kennedys in general, though, what is unique about their celebrity status is that it transcends political, economic, social, and cultural boundaries. Whether they go into elective office or other activities, such as the arts, media, business, or philanthropy, the Kennedys hold extraordinary strengths. Among other qualities, they have high name identification and access to resources (both their own and that of other people) and are able to generate favorable media coverage and position themselves as independent of conventional political processes.

During his time in Congress, for example, Patrick Kennedy raised millions for himself and his party.[16] Using his famous name, he became a major draw for political fund-raisers all across the country and helped elect dozens of members to Congress. With a personal fortune estimated at several million dollars, he clearly has access to major financial resources of his own. He is the beneficiary of two trusts, one set up by his grandmother in 1953 and another created by his father in 1959. Together with his $133,600 annual congressional salary, he earns more than $250,000 a year.[17] Long-term, money is not a problem. His father's estimated worth is $35 million, and the extended family fortune is estimated at $1 billion, much of it in real estate and proceeds from the sale of the 6-million-square-foot Merchandise Mart/Apparel Center complex in Chicago. The major beneficiaries of this fortune now is his father's generation. But according to the provisions of his grandfather's trust, once all of Joe's children except Jean Smith and Ted Kennedy pass away, the trust can be broken up and the principal distributed to remaining family members.[18] When this happens, it will push Patrick and his cousins from the category of rich to superrich.

The political significance of his family's money is that it allows Kennedy to take risks that others of lesser means are not able to do. For example, in the closing days of his 1994 bid for Congress, voters were moving to his Republican opponent in large numbers. Since Kennedy's campaign was running out of money, Patrick borrowed more than $100,000 from his personal funds to launch a last-minute air assault and hire a consultant who specialized in get-out-the-vote efforts. The same was true in 1988 during his first bid for the state legislature, when nearly all of his $93,000 expenditure was financed by personal funds. Money also allowed Kennedy and his family to hire private investigators during Patrick's first General Assembly run, the Palm Beach rape trial, and his initial congressional campaign.

The ability to draw on major financial resources gave Kennedy strategic leeway to take advantage of opportunities as they came along and reposition himself at key points in his career. For example, early in Kennedy's General Assembly service, he painted himself as a political outsider who was reform oriented and wanted to take on the establishment. However, after friends captured control of top Statehouse positions, he trumpeted his leadership endorsements and connections to get things done for the state. On the gambling issue, he opposed expansion while in the Assembly but later became a vocal proponent of a new casino for the Narragansett Indians and accepted thousands of dollars in pro-gambling contributions. He went from opposing capital punishment in 1988 to supporting it in 1994. On abortion, he switched from a general pro-choice voting record to favoring a ban on partial-birth abortions. In terms of national politics, Kennedy alternated between a public feud with Vice-President Gore in 1998 when Gephardt was considering a presidential run to a 1999 rally at which Gore extolled Kennedy's virtues. He fought bitterly with Senator Chafee, but wrote a glowing tribute to him after the senator died in 1999. Without the same degree of fame and financial resources, ordinary politicians are not able to re-create themselves when political conditions change. Instead, they are stuck with whatever public image they have had over the years.

During his time in Rhode Island, Patrick Kennedy worked tirelessly to cultivate favorable media coverage and the support of powerful journalists. In preparation for an interview at his house by columnist Bakst of the *Providence Journal*, Kennedy aide

Marcella made sure a framed copy of the front page story announcing Patrick's 1988 victory autographed by the newspaperman was hanging on the wall. Later, when another reporter visited the house, the memento was nowhere to be seen. The endless media curiosity about the Kennedys, of course, does not always work to the family's advantage. Much like a royal family, the Kennedys are under the media microscope both for good and for ill. They can attract positive coverage when they want to, but also are the object of unflattering tabloid coverage. Indeed, as the media have grown more tabloid oriented, Kennedys have not enjoyed such good coverage.

Ted Kennedy Jr. discovered this lesson the hard way. Promised a balanced 1997 *Newsweek* article on the Kennedy cousins, he was angered to see the magazine's cover story entitled "A Dynasty in Decline." "It was unfair," young Ted recalled, "The reporter promised us a fair shake, but then wrote a critical story."[19]

The luckiest aspect of Patrick Kennedy's career has been that except for talk radio hosts Buddy Cianci and Mary Ann Sorrentino, Rhode Island did not have a tabloid press to hammer him the way the *Boston Herald* or *New York Post* loved to do. In the Palm Beach rape trial of William Kennedy Smith and the babysitter sex scandal of Michael Kennedy, national tabloid reporters often condemned the entire family for allegations against single individuals. And following the tragic death of John Kennedy Jr., out-of-state television reporters crudely shouted questions at Patrick, such as, "What did John's body look like when it was brought up from the plane crash?"[20] Opinion polls on Patrick show that the congressman's political fortunes often rise and fall with the general tide of public opinion about the family, regardless of whether Patrick has anything to do with events in the news. Far too often, the press plays to common stereotypes about the Kennedy family without much evidence to back them up. Regardless of whether the coverage is positive or negative, though, there is no doubt the public and the press remain very interested in the fortunes of the next generation of the Kennedy family.

Along with money and media, Kennedys have an advantage during a long-term era when the public is cynical about public affairs. For all their faults and indiscretions, the little-known political advantage the family possesses is the public belief that Kennedys are so rich that they cannot be bought. Voters might see the Kennedys as too liberal, opportuntistic, or rich, but they have rarely been seen as corrupt. In Patrick's first legislative campaign in 1988, for example, polls at the beginning of the contest showed that 57 percent saw him as honest and trustworthy, while only 4 percent believed he was dishonest. Most Kennedy scandals have involved lifestyle problems, from drinking to womanizing to rude behavior, not cash payoffs, dereliction of duties, or compromising a public office. This is one of the reasons why the 1997 allegations of questionable campaign fund-raising against Ted, Joe, and Patrick Kennedy proved politically damaging and led to lower polling numbers for all three. These charges ran contrary to common beliefs that the Kennedys were too wealthy to stoop to the level of corruption the public sees in typical politicians. In each of Patrick Kennedy's confrontations with powerful forces, from Speaker Joe DeAngelis in Rhode Island to Speaker Newt Gingrich in Washington, Kennedy had great moral authority to condemn adversaries because the public saw him as a political white knight. Until

Kennedys lose that reservoir of goodwill about their integrity, they should continue to do well politically.

Less dependent than conventional politicians on party or ideological coalitions, both Patrick and Ted Kennedy have excelled in building personal coalitions that transcend conventional groupings. Kennedys have always been seen as partisan Democrats, but few people over the generations have worked more effectively with Republicans. For example, Ted Kennedy worked very closely with Republican Senator Orrin Hatch of Utah on crime and health care issues. In his legislative career, Patrick has followed his father's example. From the rise of his ally, John Harwood, to the Rhode Island Speakership with the help of Republicans to his own entry into Congress, Patrick has made great efforts to get to know Republicans and to work with them on defense issues, even while he was castigating them on domestic policy. Kennedy also has perfected the art of ethnic politics, with appeals to the Italian, Irish, Native American, and Portuguese communities. According to reporter MacKay, Kennedy "realized that his name was gold among a whole generation, particularly Catholics who were sons and daughters of ethnics."[21] Indeed, it is a hallmark of Kennedy strategizing to build broad, personalistic coalitions and never burn bridges. Over a period of many years, old adversaries can become new friends. Even bitter former rivals such as former Speakers DeAngelis and Matt Smith have patched things up with Kennedy in realization of Patrick's growing political power. As Kennedy ally Mark Weiner explained, "Time heals all wounds. Joe and Patrick have a pretty good relationship now. . . . Patrick has worked hard to bring Joe DeAngelis back and others who were against him."[22] On one plane trip, Kennedy even moved up to sit next to Smith and had a great conversation with him.[23]

Kennedy's career is fascinating not only for what it tells us about contemporary politics but for what it reveals about Patrick himself. In 1999, two national profiles of Kennedy appeared simultaneously. According to the *Weekly Standard*, a conservative publication, Kennedy was a spoiled, not very bright, rich kid who advanced in politics by trading shamelessly on his family name and being a "partisan bomb-thrower."[24] A day earlier, a feature in the *Boston Globe Magazine* described Patrick as the "Un-Kennedy," someone who was not bold, brash, or charismatic like his famous relatives, but a nice guy who had "all the good parts of being a Kennedy, and none of the bad."[25] Neither article, though, painted a complete portrait of Kennedy. Patrick is neither a sinner nor a saint.

With someone as young as Kennedy, it is difficult to offer definitive conclusions about his personal character or political style, which still are in the formative process. As he gains experience, he undoubtedly will file the awkward edges off of his public presentation and gain more polish. He has grown remarkably over the past decade. Yet the virtue of studying a leader's early life is that key personal qualities have not yet been masked or history rewritten to suit current needs. In Kennedy's case, what stands out from his life is hard work and outspoken defense of liberal principles combined with occasional displays of public anger and political pragmatism. From his days in the state legislature to his time in Congress, Kennedy has gained a reputation as a workhorse, someone who devotes countless hours to behind-the-scenes campaigning, legislating, and fund-raising. One reporter said of Kennedy, "He is a very hard worker. His whole life is politics. I don't think he has a life outside of politics." A Democratic colleague described him as "hard working, nice, gracious, and unassuming."[26] Kennedy described his motivation this way: "I feel personally fulfilled by being part of the work that I do. It gives me a sense of accomplishment. I am charged by what has been accomplished."[27]

Although Kennedy often is depicted as a celebrity creation, that portrait ignores the great energy Kennedy devotes to mastering the political process. He is keenly aware of his own limitations and works tirelessly to overcome them through speech coaches, media advisers, and political mentors. Kennedy himself describes these individuals as people whose job is "smoothing off the rough edges."[28] Throughout his career, Kennedy has spoken his mind bluntly in support of the downtrodden and those around the world denied basic human rights, such as in East Timor. In 2000, he called on the United States to provide a safe haven for 11-year-old Elian Gonzales on grounds that "Castro was behind the assassination of [Patrick's] uncle [President John Kennedy]."[29] At the same time, though, his expressions sometimes boil over to the point of public anger. Already in Congress, for example, there have been widely publicized blowups with Congressman Gerald Solomon over gun control and Congressman Bob Barr on Clinton's impeachment. And in Rhode Island, he has had vitriolic confrontations with Governor Lincoln Almond, Senator John Chafee, and Congressman Robert Weygand, among others. To supporters, these public outbursts are a sign of passion and youthful exuberance, while opponents see them as immature outbursts from a volatile politician. The unresolved question is how this behavior will manifest itself as Kennedy matures and moves into leadership.

Kennedys often are seen as partisan Democrats due to the fact that their voting records tend to be liberal. But what is interesting about Patrick's career is that he has been less predictable than many would think. On ideological grounds, for example, there have been several exceptions to what generally has been a liberal voting record. Most notable has been his 1994 flirtation with the centrist Democratic Leadership Council and his congressional votes in favor of a partial-birth abortion ban, the death penalty, the B-2 bomber, and other big defense programs. He also has been quite pragmatic about building alliances with Republicans at crucial moments, such as during the Gingrich era when Kennedy was not sure whether liberalism would survive as a political philosophy. Because stereotypes about the Kennedys being strong Democrats are so prevalent, Kennedy has more strategic leeway than conventional politicians who do not have such well-defined profiles. In part due to this unpredictable combination of principle and pragmatism, Kennedy often has exceeded expectations of how well he would do. In many battles in Rhode Island and Congress, opponents have underestimated Kennedy's abilities, pigeonholed him as an inflexible liberal, and been beaten in the end by an unorthodox political move. Kennedy knows how organizations work, how alliances are built, and how to use the media. These skills have allowed him to surprise opponents time and time again.

The strongest quality Patrick brings to the political process is skill at finding mentors who instruct him in the art of politics. In the Rhode Island General Assembly, for example, the members were a dedicated band of reformers who were tired of old-boy politics and undemocratic rules. Marginalized by the legislative leadership, these legislators had the time and foresight to train Patrick and utilize his potential as a polit- ical ally. In Congress, Patrick has worked closely with a variety of individuals from Congressman Dick Gephardt and Senator Jack Reed to Representative Pete Stark. Patrick took advantage of the fact that when he entered Congress, there were two other Kennedys present, Ted and Joe. Among the three of them, they had the ability to ex- tend the Kennedy network tremendously. Joe was on the crucial House Banking Com- mittee and active on housing issues. Patrick's senior legislative assistant Garrett Bliss explained that "if what I really wanted was an insight, someone with a sense of the leg- islative history in housing or banking or for the activity of the committee in those ar- eas, then I would give Jonathan [of Joe Kennedy's staff] a call." Patrick's staff was careful to keep track of how his relatives in Congress voted. "I always liked to know on hot and contentious issues where Joe and the Senator stood," Bliss noted. "If we were going to be taking a different position from their's, I gave them a heads-up about it."[30]

Patrick's connection with his father obviously was a tremendous asset for his entry into Congress. The representative long has cited his father as the most impor- tant professional role model (although his mother was more crucial in his personal development). The relationship with Ted has grown remarkably since Kennedy's teenage time when his father was not around much. Once a week, on Thursdays from 12:30 to 1:30 p.m. (or sometimes for breakfast), they have box lunch sandwiches in Ted's hideaway Senate office. "For me it's opened up, personally, a whole dynamic of our relationship that heretofore I haven't had the chance to have with him," Patrick said. "So as a son for whom his father is the most important person in his life in a lot of respects, this is a big change for me."[31] It was a relationship several of his cousins did not have due to the tragic assassinations of their fathers. Speaking at a press con- ference on gun control, Patrick explained his support of the legislation in very per- sonal terms. "My cousin Douglas got married this summer, and my father was his best man. Douglas choked up when he thanked my father, because in a way he repre- sented his own father who couldn't be there."[32] While there is mutual professional pride between father and son, occasional tensions have appeared in the relationship based on the heavy demands of his father's schedule. On election day, 1996, for ex- ample, Ted promised to come down to Rhode Island from Massachusetts at 4:00 p.m. in order to campaign for his son. Patrick had rented an RV and was visiting voting areas around the district. At the appointed time, the phone rang, it was Ted's staff calling Patrick to tell him his father was not going to make it until much later because he wanted to campaign for Senator John Kerry. According to a friend, on hearing the news, "Patrick just slumped down in his chair. He looked down and said, 'Damnit, he let me down again. I promised people he was going to be there and I can't believe he is doing this to me.'" Later that same evening, after Ted finally did show up but abruptly left before delivering a promised victory party speech, a friend noticed Patrick's distress and asked what was up with Ted. The congressman tersely warned, "Don't go there!" and refused to explain his father's premature departure. The friend concluded the father-son relationship was more tricky than the cozy public portrait let on.[33]

These strains notwithstanding, the weekly lunches are invaluable politically to Patrick because of his father's seniority and connections. Patrick's chief of staff Tony

Marcella describes the meals as "personal, private lunches," which covered everything from "family to political to legislative."[34] Sometimes, according to Bliss, it is "an interesting insight on a bill." At other times, Patrick would come back from lunch and say, "My father brought this up. Could you look into it for me?"[35] Ted's basic philosophy was simple. "Politics is about being in the right time and the right place, but also being prepared," he constantly coached.[36] However, the information exchange is not just a one-way street. In an interview, Ted noted he was the beneficiary of information given over lunch. "I get more out of that than he does. He tells me more stuff that is going on." When asked his sense of Patrick's political career, Ted said, "He's doing very well. He's got good instincts. It's common sense and some judgment and some courage. He's got them all. He's got a good feel for it. I'm very proud of him."[37] Patrick's father clearly has set high standards for his son. During the initial 1988 legislative run, Ted called daily to exhort Patrick's staff to work harder. In the 1994 congressional campaign, the senator's press secretary made regular calls to MacKay, who was covering the race, to see how Patrick was doing and trade political gossip. Once, the senator even leaned on a local labor leader who was upset with young Kennedy. Placing a personal call to the surprised union official, Senator Kennedy bluntly warned, "If you have got a beef with my son, you had better patch it up. I don't care what the problem is."[38]

The struggle to grow up in the face of the overwhelming Kennedy phenomenon has manifested itself in five crises that threatened Patrick's career: his high school experimentation with drugs, the Palm Beach rape trial of cousin William Kennedy Smith, Patrick's high-profile battle with Speaker DeAngelis, the unfavorable coverage of Michael Kennedy's sex scandal, and Patrick's 1996 fund-raising controversies. Any one of these could have terminated Kennedy's public life, but the interesting point is that in the end, he emerged stronger than before. Conventional politicians often have seen their public service ended by a single scandal. Not only did that not happen with Kennedy, but his surefootedness in dealing with each challenge strengthened his resolve and gave him valuable experience with one of the most important weapons in contemporary life, the strategic use of scandal. Now, when he (or an opponent) is accused of some misdeed, he goes on the attack. Kennedy has learned in an era dominated by scandal that the best defense is a strong offense.

Because they have achieved the status of cultural icons, observers tend to lump all Kennedys together, not respecting the fact that there are significant differences within Patrick's generation. For example, in terms of political viewpoint, Patrick Kennedy is most closely identified with Old Democrat liberal values, while his cousin, Maryland Lieutenant Governor Kathleen Kennedy Townsend, leans more to the New Democrat vision of support for volunteerism, welfare reform, a balanced budget, and economic development. At the very time when Patrick has publicly criticized centrist organizations such as the Democratic Leadership Council for betraying fundamental Democratic values, the council's president Al From calls Townsend "a model for New Democrats."[39] In a family as large as the Kennedys with varied life experiences, there is no reason to assume they will share the same values, beliefs, or political style. Currently, there are 26 surviving members of the third generation and 50 of the fourth generation. These two generations of Kennedys, who are spread throughout the country and have varied interests, are likely to segment into separate domains, with different leaders in various walks of life. Ted Kennedy Jr. works on lead abatement liability issues. Kara Kennedy Allen has gained prominence through the Very Special Arts program. Tim Shriver heads Special Olympics. Maria Shriver and Douglas Kennedy work for media organizations. Caroline Kennedy has written books on law and privacy. Christopher Kennedy runs the Merchandise Mart business in Chicago. Joe Kennedy Jr., now retired from politics, has gone back to Citizen's Energy. Robert Kennedy Jr. is an environmental activist.[40]

The plane crash of John Kennedy Jr. generated endless stories about a possible Kennedy curse. The long series of tragedies afflicting the family is legendary: Joe Kennedy's death in a World War II plane accident, Rosemary Kennedy's retardation, Jack and Robert Kennedy's assassinations, David Kennedy's drug overdose and death, the William Kennedy Smith rape trial, and Michael Kennedy's sex scandal and skiing accident. Yet in the case of JFK Jr.'s crash, pilot error was the main culprit. Family members did not want to fly with him because he was inexperienced and suffered from dyslexia, a malady that causes people to misread numbers and get confused between left and right.[41] The large number of airplane accidents that have afflicted the family arises because, with their prominent status, money, and chance to travel around the world, Kennedys spend a lot of time in private planes, placing them at greater than average risk. The other way celebrityhood exposes the family to inordinate danger is through the high expectations and unrealistic hopes that many Americans have toward them. These stereotypes about who the Kennedys are and how they act place unusual pressures on family members, which in some cases have led to substance abuse and self-destructive behavior. As long as the public and media have such obsessive interest in all things Kennedy, their celebrityhood creates weird dynamics in terms of how people treat them. Dining with a friend in a Providence restaurant, Patrick Kennedy was approached by a stranger who offered his friend $300 in cash on the spot if he would let her sit at the table. Kennedy later joked that his friend should have taken the money and then moved with Patrick to another table.[42]

Kennedy critics complain about the cousins' ability to use celebrityhood for social and political gain. But Kennedys are celebrities as much for how Americans treat them as for their own actions. With the public hungry for any tidbit of information, the Kennedys are forced into celebrityhood whether they want it or not. Entering politics was actually the toughest choice Patrick Kennedy had to make. It put him before the public and invited unfair comparisons with his forebears. At times, Kennedy has questioned whether he is "Kennedy enough" to meet people's expectations.[43] The authentic nature of his struggles in our confessional media era gives him a unique credibility with ordinary voters. Though he is a Kennedy and has many advantages stemming from fame, he too has dealt with adversity and overcome personal problems.

In the end, what is most notable about the Kennedys and what helps to explain their extraordinary staying power in the public eye is their ability to dream big. Early in Patrick Kennedy's career, he was asked on statewide television whether he would like to run for president someday. The then 26-year-old state representative who just a few years earlier had graduated from Providence College calmly replied, "Yes."[44] None of the interviewers blanched. Not Jim Taricani, the investigative reporter for WJAR-TV, who spent much of his time covering Mafiosi racketeers, nor Dyana Koelsch, the political reporter whose beat was the Statehouse, nor columnist Charlie Bakst. Not a single one of these veteran questioners of Rhode Island newsmakers accused the speaker of megalomania. This was in spite of the fact that Rhode Island was the smallest state in the union and a place that normally appeared in the national press as the measuring rod for passing icebergs or insect plagues.[45] Not once in its history had the state produced a presidential candidate. In fact, because of its puny four electoral college votes, Rhode Island had not even generated a serious vice-presidential candidate. Yet in 1994, a young politician whose voice still cracked from time to time was proclaiming his presidential ambitions, and no one scoffed. The reason was clear. The speaker was not the typical ambitious politician of a small state. He was Patrick Kennedy, the youngest scion of the famous Kennedy family. This young man was the only person in Rhode Island who could seriously imagine running for the highest office in the land. The unbridled ambition demonstrated by the representative was a vivid reminder of a remark Barbara Tannenbaum had made about the Kennedys. The family, she pointed out, "always ends up on its feet somehow." She said of Patrick, "I don't think he saw himself as having a limit." Mud could be thrown. Past behavior could be challenged. The Kennedys could be criticized. But politically, the family always could dream of a brighter future. It comes from a sense of "never having been stopped," she said.[46]

Notes

PREFACE

1. Bob Barr, "Impeaching William Jefferson Clinton," *Congressional Record*, December 18, 1998.
2. Francis Clines, "A 'Dreadful Day' Unfolds On and Off House Floor," *New York Times*, December 19, 1998, p. A1; John Mulligan, "Kennedy-Barr Battle Shows Strain of Debate," *Providence Journal*, December 19, 1998, p. A1; Rebecca Carr, "Ugly Words: Barr Tangles with a Kennedy," *Atlanta Journal and Constitution*, December 19, 1998, p. 1A.
3. David Canon, *Athletes, Actors, and Astronauts* (Chicago: University of Chicago Press, 1990); Joseph Schlesinger, *Ambition and Politics: Political Careers in the United States* (Chicago: Rand McNally, 1966).

CHAPTER 1

1. Carol Liston, "2nd Son for Ted," *Boston Globe*, July 15, 1967, p. 1. Also see Maxine Cheshire, "Kennedys Wary of the 'Caroline,'" *Boston Globe*, July 13, 1967, p. 31.
2. Carol Liston, "2nd Son For Ted," *Boston Globe*, July 15, 1967, p. 1.
3. Doris Kearns Goodwin, *The Fitzgeralds and the Kennedys* (New York: St. Martin's Press, 1987), pp. 226, 230, 410.
4. "Not Like a Kennedy, But . . . Patrick Naps for Newsmen," *Boston Globe*, July 19, 1967; "Meet Patrick Joseph Kennedy," *Boston Globe*, July 18, 1967, p. 1.
5. Gloria Negri, "Cardinal Baptizes Patrick," *Boston Globe*, July 30, 1967, p. 2.
6. Doug Riggs, "The Kennedy Complex," *Providence Journal Magazine*, October 14, 1990, p. M6.
7. Robert Shrum, interview by author, May 26, 1996; "Son Ill; Kennedy Cancels Flight," *Washington Post*, March 30, 1980, p. A16.
8. Larry Thompson, "Health," *Washington Post*, August 25, 1987, p. Z10.
9. Patrick Kennedy, interview by *Providence Journal* columnist M. Charles Bakst for WLNE-TV feature, October 14, 1994.
10. Bob Hohler, "Striving to Find His Voice; R.I.'s Kennedy Starts Slowly," *Boston Globe*, June 19, 1995, p. 1. The bully story comes from Kevin Sullivan, "The Morning After," *Rhode Island Monthly*, August 1991, p. 74.
11. Patrick Kennedy and Gail McKnight, "Kennedy Touch Football; The Family Tradition Lives On with a New Generation," *USA Today*, November 19, 1989, p. 14.
12. John Mulligan, "The Next Step," *Providence Journal Magazine*, February 19, 1995, p. 8M; Judith Gaines, "A Kennedy Learns the Fame Can Hurt," *Boston Globe*, April 11, 1991, p. 40.
13. Douglas Kennedy, interview by author, July 18, 1996.
14. Roger Piantadosi, "Style," *Washington Post*, July 7, 1977, p. D2.
15. Burton Hersh, *The Education of Edward Kennedy* (New York: William Morrow, 1972), p. 146.
16. Doug Riggs, "The Kennedy Complex," *Providence Journal Magazine*, October 14, 1990, p. M6.
17. Marci McDonald, "The Kennedy Dynasty: A New Generation Arrives on the Public Stage," *Macleans*, November 28, 1988, p. 30.
18. Mike Capuzzo, "Teddy's Son Angrily Defends Kennedy Name," *Toronto Star*, April 28, 1991, p. D4.
19. Patrick Kennedy, interview by *Providence Journal* columnist M. Charles Bakst for WLNE-TV feature, October 14, 1994, author's private archive.
20. Ibid.
21. John Mulligan, interview by author, August 25, 1999.
22. Robert Shrum, interview by author, May 26, 1996.
23. Patrick Kennedy, interview by *Providence Journal* columnist M. Charles Bakst for WLNE-TV feature, October 14, 1994, author's private archive.
24. Barbara Tannenbaum, interview by author, December 21, 1995; John Mulligan, "The Next Step," *Providence Journal Magazine*, February 19, 1995, p. 8M; John Mulligan, interview by author, August 25, 1999.
25. Douglas Kennedy, interview by author, July 18, 1996.
26. Jack McConnell, interview by author, August 24, 1999.
27. Bob Hohler, "The UnKennedy," *Boston Globe Magazine*, June 6, 1999, p. 39.

28. Patrick Kennedy, interview by *Providence Journal* columnist M. Charles Bakst for WLNE-TV feature, October 14, 1994.
29. Ibid.
30. John J. O'Connor, "Ted Kennedy Jr. Story: A Family Biography," *New York Times*, November 24, 1986, p. C17; Bob Morris, "Courage Was the Armor in Battle with Cancer," *Orlando Sentinel Tribune*, December 30, 1991, p. B1.
31. Larry Tye, "'National Crusade' Hits Kennedys Close to Home," *Boston Globe*, August 4, 1998, p. A9.
32. Lee Dykas, "Kennedy Recalls Learning about His Brother's Cancer," *Providence Journal*, November 16, 1989, p. E17.
33. Marcia Chellis, *Living with the Kennedys: The Joan Kennedy Story* (New York: Simon and Schuster, 1985), p. 48.
34. Dykas, "Kennedy Recalls."
35. Joan Braden, "Joan Kennedy Tells Her Own Story," *McCall's* 105, no. 11 (August 1978): 120–21, 190, 193.
36. Ibid, pp. 190, 193.
37. Kevin Sullivan, "The Morning After," *Rhode Island Monthly*, August 1991, p. 72.
38. Ibid., p. 74.
39. Patrick Kennedy, interview by *Providence Journal* columnist M. Charles Bakst for WLNE-TV feature, October 14, 1994.

40. M. Charles Bakst, "Campaign '88: The Democrats in Atlanta," *Providence Journal*, July 21, 1988, p. A8.
41. Robert Shrum, interview by author, May 26, 1996.
42. Douglas Kennedy, interview by author, July 18, 1996.
43. Tom Morganthau "Teddy Makes a Father's Decision," *Newsweek*, December 13, 1982, p. 32
44. Robert Shrum, interview by author, May 26, 1996; Tom Morganthau, "Teddy Makes a Father's Decision," *Newsweek*, December 13, 1982, p. 32; Scott MacKay, "Kennedy Mystique Becomes a Factor in Providence Politics," *Providence Journal*, July 10, 1988, p. A1.
45. Burton Hersh, *The Shadow President: Ted Kennedy in Opposition* (South Royalton, V. Steerforth Press, 1997), p. 64. See also Adam Clymer, *Edward M. Kennedy: A Biography* (New York: William Morrow, 1999).
46. Joan Braden, "Joan Kennedy Tells Her Own Story," *McCall's* 105, no. 11 (August 1978): 120–21, 190, 193.
47. E. Graydon Carter, "People," *Time*, December 20, 1982, p. 67.
48. Patrick Kennedy, interview by *Providence Journal* columnist M. Charles Bakst for WLNE-TV feature, October 14, 1994.

CHAPTER 2

1. Lynn Langway, "Newsmakers," *Newsweek*, January 10, 1983, p. 37; "Style," *Washington Post*, January 21, 1983, p. D3.
2. Chellis, *Living with the Kennedys*, p. 238.
3. Patrick Kennedy, interview by *Providence Journal* columnist M. Charles Bakst for WLNE-TV feature, October 14, 1994, author's private archive.
4. Donnie Radcliffe, "Style," *Washington Post*, March 30, 1982, p. B2.
5. Patrick Kennedy, interview by *Providence Journal* columnist M. Charles Bakst for WLNE-TV feature, October 14, 1994, author's private archive.
6. Chellis, *Living with the Kennedys*, p. 196.
7. Iris Krasnow, "Memories of Rose," *Life Magazine*, July 1990, p. 34.
8. Patrick Kennedy, interview by *Providence Journal* columnist M. Charles Bakst for WLNE-TV feature, October 14, 1994, author's private archive.
9. See Fessenden School publications, "The Time to Be," inside front cover, and "Information Bulletin," inside front cover.
10. Cathleen McGuigan, "Newsmakers," *Newsweek*, June 13, 1983, p. 35.

11. David Cobb, personal correspondence, May 16, 1997.
12. D. Morgan McVicar, "More Troubles for Kennedys, Questions Still Linger on Patrick's Drug Use," *Providence Journal*, December 10, 1991, p. A1.
13. Ibid.
14. Patrick Kennedy, interview by *Providence Journal* columnist M. Charles Bakst for WLNE-TV feature, October 14, 1994, author's private archive.
15. Scott MacKay, "Patrick Kennedy Admits Drug Rehab, Sought Help While a Student Six Years Ago," *Providence Journal*, December 9, 1991, p. A1; Scott MacKay, "Constituents Concerned But Willing to Give a Second Chance," *Providence Journal*, December 10, 1991, p. A1.
16. John Mulligan, "The Next Step," *Providence Journal Magazine*, February 19, 1995, p. 8M.
17. Patrick Kennedy, interview by *Providence Journal* columnist M. Charles Bakst for WLNE-TV feature, October 14, 1994, author's private archive; background source: Scott McKay, "Kennedy Tells of Depression," *Providence Journal,* March 1, 2000, p. A1.
18. Norma Nathan, "The Eye," *Boston Herald*,

July 15, 1986, p. 6; Gerald Sullivan and Michael Kenney, *The Race for the Eighth* (New York: Harper and Row, 1987), pp. 149–50.

19. Patrick Kennedy, interview by *Providence Journal* columnist M. Charles Bakst for WLNE-TV feature, October 14, 1994, author's private archive.

20. Norma Nathan, "The Eye," *Boston Herald,* July 15, 1986, p. 6.

21. *The Hoya,* Georgetown University student newspaper, August 26, 1986, pp. 2, 10, and August 29, 1980, p. 7.

22. Mary Carroll Johansen, "Freshman Class Most Select Ever," *The Hoya,* August 29, 1986, p. 7; Georgetown University "Undergraduate Prospectus."

23. Patrick Kennedy, interview by author, September 6, 1995.

24. John Mulligan, "The Next Step," *Providence Journal Magazine,* February 19, 1995, p. 8M.

25. Doug Riggs, "The Kennedy Complex," *Providence Journal Magazine,* October 14, 1990, p. M6.

26. Donnie Radcliffe, "Washington Ways," *Washington Post,* February 2, 1982, p. C1.

27. Robert Shrum, interview by author, May 26, 1996.

28. Fern Schumer Chapman, "Joe Kennedy, the Poor Man's Oil Tycoon," *Fortune,* July 23, 1984, p. 98.

29. *Washington Post,* "Which Kennedy's First?" December 9, 1985, p. A4; "Political Rivalry between Kennedys Reported," *Los Angeles Times,* December 9, 1985, p. 29. Also see Sullivan and Kenney, *Race for the Eighth,* pp. 11–15.

30. Wayne Woodlief, "Kennedy Clan 'Strained' by New-Generation Pols," *Boston Herald,* De-

cember 8, 1985, p. 12. Also see Michele Ingrassia, "The Kids: The Next Generation of Kennedys Has Come of Age," *Newsday,* November 25, 1988, p. 2.

31. Paul Herrnson, *Congressional Elections,* 2d ed. (Washington, D.C.: Congressional Quarterly, 1998).

32. Joseph LaPlante, "Kennedy Kicks Off Run for Congress," *Providence Journal,* January 20, 1986, p. A1.

33. Sullivan and Kenney, *Race for the Eighth,* 1987, pp. 56–57.

34. Michele Ingrassia, "The Kids: The Next Generation of Kennedys Has Come of Age," *Newsday,* November 25, 1988, p. 2.

35. Sullivan and Kenney, *Race for the Eighth,* pp. 127–29.

36. Ibid., p. 162.

37. Ibid., p. 209.

38. Ibid., pp. 216–18.

39. Michael Shnayerson, "Bobby's Kids," *Vanity Fair,* August 1997, pp. 108–19, 161–65.

40. Michele Ingrassia, "The Kids: The Next Generation of Kennedys Has Come of Age," *Newsday,* November 25, 1988, p. 2.

41. Patrick Kennedy, interview by author, September 6, 1995.

42. Scott MacKay, "Kennedy Mystique Becomes a Factor in Providence Politics," *Providence Journal,* July 10, 1988, p. A1.

43. Joan Kennedy, interview by author, June 22, 1998.

44. Patrick Kennedy, interview by author, September 6, 1995.

45. M. Charles Bakst, "Kennedy Gears Up for U.S. House Bid," *Providence Journal,* March 14, 1993, p. I1.

46. Barbara Tannenbaum, interview by author, December 21, 1995.

CHAPTER 3

1. Scott MacKay, "Kennedy Mystique Becomes a Factor in Providence Politics," *Providence Journal,* July 10, 1988, p. A1.

2. *Providence College Bulletin,* 1995, inside cover.

3. *Princeton Review: The Best 309 Colleges* (New York: Random House, 1995), pp. 466–67.

4. Chris Shaban, interview by author, January 6, 1996.

5. Scott Avedisian, interview by author, January 2, 1996.

6. Father Joseph Lennon, "The Worth of Catholic Education," *The Cowl,* November 4, 1987, p. 4.

7. Scott MacKay, "Kennedy Mystique Becomes a Factor in Providence Politics," *Providence Journal,* July 10, 1988, p. A1.

8. Peter Dujardin, "Abortion Topic Dominates

Student Debate," *The Cowl,* February 28, 1990, p. 1.

9. Scott Avedisian, interview by author, January 2, 1996.

10. Chris Shaban, interview by author, January 6, 1996.

11. James Vallee, interview by author, August 13, 1996.

12. Scott Avedisian, interview by author, January 2, 1996; Chris Shaban, interview by author, January 6, 1996.

13. Doug Riggs, "The Kennedy Complex," *Providence Journal Magazine,* October 14, 1990, p. M6.

14. Lee Dykas, "Working to Erase the Stigma of Suicide," *Providence Journal,* May 10, 1989, p. B1.

15. Doug Riggs, "The Kennedy Complex," *Providence Journal Magazine*, October 14, 1990, p. M6.
16. James Vallee, interview by author, August 13, 1996.
17. John Tabella, interview by author, August 2, 1995.
18. M. Charles Bakst, "R.I. Politics: Good Will, Political Tidbits Abound at Bipartisan Fete for Melucci," *Providence Journal*, October 4, 1987, p. C2. Bakst's recollections on meeting Kennedy are taken from an August 6, 1999, interview by the author.
19. Tom O'Grady, "PC Young Democrats," letter to the editor, *The Cowl* February 3, 1988, p. 7; Thomas O'Grady, "PC Young Democrats Begin Weekly Forum," *The Cowl*, February 10, 1988, p. 2; Robert McGehee, "R.I. General Treasurer Speaks to PC's Young Democrats," *The Cowl*, February 24, 1988, p. 1. Also see "200 Join Young Republicans at PC," *The Cowl*, September 16, 1987, p. 3; and Chris Shaban, "PC Young Republicans: A Step Beyond Ideology," *The Cowl*, December 9, 1987, p. 7.
20. Jonathan Karp, "Rhode Islanders for Dukakis Gear for R.I., N.H. Primaries," *Providence Journal*, December 6, 1987, p. C4; "People," *Providence Journal*, February 3, 1988, p. C7. Also see M. Charles Bakst, Katherine Gregg, and Kevin Sullivan, "Political Scene: Presidential News," *Providence Journal*, January 23, 1988, p. A5.
21. Jonathan Karp, p. C4.
22. Chris Shaban, interview by author, January 6, 1996.
23. Scott Avedisian, interview by author, January 2, 1996.
24. M. Charles Bakst, "Kennedy Touts Dukakis Bid with No Regrets," *Providence Journal*, March 6, 1988, p. C2.
25. Ibid; M. Charles Bakst, interview by author, August 6, 1999.
26. Delegate vote totals, *Providence Journal*, March 9, 1988, p. A12.
27. Patrick Kennedy, interview by author, September 6, 1995.
28. Kevin Sullivan, "Rhode Island Will Have 28 Delegates to the July 18–21 Democratic National Convention in Atlanta," *Providence Journal*, July 5, 1988, p. A1.
29. John Tabella, interview by author, August 2, 1995.

CHAPTER 4

1. Jack Skeffington, interview by author, August 2, 1995.
2. Ibid. For a discussion of state elections, see Malcolm Jewell and David Olson, *Politial Parties and Elections in American States*, 3d ed. (Chicago: Dorsey, 1988).
3. Ray Rickman, interview by author, August 14, 1995.
4. "Kennedy's Son Has Operation," *Chicago Tribune*, April 22, 1988, p. C20.
5. Chuck Conconi, "Personalities: Patrick Kennedy Goes Home," *Washington Post*, May 9, 1988, p. B3.
6. Jack Skeffington, interview by author, August 2, 1995.
7. Doug Riggs, "The Kennedy Complex," *Providence Journal Magazine*, October 14, 1990, p. M6.
8. Robert Shrum, interview by author, May 26, 1996.
9. James Vallee, interview by author, August 13, 1996.
10. Jack Skeffington, interview by author, August 2, 1995.
11. Ibid.
12. Patrick Kennedy, interview by author, September 6, 1995.
13. Doug Riggs, "The Kennedy Complex," *Providence Journal Magazine*, October 14, 1990, p. M6.
14. Scott MacKay, "Patrick Kennedy Eyes State Representative Job: May Challenge Veteran Skeffington in the 9th District," *Providence Journal*, June 7, 1988, p. B7.
15. Jack Skeffington, interview by author, August 2, 1995.
16. Scott MacKay, "Kennedy Mystique Becomes a Factor in Providence Politics," *Providence Journal*, July 10, 1988, p. A1.
17. John Tabella, interview by author, August 2, 1995.
18. Chris Nocera, interview by author, August 8, 1995.
19. John Tabella, interview by author, August 2, 1995.
20. Scott MacKay, "Key Democrats Turn Out to Support Skeffington," *Providence Journal*, July 29, 1988, p. C1.
21. John Tabella, interview by author, August 2, 1995.
22. Ibid.
23. "A Campaign Plan for the Skeffington Reelection Effort," confidential document, July 1988; "A Survey of 9th Representative District Primary Voter Attitudes," July 1988, author's private archive.
24. Tony Pesaturo, interview by author, August 18, 1995.
25. "A Campaign Plan for the Skeffington Reelection Effort," July 1988, author's private archive.

26. Ibid.
27. Tony Pesaturo interview by author, August 18, 1995.
28. Tony Pesaturo interview by author, August 2, 1995.
29. Background source.
30. John Tabella, interview by author, August 2, 1995.
31. Scott MacKay, "Kennedy's Earnings $22,309 Last Year," *Providence Journal*, August 16, 1988, p. B1.
32. Chris Nocera, interview by author, August 8, 1995; John Tabella, interview by author, August 2, 1995.
33. Chris Nocera, interview by author, August 8, 1995.
34. Ibid.
35. Ibid.
36. Barbara Tannenbaum, interview by author, December 21, 1995.
37. Chris Nocera, interview by author, August 8, 1995.
38. John Tabella, interview by author, August 2, 1995.
39. Chris Nocera, interview by author, August 8, 1995.
40. Ibid.
41. Laura Meade, "Skeffington Backs Shopkeeper Arrested in Slaying, Asks Return of Death Penalty," *Providence Journal*, July 26, 1988, p. A11.
42. Tony Pesaturo, interview by author, August 2, 1995.
43. John Tabella, interview by author, August 2, 1995.
44. Ibid.
45. James O'Neill, "Patrick Kennedy's Manager Files Charges against Skeffington Aides," *Providence Journal*, August 25, 1988, p. C1.
46. Ibid.
47. Lee Dykas, "Skeffington Tilted Off Balance by Kennedy's Vandalized Signs," *Providence Journal*, August 31, 1988, p. D1.
48. John Tabella, interview by author, August 2, 1995.

49. Tony Pesaturo, interview by author, August 2, 1995.
50. Robert Corriea, "Elections Board Declines a Hearing on Kennedy's Impropriety Allegations," *Providence Journal*, September 6, 1988, p. B1.
51. Chris Nocera, interview by author, August 8, 1995.
52. John Tabella, interview by author, August 2, 1995.
53. Robert Corriea, "Elections Board Declines a Hearing on Kennedy's Impropriety Allegations," *Providence Journal*, September 6, 1988, p. B1.
54. Jack Skeffington, interview by author, August 2, 1995.
55. Dan Barry, "Kennedy Investigator's Knock on Door Was Cold Comfort for Challenged Voter," *Providence Journal*, September 7, 1988, p. D1.
56. Skeffington direct mail brochure, undated, author's private archive.
57. John Tabella, interview by author, August 2, 1995.
58. Ibid.
59. Tony Pesaturo, interview by author, August 2, 1995.
60. Ibid.
61. Ibid.
62. Jack Skeffington, interview by author, August 2, 1995. Also see Scott MacKay, "'Perfect Gentleman' an Icon, Reluctantly," *Providence Journal*, July 18, 1999, p. A1.
63. Barbara Tannenbaum, interview by author, December 21, 1995.
64. Patrick Kennedy campaign video, "Our Vote Is Working," 1990, author's private archive.
65. M. Charles Bakst, "Patrick Kennedy Won the Election; Now His Job Is to Show He Earned It," *Providence Journal*, September 18, 1988, p. C2.
66. Alpha Research Associates' Exit Poll Results, September 14, 1988, author's private archive.
67. John Tabella, interview by author, October 11, 1995.

CHAPTER 5

1. Ray Rickman, interview by author, August 14, 1995.
2. Joe DeAngelis, interview by author, August 1, 1995.
3. Rhode Island, *Journal of the House of Representatives*, January 3, 1989, p. H.J. 7.
4. Ray Rickman, interview by author, August 14, 1995.
5. Elmer Cornwell, interview by author, September 8, 1995. A discussion of state legislatures

can be found in Sarah McCally Morehouse, *State Politics, Parties, and Policy* (New York: Holt, Rinehart, and Winston, 1981).
6. Elmer Cornwell, interview by author, September 8, 1995; George Caruolo, interview by author, September 20, 1995.
7. Linda Kushner, interview by author, August 23, 1995.
8. John Harwood, interview by author, September 20, 1995.

9. Ibid.
10. George Caruolo, interview by author, September 20, 1995.
11. Joe DeAngelis, interview by author, August 1, 1995.
12. Ibid.
13. Tom Lamb, interview by author, August 21, 1995.
14. Chris Boyle, interview by author, August 28, 1995.
15. Elmer Cornwell, interview by author, September 8, 1995.
16. Chris Boyle, interview by author, August 28, 1995.
17. Ibid.; Rodney Driver, interview by author, August 16, 1995.
18. Linda Kushner, interview by author, August 23, 1995.
19. Tom Lamb, interview by author, August 21, 1995.
20. George Caruolo, interview by author, September 20, 1995.
21. John Tabella, interview by author, August 2, 1995; Ray Rickman, interview by author, August 14, 1995.
22. Chris Nocera, interview by author, August 8, 1995.
23. Scott Avedisian, interview by author, January 2, 1996. For the general value of constituency service, see Morris Fiorina, *Congress: Keystone of the Washington Establishment* (New Haven: Yale University Press, 1977).
24. Patrick Kennedy "Five Reasons To Feel Unashamed About Being a Liberal," *Providence Journal Magazine* January 29, 1989, p. M5.

25. Linda Kushner, personal journal, February 8, 1989, pp. 28–29, author's private archive.
26. Ibid.
27. "Gun Legislation Planned," *Providence Journal*, February 10, 1989, p. A3; Kevin Sullivan, "Lawmakers Want to Make Buying Guns Harder," *Providence Journal*, February 11, 1989, p. A4.
28. Kevin Sullivan, "Assembly Gun-Control Battle May Not Be Over," *Providence Journal*, May 5, 1989, p. A12; Kevin Sullivan, "'89 General Assembly Produced Great Plays But Lackluster Record," *Providence Journal*, July 9, 1989, p. A12.
29. Joe DeAngelis, interview by author, August 1, 1995. Also see Robert Erikson, Gerald Wright, and John McIver, *Statehouse Democracy* (New York: Cambridge University Press, 1993).
30. Linda Kushner, interview by author, August 23, 1995.
31. "Power Plant Siting Bill Tabled for Clarification," *Providence Journal*, May 26, 1990, p. A4.
32. Katherine Gregg and Christopher Beall, "House Action Exempts Newbay, Kennedy Amendment Generates Hot Debate," *Providence Journal*, May 31, 1990, p. A3.
33. Linda Kushner, interview by author, August 23, 1995.
34. Ray Rickman, interview by author, August 14, 1995.
35. Scott MacKay and John Mulligan, "Kennedy Cancels Hope," *Providence Journal*, June 23, 1990, p. A3.
36. Chris Nocera, interview by author, August 8, 1995.

CHAPTER 6

1. Scott MacKay, interview by author, August 10, 1999.
2. Charles Maher, interview by author, August 22, 1995.
3. Ibid.; Richard DuJardin, "Gelineau Reflects on 25-Year Tenure as Bishop," *Providence Journal*, April 27, 1997, pp. D1, D7.
4. Charles Maher, interview by author, August 22, 1995.
5. Barbara Tannenbaum, interview by author, December 21, 1995.
6. Ray Rickman, interview by author, August 14, 1995. A discussion of religion and politics can be found in Kenneth Wald, *Religion and Politics in the United States*, 3d ed. (Washington, D.C.: Congressional Quarterly Press, 1997).
7. Chris Nocera, interview by author, August 8, 1995.
8. Bishop Louis Gelineau, interview by author, May 15, 1997.

9. Chris Nocera, interview by author, August 8, 1995.
10. Linda Kushner, interview by author, August 23, 1995.
11. Chris Nocera, interview by author, August 8, 1995.
12. Charles Maher, interview by author, August 22, 1995.
13. Chris Nocera, interview by author, August 8, 1995.
14. Charles Maher, interview by author, August 22, 1995.
15. Ibid.
16. Ibid.
17. Steven Eisenstadt, "Diocese Overrules Parents, Cancels Rep. Kennedy Talk," *Providence Journal*, May 10, 1990, p. A1.
18. Ibid.
19. Chris Nocera, interview by author, August 8, 1995.

CHAPTER 7

1. Patrick Kennedy campaign video, *Our Vote Is Working*, 1990, author's private archive.
2. Kevin Sullivan, "The Littlest Kennedy," *Boston Phoenix*, March 22, 1991, pp. 9–10; Kevin Sullivan, "The Morning After," *Rhode Island Monthly*, August 1991, p. 72.
3. John Tabella, interview by author, October 11, 1995.
4. Ray Rickman, interview by author, August 14, 1995.
5. John Tabella, interview by author, October 11, 1995.
6. Joe DeAngelis, interview by author, August 1, 1995.
7. Ibid.
8. George Caruolo, interview by author, September 20, 1995.
9. Linda Kushner, interview by author, August 23, 1995.
10. Ray Rickman, interview by author, August 14, 1995.
11. Joe DeAngelis, interview by author, August 1, 1995.
12. Ibid.
13. Chris Boyle, interview by author, August 28, 1995.
14. Elmer Cornwell, interview by author, September 8, 1995.
15. Ibid.
16. Scott MacKay, "Rep. Patrick Kennedy Presses for Reforms in Budget Process," *Providence Journal*, January 1, 1991, p. D9.
17. Joe DeAngelis, interview by author, August 1, 1995.
18. Chris Boyle, interview by author, August 28, 1995.
19. Joe DeAngelis, interview by author, August 1, 1995.
20. Bruce Sundlun, interview by author, August 30, 1995.
21. Robert Shrum, interview by author, November 7, 1997.
22. Joseph Paolino, visit to the author's Brown University class, March 14, 1991.
23. Bruce Sundlun, interview by author, August 30, 1995.
24. Ibid.
25. Ibid.
26. Elmer Cornwell, interview by author, September 8, 1995.
27. Bruce Sundlen, interview by author, August 30, 1995.
28. Chris Boyle, interview by author, August 28, 1995.
29. George Caruolo, interview by author, September 20, 1995.
30. Ibid.
31. John Harwood, interview by author, September 20, 1995.
32. Bruce Sundlun, interview by author, August 30, 1995.
33. Joe DeAngelis, interview by author, August 1, 1995.
34. Bruce Sundlun, interview by author, August 30, 1995.
35. Elmer Cornwell, interview by author, September 8, 1995.
36. Chris Nocera, interview by author, August 8, 1995.
37. Ray Rickman, interview by author, August 14, 1995.
38. Jeffrey Hiday, "Democrats Hesitant on Mancini Credit Union Issue," *Providence Journal*, February 14, 1991, p. A9.
39. Ray Rickman, interview by author, August 14, 1995.
40. Scott MacKay, "DeAngelis's Critics Say Public on Their Side," *Providence Journal*, February 6, 1991, p. A9.
41. Ray Rickman, interview by author, August 14, 1995.
42. Linda Kushner, personal journal, 1991; Linda Kushner, interview by author, August 23, 1995.
43. Ray Rickman, interview by author, August 14, 1995.
44. Ibid.
45. Linda Kushner, interview by author, August 23, 1995.
46. Joe DeAngelis, interview by author, August 1, 1995.
47. M. Charles Bakst, "DeAngelis in House Hot Seat," *Providence Journal*, February 17, 1991, p. C1.
48. Joe DeAngelis, interview by author, August 1, 1995.
49. "DeAngelis Resignation Not Warranted, Teitz," *Providence Journal*, February 23, 1991, p. B9. Also, author's lunch with Patrick Kennedy, February 27, 1991, at Brown University Faculty Club.
50. Kevin Sullivan, "The Littlest Kennedy," *Boston Phoenix*, March 22, 1991, pp. 9–10.
51. Joe DeAngelis, interview by author, August 1, 1995.
52. Ibid.
53. Russell Garland and Scott MacKay, "TV Drama," *Providence Journal*, March 30, 1991, p. A3.
54. Kevin Sullivan, "The Littlest Kennedy," *Boston Phoenix*, March 22, 1991, pp. 9–10.

CHAPTER 8

1. Kathleen O'Brien, interview by author, July 15, 1996.
2. James Vallee, interview by author, August 13, 1996.
3. Doug Riggs, "The Kennedy Complex," *Providence Journal Magazine*, October 14, 1990, p. M6.
4. Fox Butterfield, "Views of the Kennedy House," *New York Times*, April 10, 1991, p. A16.
5. Judith Gaines, "A Kennedy Learns the Fame Can Hurt," *Boston Globe*, April 11, 1991, p. 40; John Elvin, "Society's to Blame," *Washington Times*, May 20, 1991, p. A6. For a more general view of scandal coverage, see Howard Kurtz, *Spin Cycle* (New York: Free Press, 1998).
6. Janet Cawley and Ray Gibson, "'69 Tragedy Echoed in Kennedy Case," *Chicago Tribune*, June 9, 1991, p. C23.
7. Hersh, *Shadow President*, p. 89.
8. Larry Tye, "Reports from Witnesses Conflict in Data on Smith Rape Inquiry," *Boston Globe*, May 15, 1991, p. 1.
9. Timothy Clifford, "Teddy Regrets Trip to Palm Beach Bar," *Newsday*, December 7, 1991, p. 5.
10. Frank Cerabino, "Did Fateful Night End with a Kiss?" *Orlando Sentinel Tribune*, May 25, 1991, p. A1.
11. David Kaplan, "The Trial You Won't See," *Newsweek*, December 16, 1991, p. 18.
12. "Kennedy Menu," *St. Petersburg Times*, July 2, 1991, p. 4A.
13. Chris Nocera, interview by author, August 8, 1995.
14. Ibid.
15. "A New Melodrama for Kennedy, Alcohol Factor in Alleged Rape at Palm Beach Retreat," *Providence Journal*, April 2, 1991, p. A1.
16. Scott MacKay, "Patrick Kennedy Lambastes 'Tabloids'," *Providence Journal*, April 4, 1991, p. B5.
17. Chris Nocera, interview by author, August 8, 1995.
18. Scott MacKay, "Patrick Kennedy Lambastes 'Tabloids'," *Providence Journal*, April 4, 1991, p. B5.
19. Joe DeAngelis, interview by author, August 1, 1995.
20. Kevin Sullivan, "The Morning After," *Rhode Island Monthly*, August 1991, p. 72.
21. Larry Martz with Peter Katel, "What Happened in Palm Beach?" *Newsweek*, April 15, 1991, p. 32.
22. Mike Capuzzo, "Teddy's Son Angrily Defends Kennedy Name," *Toronto Star*, April 28, 1991, p. D4.
23. Karen Lee Ziner, "Patrick Kennedy Recalls Fateful Hours, Deposition Details Events on Night of Alleged Rape," *Providence Journal*, May 18, 1991, p. A1.
24. Gloria Borger and Missy Daniel, "A Question of Survival," *U.S. News & World Report*, May 27, 1991, p. 24.
25. Felice Freyer, "Patrick Kennedy: 'I Want All the Facts to Come Out,'" *Providence Journal*, April 8, 1991, p. A1.
26. John Cassidy, "Kennedys' Fury over Rape-Case Circus," *London Sunday Times*, August 4, 1991, p. 1.
27. Kevin Sullivan, "The Morning After," *Rhode Island Monthly*, August 1991, p. 72.
28. Barbara Tannenbaum, interview by author, December 21, 1995.
29. Judith Gaines, "Patrick Kennedy Mum on Family View of Smith," *Boston Globe*, July 26, 1991, p. 4.
30. Fox Butterfield, "Friends See Fragmenting of Kennedys," *New York Times*, April 8, 1991, p. A8.
31. Barbara Tannenbaum, interview by author, December 21, 1995.
32. David Margolick, "Private Investigator's Pursuit of a Police Detective Pays Off for Simpson," *New York Times*, August 21, 1995, p. A8; For a discussion of Ted Kennedy's use of private investigators, see Douglas Frantz, "Plenty of Dirty Jobs in Politics and a New Breed of Diggers," *New York Times*, July 6, 1999, p. A1.
33. Chris Nocera, interview by author, August 8, 1995.
34. Scott MacKay, "Poll Reflects Positively on Rep. Kennedy in Matter of His Cousin's Rape Case," *Providence Journal*, November 6, 1991, p. B3.
35. Barbara Tannenbaum, interview by author, December 21, 1995.
36. "Kennedy and Son Testify at Smith Trial," *Minneapolis Star Tribune*, December 7, 1991, p. 7A; Mary Jordan, "Kennedy Questioning Elicits Reminiscence of Tragedies," *Washington Post*, December 7, 1991, p. A1.
37. "Smith Found Innocent of Rape Charge," *St. Louis Post-Dispatch*, December 12, 1991, p. 1A.
38. Scott MacKay, "Patrick Kennedy Admits Drug Rehab," *Providence Journal*, December 9, 1991, p. A1.
39. John Tabella, interview by author, August 2, 1995.

40. Scott MacKay, "Patrick Kennedy Tells Constituents He's Drug-Free," *Providence Journal*, December 11, 1991, p. A1.

41. Ibid.

42. Chris Nocera, interview by author, August 8, 1995.

43. Patrick Kennedy, conversation with author, 1990.

44. John Tabella, interview by author, August 2, 1995.

45. Chris Nocera, interview by author, August 8, 1995.

46. John Larrabee, "Kennedy Spotlight Never Dims," *USA Today*, May 23, 1991, p. 3A.

47. W. John Moore, "From the K Street Corridor," *National Journal*, November 16, 1991, p. 2813.

48. Chris Nocera, interview by author, August 8, 1995.

49. Robert Foley, interview by author, July 19, 1996.

50. Patrick Kennedy, interview by *Providence Journal* columnist M. Charles Bakst for WLNE-TV feature, October 14, 1994, author's personal archive.

51. Chris Nocera, interview by author, August 8, 1995.

52. Rhode Island International Trade Corporation, Original Articles of Incorporation, Secretary of State Corporations Division, Corporate ID 66121, November 21, 1991.

53. 1992 Annual Report, Secretary of State Corporations Division, Corporate ID 05-0463100, February 27, 1992.

54. Barbara Tannenbaum, interview by author, December 21, 1995.

55. John Tabella, interview by author, August 2, 1995.

56. Robert Foley, interview by author, July 19, 1996.

57. Chris Nocera, interview by author, August 8, 1995.

58. Robert Foley, interview by author, July 19, 1996.

59. Chris Nocera, interview by author, August 8, 1995.

60. Tony Marcella, interview by author, October 5, 1995.

61. John Tabella, interview by author, October 11, 1995.

62. Robert Foley, interview by author, July 19, 1996.

63. Ibid.

64. Ibid.

CHAPTER 9

1. Joe DeAngelis, interview by author, August 1, 1995.

2. Rhode Island, *Journal of the House of Representatives*, January 7, 1992, pp. H.J. 2, 3.

3. Vartan Gregorian, *Carved in Sand: Report on the Collapse of the Rhode Island Share and Deposit Indemnity Corporation*, March 14, 1991, author's personal archive.

4. Darrell M. West, Thomas J. Anton, and Jack Combs, *Public Opinion in Rhode Island, 1984–1993*, (Providence, R.I.: Brown University, 1994).

5. Ray Rickman, interview by author, August 14, 1995.

6. Elmer Cornwell, interview by author, September 8, 1995.

7. Chris Boyle, interview by author, August 28, 1995.

8. Linda Kushner, interview by author, August 23, 1995.

9. Chris Boyle, interview by author, August 28, 1995.

10. Ibid.

11. Ibid.

12. Ibid.

13. George Caruolo, interview by author, September 20, 1995.

14. Rodney Driver, interview by author, August 16, 1995.

15. Robert Weygand, interview by author, August 24, 1998.

16. John Harwood, interview by author, September 20, 1995.

17. George Caruolo, interview by author, September 20, 1995.

18. John Harwood, interview by author, September 20, 1995.

19. George Caruolo, interview by author, September 20, 1995.

20. Ibid.

21. Ibid.

22. Joe DeAngelis, interview by author, August 1, 1995.

23. George Caruolo, interview by author, September 20, 1995.

24. Robert Weygand, interview by author, August 24, 1998.

25. Tony Marcella, interview by author, October 5, 1995.

26. George Caruolo, interview by author, September 20, 1995.

27. Elmer Cornwell, interview by author, September 8, 1995.

28. George Caruolo, interview by author, September 20, 1995.

29. Chris Nocera, interview by author, August 8, 1995.

CHAPTER 10

1. Scott MacKay, "Rep. Kennedy Moves to Machtley's District, Mulls Run for Congress," *Providence Journal*, March 4, 1993, p. D11. A more general discussion of congressional campaigning can be found in Herrnson, *Congressional Elections*; Gary Jacobson, *The Politics of Congressional Elections*, 4th ed. (New York: Longman, 1997).

2. John Mulligan, "St. Germain Finds Well Has Run Dry," *Providence Journal*, November 9, 1988, p. A1; Michael Kranish, "R.I. Lawmaker May Face New Misconduct Probe," *Boston Globe*, November 2, 1988, p. 46.

3. D. West, T. Anton, and J. Combs, *Public Opinion in Rhode Island, 1984–1993*.

4. WJAR-TV, *Election Night Coverage*, November 3, 1992.

5. Patrick Kennedy, interview by author, September 6, 1995.

6. Scott MacKay, "Rep. Kennedy Moves to Machtley's District, Mulls Run for Congress," *Providence Journal*, March 4, 1993, p. D11. Also see Richard Fenno, *Home Style: House Members in their Districts* (Boston: Little, Brown, 1978).

7. John Mulligan, "Kennedy Fund-Raiser Lures Powerful," *Providence Journal*, July 21, 1993, p. D4.

8. John Mulligan, Russell Garland, James O'Neill, and Scott MacKay, "Dems Help Kennedy," *Providence Journal*, August 7, 1993, p. A3.

9. George Caruolo, interview by author, September 20, 1995.

10. John Harwood, interview by author, September 20, 1995.

11. Patrick Kennedy, interview by author, September 6, 1995.

12. Ibid.

13. John Mulligan, "Kennedy Fund-Raiser Lures Powerful," *Providence Journal*, July 21, 1993, p. D4.

14. Scott Wolf, interview by author, August 24, 1995.

15. Ibid.

16. Guy Dufault, interview by author, December 7, 1995.

17. Robert Weygand, interview by author, August 24, 1998.

18. Guy Dufault, interview by author, December 7, 1995.

19. John Mulligan, "The Next Step," *Providence Journal Magazine*, February 19, 1995, p. 8M.

20. Ibid.

21. Tony Marcella, interview by author, October 5, 1995.

22. Scott MacKay, "Kennedy Kicks Off with Cast of Thousands," *Providence Journal*, May 7, 1994, p. A1.

23. Guy Dufault, interview by author, December 7, 1995. For the role of money in congressional elections, see Gary Jacobson, *Money in Congressional Elections* (New Haven: Yale University Press, 1980).

24. Kevin Vigilante, interview by author, December 21, 1995. Also see Sandy Maisel, *From Obscurity to Oblivion* (Knoxville: University of Tennesee Press, 1982).

25. Kevin Vigilante, interview by author, December 21, 1995.

26. Patrick Kennedy, interview by author, September 6, 1995.

27. David Axelrod, interview by author, August 25, 1995.

28. Tubby Harrison, interview by author, July 31, 1995.

29. Larry Berman, appearance at Brown University Election Debriefing, November 19, 1994.

30. David Axelrod, interview by author, August 25, 1995.

31. Larry Berman, appearance at Brown University Election Debriefing, November 19, 1994.

32. David Axelrod, interview by author, August 25, 1995.

33. Larry Berman, appearance at Brown University Election Debriefing, November 19, 1994. Also see Darrell M. West, *Air Wars: Television Advertising in Election Campaigns, 1952–1996*, 2d ed. (Washington, D.C.: Congressional Quarterly Press, 1997).

34. David Axelrod, interview by author, August 25, 1995.

35. Ibid.

36. Paul Moore, appearance at Brown University Election Debriefing, November 19, 1994.

37. Guy Dufault, interview by author, December 7, 1995.

38. Josh Seftel, *Taking on the Kennedys*, PBS P.O.V. Documentary, May 28, 1996.

39. Kevin Vigilante, interview by author, December 21, 1995.

40. Hersh, *Education of Edward Kennedy*, pp. 176–77, 179; Murray Levin, *Kennedy Campaigning* (Boston: Beacon Press, 1966), pp. 63, 145, 195.

41. David Axelrod, interview by author, August 25, 1995.

42. Kevin Vigilante, interview by author, December 21, 1995.

43. Paul Moore, appearance at Brown University Election Debriefing, November 19, 1994.

44. Larry Berman, appearance at Brown University Election Debriefing, November 19, 1994.

45. Scott MacKay, appearance at Brown University Election Debriefing, November 19, 1994.
46. Background source.
47. Tony Marcella, interview by author, October 5, 1995.
48. Tony DePaul, "PC Students Play Politics in Campus Proxy Debate," *Providence Journal*, March 30, 1988, p. D1; "PC Students Present Candidates' Views," *The Cowl*, April 13, 1988, p. 1.
49. Chris Shaban, interview by author, January 6, 1996; moderator Patrick Gallagher, interview by author, January 9, 1996.
50. Brendan Curran, "PC's Young Political Parties To Face Off," *The Cowl*, November 15, 1989, p. 1.
51. Author transcript of Channel 6 debate, October 9, 1994.
52. Ibid.
53. Scott MacKay, "Vigilante Scores Kennedy on Failure to Disclose Taxes," *Providence Journal*, October 8, 1994, p. 1A.
54. Josh Seftel, *Taking on the Kennedys*, PBS P.O.V. Documentary, May 28, 1996.
55. Larry Berman, appearance at Brown University Election Debriefing, November 19, 1994.
56. Ibid.
57. Scott MacKay, appearance at Brown University Election Debriefing, November 19, 1994.
58. Guy Dufault, interview by author, December 7, 1995.
59. David Axelrod, interview by author, August 25, 1995.
60. Kevin Vigilante, interview by author, December 21, 1995.
61. Josh Seftel, *Taking on the Kennedys*, PBS P.O.V. Documentary, May 28, 1996.
62. John Mulligan, "The Next Step," *Providence Journal Magazine*, February 19, 1995, p. 8M.
63. Alissa Silverman, "Brother's Keeper?" *Providence Phoenix*, June 6, 1997, p. 6; Josh Seftel, *Taking on the Kennedys*, PBS P.O.V. Documentary, May 28, 1996.
64. Josh Seftel, *Taking on the Kennedys*, PBS P.O.V. Documentary, May 28, 1996.
65. Kevin Vigilante, interview by author, December 21, 1995.
66. Scott MacKay, "Vigilante," *Providence Journal*, October 27, 1994, p. A18.
67. Tony Marcella, interview by author, October 5, 1995.
68. Larry Berman, appearance at Brown University Election Debriefing, November 19, 1994.
69. Guy Dufault, interview by author, December 7, 1995.
70. Ibid.
71. Ibid.

CHAPTER 11

1. Patrick Kennedy, interview by author, September 6, 1995.
2. Ibid. Also see Ed Gillespie and Bob Schellhas, ed., *Contract with America* (New York: Times Books, 1994); William Connelly and John Pitney, "The House Republicans: Lessons for Political Science," in *New Majority or Old Minority*, ed. Nicol Rae and Colton Campbell (Lanham, Md. Rowman and Littlefield, 1999).
3. Ibid.
4. Patrick Kennedy, interview by author, September 6, 1995.
5. Tony Marcella, interview by author, October 5, 1995.
6. Ibid.
7. Patrick Kennedy, interview by author, September 6, 1995. See Allan Cigler and Burdett Loomis, *Interest Group Politics*, 5th ed. (Washington, D.C.: Congressional Quarterly Press, 1998).
8. Tony Marcella, interview by author, October 5, 1995.
9. John Mulligan, interview by author, August 25, 1999.
10. Michael Crowley, "When Kennedys Collide," *Boston Phoenix*, February 28, 1997, pp. 10–11. Also see John Mulligan, "The Next Step," *Providence Journal Magazine*, February 19, 1995, p. 8M.
11. Bob Hohler, "Striving To Find His Voice; R.I.'s Kennedy Starts Slowly," *Boston Globe*, June 19, 1995, p. 1.
12. Chris Black, "Rep. Patrick Kennedy Marks a Milestone," *Boston Globe*, July 14, 1997, p. A7.
13. Tony Marcella, interview by author, October 5, 1995.
14. Tubby Harrison, interview by author, July 31, 1995.
15. Patrick Kennedy, interview by author, September 6, 1995.
16. Ibid.
17. John Mulligan, "The Next Step," *Providence Journal Magazine*, February 19, 1995, p. 8M.
18. Patrick Kennedy, interview by author, September 6, 1995.
19. John Mulligan, "The Next Step," *Providence Journal Magazine*, February 19, 1995, p. 8M.
20. Tony Marcella, interview by author, October 5, 1995.
21. Mike Mello, interview by author, September 6, 1995.
22. Guy Dufault, interview by author, December 7, 1995.

23. Ibid.
24. Jack Reed, interview by author, February 20, 1996.
25. Ibid. Also see David Rohde, *Parties and Leaders in the Postreform House* (Chicago: University of Chicago Press, 1991); Richard Fenno, *The Making of Senator Dan Quayle* (Washington, D.C.: Congressional Quarterly Press, 1989).
26. Jack Reed, interview by author, February 20, 1996.
27. Patrick Kennedy, interview by author, September 6, 1995.
28. Ibid.
29. Douglas Koopman, *Hostile Takeover: The House Republican Party, 1980–1995* (Lanham, Md.: Rowman and Littlefield, 1996).
30. Garrett Bliss, interview by author, May 13, 1997.
31. Jack McConnell, interview by author, August 24, 1999.
32. Patrick Kennedy, interview by author, September 6, 1995.
33. Ibid.
34. Tony Marcella, interview by author, October 5, 1995.
35. Candy Crowley, "Washington Experiences Scarcity of Liberals," *Inside Politics*, CNN, January 18, 1995, Transcript # 745-5.
36. Tony Marcella, interview by author, October 5, 1995.
37. Jack Reed, interview by author, February 20, 1996.
38. Jack Reed, interview by author, February 20, 1996.
39. Ibid.
40. Ibid.

41. Patrick Kennedy, interview by author, September 6, 1995.
42. Ibid.
43. Ibid.
44. Patrick Kennedy, *Rhode Island Weekly*, Cox Communications cable television show, September 6, 1995.
45. Garrett Bliss, interview by author, May 13, 1997.
46. Patrick Kennedy, *Rhode Island Weekly*, Cox Communications cable television show, September 6, 1995.
47. Ibid.
48. Ibid.
49. Tony Marcella, interview by author, October 5, 1995.
50. Ibid.
51. Jack Reed, interview by author, February 20, 1996.
52. Tony Marcella, interview by author, October 5, 1995.
53. Ibid.
54. Ibid.
55. Jack Reed, interview by author, February 20, 1996.
56. Ibid.
57. Ibid.
58. John Mulligan, "Kennedy Suffers Political Setback in Planned Elimination of Seawolf," *Providence Journal*, June 16, 1995, p. A9.
59. Larry Berman, interview by author, July 27, 1995.
60. Jack Reed, interview by author, February 20, 1996.
61. David Axelrod, interview by author, August 25, 1995.

CHAPTER 12

1. Justin Coleman, "A Season inside Channel 10," Brown University independent study, December 19, 1996.
2. Larry Berman, classroom visit, Brown University, November 18, 1996.
3. Background source.
4. D. West, *Air Wars*.
5. Christopher Rowland, "Kennedy's PAC Makes Him a Big-Time Fund-Raiser," *Providence Journal*, October 5, 1996, p. A1. The overall contribution figures come from Leslie Wayne, "Congress Uses Leadership PAC's to Wield Power," *New York Times*, March 13, 1997, p. A25.
6. Christopher Rowland, "Kennedy's PAC Makes Him a Big-Time Fund-Raiser," *Providence Journal*, October 5, 1996, p. A1.
7. Larry Berman, classroom visit, Brown University, November 18, 1996.

8. Russell Garland, "No Longer a Newcomer," *Providence Journal*, October 16, 1996, p. A1.
9. Larry Berman, classroom visit, Brown University, November 18, 1996.
10. M. Charles Bakst, "On the Road for the Democratic Party: Patrick Kennedy's Excellent Adventure," *Providence Journal*, October 27, 1996, p. D1.
11. Ibid.
12. Ibid.
13. Ibid.
14. Dyana Koelsch, "Interview with Patrick Kennedy," *Five at Five* WJAR-TV, October 25, 1996.
15. Larry Berman, classroom visit, Brown University, November 18, 1996.
16. Scott MacKay, "Kennedy Flies to Missouri, But Finds Party's Already Over," *Providence Journal*, November 7, 1996, p. A1.

17. Ibid.

18. M. Charles Bakst, "On the Road for the Democratic Party: Patrick Kennedy's Excellent Adventure," *Providence Journal*, October 27, 1996, p. D1.

19. Larry Berman, classroom visit, Brown University, November 18, 1996.

20. Patrick Kennedy, interview by author, September 6, 1995.

21. Russell Garland, "No Longer a Newcomer," *Providence Journal*, October 16, 1996, p. A1. Also see Jack White, *Newsmakers Interview*, WPRI-TV, October 6, 1996.

22. Larry Berman, classroom visit, Brown University, November 18, 1996.

23. Background source.

24. M. Charles Bakst, "In Abortion Debate, Chafee and Reed Steady for Choice," *Providence Journal*, March 27, 1997, p. B1.

25. Michael Brown, "Kennedy Attacks the Church," *Providence Visitor*, October 31, 1996, p. 1.

26. Laura Meade Kirk, "Bishop Gelineau Recalled as 'A People's Bishop,'" *Providence Journal*, June 12, 1997, p. A21.

27. *Six O'Clock News*, WJAR-TV, June 11, 1997.

28. John Mulligan, "Weygand, Kennedy Oppose Budget Deal," *Providence Journal*, May 21, 1997, p. A3.

29. M. Charles Bakst, "On Indian Issue, Kennedy Is Alone; Partisan, At Ease," *Providence Journal*, November 19, 1996, p. B1.

30. Russell W. Field Jr., "We Will Continue to Serve Our Community," *Providence Journal*, February 24, 1997, p. B5.

31. Larry Berman, interview by author, February 11, 1997.

32. *Six O'Clock News*, WJAR-TV, February 10, 1997.

33. Garrett Bliss, interview by author, May 13, 1997.

34. Scott MacKay, "Kennedy Promotes Caruolo Hospital Bill," *Providence Journal*, March 13, 1997, p. G1.

35. Martin Gottlieb and Kurt Eichenwald, "Biggest Hospital Operator Attracts Federal Inquiries," *New York Times*, March 28, 1997, p. A1; Kurt Eichenwald, "A Health Care Giant's Secret Payments Taint a Texas Deal," *New York Times*, March 29, 1997, p. 25; Kurt Eichenwald, "F.B.I. Reported Examining Hospital Operator in Ohio," *New York Times*, April 1, 1997, p. D2.

36. Brian Jones, "How Do You Negotiate with Your Future Bosses?" *Providence Journal*, June 15, 1997, p. F1–2.

37. *Six O'Clock News*, WJAR-TV, May 30, 1997.

38. Brian Jones, "Almond Vows to Veto Hospital Limits," *Providence Journal*, June 19, 1979, p. A1, 15.

39. Amy Keller, "Sen. Frist's Net Worth Takes a Hit," *Roll Call*, August 11, 1997, p. 1

40. Felice Freyer, "Fight against For-Profit Hospitals Intensifies," *Providence Journal*, June 10, 1997, p. B1.

41. Christopher Rowland, "Hospital CEO Protests For-Profit Limitations," *Providence Journal*, June 12, 1997, p. B1, 3.

42. Congressman Patrick J. Kennedy news release, "Kennedy: Poll Results Make It Clear That Restrictions on For-Profit Hospitals Are in the Best Interest of Rhode Islanders," June 25, 1997.

43. Scott MacKay, "Almond Vetoes Hospital Bill," *Providence Journal*, July 8, 1997, p. A1.

44. Ibid.

45. Brown University press release, "R.I. Voters Praise Renaissance of Downtown Providence, Support Bill That Would Limit Takeovers of Hospitals by For-Profit Health-Care Companies," June 25, 1997.

46. Scott MacKay, "Kennedy Continues Blasting His Foes," *Providence Journal*, March 8, 1997, p. A3.

47. Ibid; Keith Lang, interview by author, May 9, 1997.

48. Scott MacKay, "Kennedy Continues Blasting His Foes," *Providence Journal*, March 8, 1997, p. A3.

49. John Mullligan, Scott MacKay, and Christopher Rowland, "Pneumonia Gets Chafee's Attention," *Providence Journal*, December 9, 1996, p. B1.

50. Larry Berman, interview by author, August 31, 1995.

51. Nancy Mayer, interview by author, June 29, 1998.

52. Tony Pesaturo, interview by author, November 25, 1996, March 24, 1997.

53. WPRI-TV news release, October 16, 1996.

54. WJAR-TV broadcast, October 25, 1996.

55. M. Charles Bakst, "Don't Bet on Chafee Packing It In for 2000 Race," *Providence Journal*, August 15, 1996, p. A8.

56. Ibid.

57. John Chafee, interview by author, June 30, 1998. The background on Gorton's problems with Native Americans comes from Drummond Ayres, "Gorton Faces Challenge from Washington Tribes," *New York Times*, April 15, 1999, p. A18.

58. Keith Lang, interview by author, May 9, 1997.

59. John Chafee, interview by author, June 30, 1998.

60. Keith Lang, interview by author, May 9, 1997.

61. *Six O'Clock News*, WJAR-TV, May 30, 1997.

62. M. Charles Bakst, "Chafee vs. Kennedy: A Race You'd Love to See," *Providence Journal*, September 29, 1996, p. D1.
63. *Six O'Clock News*, WJAR-TV, May 30, 1997. Also aired on *10 News Conference*, WJAR-TV, June 1, 1997, 7:20 a.m. segment.
64. John Mulligan, "Kennedy Takes a Stand for Tribal Civil Rights," *Providence Journal*, May 1, 1997, p. A1. Also see John Mulligan, "Lawmakers Square Off over Tribe's Gambling Enterprises," *Providence Journal*, May 2, 1997, p. A6.
65. M. Charles Bakst, "Chafee vs. Kennedy: A Race You'd Love to See," *Providence Journal*, September 29, 1996, p. D1.
66. Ibid.
67. Ibid.
68. John Mulligan, "Kennedy Takes a Stand for Tribal Civil Rights," *Providence Journal*, May 1, 1997, p. A1; Michelle Dally Johnston, "The Last Boy Scout," *Rhode Island Monthly*, April 1997, p. 107.
69. M. Charles Bakst, "Chafee vs. Kennedy: A Race You'd Love to See," *Providence Journal*, September 29, 1996, p. D1.
70. Ibid.
71. Tony Pesaturo, interview by author, November 25, 1996.
72. Keith Lang, interview by author, May 9, 1997.
73. John Chafee, interview by author, June 30, 1998.
74. Peter Lord, "In D.C.: Hot Air over Clean Air," *Providence Journal*, June 5, 1997, p. A1.
75. John Chafee, interview by author, June 30, 1998.
76. Keith Lang, interview by author, May 9, 1997.

CHAPTER 13

1. Richard Berke, "Democratic Party Is Unable to Pay '96 Election Bills," *New York Times*, March 27, 1997, p. A1.
2. Michael Frisby and David Rogers, "Businessman's Access to White House Leads to a Security Inquiry," *Wall Street Journal*, March 17, 1997, p. 1.
3. David Rosenbaum, "Oilman Says He Got 'Access' by Giving Democrats Money," *New York Times*, September 19, 1997, p. A1.
4. Tim Weiner, "C.I.A. to Examine Possible Links of Agency to a Democratic Donor," *New York Times*, March 18, 1997, p. A1.
5. Michael Kranish, "Financier's Connections to Kennedy Come to Light: Tamraz Raised Funds, Hired Senator's Wife," *Boston Globe*, March 21, 1997, p. A1.
6. Elsa Walsh, "Kennedy's Hidden Campaign," *New Yorker*, March 31, 1997, pp. 66–81.
7. Michael Kranish, "Financier's Connections to Kennedy Come to Light: Tamraz Raised Funds, Hired Senator's Wife," *Boston Globe*, March 21, 1997, p. A1.
8. David Rosenbaum, "Oilman Says He Got 'Access' by Giving Democrats Money," *New York Times*, September 19, 1997, p. A1.
9. R. G. Ratcliffe, "Political Advisers Help Craft Strategy for Gtech," *Houston Chronicle*, March 9, 1997, p. 27.
10. Federal Election Commission, April 15, 1996 Quarterly Report, filed July 3, 1996, p. 5 of Itemized Disbursements.
11. Michael Kranish, "'94 Donations of $36,000 to Sen. Kennedy Called Illegal," *Boston Globe*, May 22, 1997, p. A1.
12. Michael Kranish, "Investigation Links Kennedy Donors, Late Commerce Chief," *Boston Globe*, May 23, 1997, p. A7.
13. John Mulligan, "Kennedy Returned $2,000 Gift to Tamraz," *Providence Journal*, September 19, 1997, p. A1.
14. John Mulligan, "Rep. Kennedy Returns $5,000 Tied to Buddhist Temple," *Providence Journal*, September 5, 1997, p. A5; John Mulligan, "Kennedy Explains His Rationale in Returning Money Raised at Temple," *Providence Journal*, September 9, 1997, p. A4. For the discussion of Hsia's indictment, see John Mulligan, "Patrick Kennedy among Those Misled to File False Statements," *Providence Journal*, February 19, 1998, p. A3; Eliza Newlin Carney, "Cashing In on Camelot," *National Journal*, February 21, 1998, pp. 400–403.
15. Sheila Rauch Kennedy, *Shattered Faith* (New York: Pantheon Books, 1997).
16. Ibid., pp. 10–11.
17. Stephen Kurkjian and Kate Zernike, "Baby Sitter Declines to Assist DA in Probe of Michael Kennedy," *Boston Globe*, May 23, 1997, p. A1.
18. Eileen McNamara, "Ideal Kennedys: The Women," *Boston Globe*, April 30, 1997, p. B1.
19. Frank Phillips and Don Aucoin, "Rep. Kennedy's Lead Vanishes in Poll," *Boston Globe*, April 30, 1997, p. A1.
20. "'I'm Sorry,' Kennedy Tells Mass. Convention," *Providence Journal*, June 8, 1997, p. A3.
21. Ibid.
22. Stephen Kurkjian and Kate Zernike, "DA Asks Kennedy for Credit Card Slips," *Boston Globe*, June 10, 1997, p. B1.
23. Scot Lehigh, "Apology Viewed as Political, Poll Shows," *Boston Globe*, June 20, 1997, p. B4.

24. Richard Pyle, "JFK Jr. Labels His Cousins 'Poster Boys for Bad Behavior,'" *Boston Globe*, August 11, 1997, p. A1. See John Kennedy's Editor's Letter, "Don't Sit under the Apple Tree," *George*, September 1997, pp. 26–28.
25. Michael Vallente, *Tom and Mike* WHJJ radio, August 11, 1997.
26. Adrian Walker, "Rep. Kennedy Fires Back at Cousin," *Boston Globe*, August 12, 1997, p. A1.
27. Scott MacKay, "Kennedy Withdraws from Governor's Race," *Providence Journal*, August 29, 1997, p. A1; Scot Lehigh and Don Aucoin, "Aides Say Controversy Took Toll on Kennedy," *Boston Globe*, August 30, 1997, p. A6.
28. Michael Shnayerson, "Bobby's Kids," *Vanity Fair*, August 1997, p. 165.
29. "JFK Jr. Says His Family's 'Difficulties' Sell Papers," *Boston Globe*, May 23, 1997, p. B10.
30. Joke cited on World Wide Web home page of the *Los Angeles Times*, May 8, 1997 (http://www.latimes.com).
31. "The Kennedy Mystique," *Boston Globe*, August 13, 1997, p. A18.
32. Keith Lang, interview by author, May 9, 1997.
33. *A Lively Experiment*, WSBE-TV, August 14, 1997.
34. M. Charles Bakst, "Joe Kennedy's Campaign Should Be a Warning to Patrick," *Providence Journal*, September 7, 1997, p. B1.
35. Mike Mello, classroom visit, Brown University, September 16, 1997.
36. Ibid.
37. Brown University Survey, press release, September 24, 1997. Also see Jody McPhillips, "Voters Are Happier with Elected Officials," *Providence Journal*, September 25, 1997, p. B1.
38. M. Charles Bakst, "Dropping in Polls, Kennedy Needs to Rethink His Message," *Providence Journal*, October 5, 1997, p. B1.
39. M. Charles Bakst, interview by author, August 6, 1999.
40. Michael Janofsky, "Favorite Game for Kennedys Took Deadly Turn on Slopes," *New York Times*, January 2, 1998, p. A1; Scot Lehigh, "Risk-Taking Roots Run Deep in Family," *Boston Globe*, January 2, 1998, p. A1.
41. Frank Phillips and Scot Lehigh, "Joe Kennedy, After Year of Turmoil, Walks Away: Will Not Seek Reelection, Plans to Run Energy Firm," *Boston Globe*, March 14, 1998, p. A1.
42. Tony Marcella, interview by author, March 17, 1998.
43. *Six O'Clock News*, WJAR-TV, March 14, 1998, and WLNT-TV, *Six O'Clock News*, March 14, 1998.
44. Tony Marcella, interview by author, August 31, 1998.
45. Nancy Mayer, interview by author, June 29, 1998.
46. Ibid.
47. Nancy Mayer, interview by author, December 12, 1997.
48. John Mulligan, "Kennedy Takes Paradoxical Casino Stand," *Providence Journal*, April 25, 1998, p. A1.
49. May Rae Bragg, "Kennedy Reminisces about Life in the Famed Political Clan," *Dubuque Telegraph Herald*, September 14, 1997, p. A3.
50. *A Lively Experiment*, Channel 36, December 11, 1997. Also see M. Charles Bakst, "Mayer to Challenge Kennedy in 1998? Interesting If True," *Providence Journal*, December 24, 1997, p. B1.
51. Nancy Mayer, interview by author, December 12, 1997.
52. John Chafee, interview by author, June 30, 1998.
53. *A Lively Experiment*, Channel 36, January 8, 1998.
54. Nicholas Graham, interview by author, June 23, 1998.
55. Ibid.
56. *10 News Conference*, WJAR-TV, February 8, 1998, 7:15 a.m. segment.
57. Ibid. 10:15 a.m. segment.
58. Brown University survey, press release, January 27, 1998.
59. Nancy Mayer, interview by author, June 29, 1998.
60. Ibid.
61. Larry Berman, classroom visit, Brown University, November 19, 1998.
62. Barry Massey, "Dems Help N.M. Candidate for House," Associated Press wire, June 22, 1998.
63. Norah O'Donnell, "Patrick, House's Lone Kennedy, Seems Headed for Plum Posts," *Roll Call*, April 2, 1998, p. 1.
64. Tony Marcella, interview by author, March 17, 1998.
65. Nicholas Graham, interview by author, June 23, 1998.
66. Michael Kranish, "N.E. Campaign Coffers Get Nontraditional Use," *Boston Globe*, June 8, 1998, p. A1; Eliza Newlin Carney, "Cashing In on Camelot," *National Journal*, February 21, 1998, pp. 400–403.
67. "Gala Marks Muhlenberg College's 150 Years," *Morning Call*, May 12, 1998, p. B2.
68. Dick Gephardt, remarks at Patrick Kennedy Reelection announcement rally in Providence, June 22, 1998.

69. Patrick Kennedy, remarks at his reelection announcement rally in Providence, June 22, 1998.
70. Joan Kennedy, interview by author, June 22, 1998.

71. Katherine Gregg, "The Kennedy from Rhode Island," *Providence Journal*, October 10, 1994, p. A1.
72. Tony Marcella, interview by author, August 31, 1998.

CHAPTER 14

1. Anonymous, *Primary Colors* (New York: Warner Books, 1996), pp. 27–28. Also see David Shribman, "Gephardt's Kennedy Strategy," *Fortune*, October 13, 1997, p. 56.
2. Seymour Hersh, *The Dark Side of Camelot* (Boston: Little, Brown, 1997).
3. Jo Mannies, "Kennedy Magnetism Put on Display Here," *St. Louis Post-Dispatch*, October 13, 1997, p. 2B.
4. M. Charles Bakst, "Kennedy's Friend Gephardt Races into an Uncertain Future," *Providence Journal*, December 7, 1997, p. D1.
5. Jo Mannies, "Kennedy Magnetism Put on Display Here," *St. Louis Post-Dispatch*, October 13, 1997, p. 2B.
6. David Maraniss, *First in His Class* (New York: Simon & Schuster, 1995), pp. 9–20.
7. John Mulligan, "Most of R.I. Delegation Falls in Line on Budget," *Providence Journal*, August 2, 1997, p. A6.
8. Tony Marcella, interview by author, August 31, 1998.
9. Erika Niedowski, "Kennedy Clan at Odds over Budget," *The Hill*, August 6, 1997, p. 1.
10. John Mulligan, "Most of R.I. Delegation Falls in Line on Budget," *Providence Journal*, August 2, 1997, p. A6.
11. Federal News Service, transcript of Republican press conference, August 1, 1997.
12. Patrick Kennedy, "America Needs 'True' Democrats," *Wall Street Journal*, August 7, 1997, p. A15. Also see Jill Zuckman, "In Gephardt-Kennedy Tie, A Primary Bond," *Boston Globe*, August 24, 1997, p. A6.
13. Robert Walsh, interview by author, July 28, 1999.
14. John Yang, "Looking Back to Theodore Roosevelt, Gephardt Calls for 'New Progressivism,'" *Washington Post*, December 3, 1997, p. A16. Also see Bob Hohler, "Gephardt Takes on Other Top Democrats," *Boston Globe*, December 3, 1997, p. A3.
15. Jill Zuckman, "Astraddle the Squabble," *Boston Globe*, December 12, 1997, p. A1.
16. Richard Berke, "Gephardt Criticizes Politics of Small Ideas; White House Fumes," *New York Times*, December 3, 1997, p. A28.
17. Russell Garland, "Gephardt Makes the Rounds," *Providence Journal*, December 4, 1997, p. B1.

18. Juliet Eilperin, "Line-Item Threats and Fast-Track Votes Go Together," *Roll Call*, November 10, 1997, p. 1.
19. Larry Berman, classroom visit, Brown University, November 19, 1998.
20. Robert Weygand, interview by author, August 24, 1998.
21. Ibid.
22. John Mulligan, "Indian Gambling Issue Spurs Weygand-Kennedy Turf Battle," *Providence Journal*, June 18, 1998, p. A1.
23. Robert Weygand, interview by author, August 24, 1998.
24. Ibid.
25. Tony Marcella, interview by author, August 31, 1998.
26. John Mulligan, "'Pulse Is Very, Very Weak' on Tribal Gambling Bill," *Providence Journal*, June 26, 1998, p. A1.
27. M. Charles Bakst, "Al Gore in R.I.: Briefed, Detached and On Message," *Providence Journal*, July 2, 1998, p. B1. Also see Terry Neal and Ceci Connolly, "Kennedy Left Out in R.I.," *Washington Post*, July 5, 1998, p. A10.
28. Norah O'Donnell, "Kennedy Charges Presidential Politics Led to R.I. Snub," *Roll Call*, July 6, 1998.
29. Ibid.
30. M. Charles Bakst, "Al Gore in R.I.: Briefed, Detached and On Message," *Providence Journal*, July 2, 1998, p. B1.
31. John Rother, interview by author, July 1, 1998.
32. *A Lively Experiment*, WSBE-TV July 2, 1998.
33. Robert Weygand, interview by author, August 24, 1998.
34. John Mulligan, "Clinton's Admission Disappoints Kennedy," *Providence Journal*, August 25, 1998, p. A6.
35. Larry Berman, classroom visit, Brown University, November 19, 1998.
36. John Mulligan, "Kennedy: No Penalty for Clinton," *Providence Journal*, October 2, 1998, p. A1.
37. John Mulligan, "Kennedy, Weygand Bicker over Impeachment Probe," *Providence Journal*, October 7, 1998, p. A1.
38. Tony Marcella, interview by author, November 15, 1999. Also see "Patrick Kennedy's Quest to Make a Difference Where It Counts," *Caring Magazine*, October 1999, pp. 34–44.

39. Background source. Also see Anne Kornblut, "Kennedy 'No' Doesn't End Speculation, *Boston Globe*, March 18, 1999, p. A4.
40. Dick Gephardt, comments as relayed through deputy press secretary Sue Harvey, September 9, 1999.
41. M. Charles Bakst, "Kennedy Choice: A Moment in Time, Kudos from Gore," *Providence Journal*, November 20, 1988, p. A14.
42. Christopher Rowland and John Mulligan, "Kennedy Rules Out a Run against Chafee," *Providence Journal*, November 20, 1998, p. A1.
43. Karin Johanson, interview by author, August 12, 1999.
44. John Lewis, interview by author, February 16, 1999. The Gore comments were made at a Providence Democratic rally on June 11, 1999.
45. Tony Marcella, interview by author, August 31, 1998.
46. Larry Berman, classroom visit, Brown University, November 19, 1998.
47. John Lewis, interview by author, February 16, 1999.
48. Bob Hohler, "Kennedy Compound Doors Open to $100,000 Democratic Donors," *Boston Globe*, April 6, 1999, p. A3.
49. Robert Schlesinger, "Patrick Kennedy's Recipe for Success at DCCC: Money + Message = More Members," *The Hill*, March 17, 1999, p. 1.
50. John Mulligan, "Kennedy Musters Democrats' Muscle," *Providence Journal*, December 18, 1998, p. A1.
51. CNN live coverage, December 18, 1998, 9:25 a.m., transcript # 98121805V54.
52. John Mulligan, "Kennedy Backs Off Strategy Against GOP," *Providence Journal*, May 13, 1999, p. A9.
53. John Mulligan, "Gun Vote Clouds Once Sure-Fire Issue," *Providence Journal*, June 21, 1999, p. A1.
54. Ibid.
55. Jim Nicholson, "We Continue to Listen to Rural Americans," *Providence Journal*, June 28, 1999, p. B6.
56. John Mercurio, "GOP Seizes on DCCC Head's 'Rural' Comment," *Roll Call*, June 28, 1999. Also see John Mercurio, "Democrats Respond to GOP Attacks About Rural Districts," *Roll Call*, July 5, 1999.
57. Ibid.
58. Karin Johanson, interview by author, August 12, 1999.
59. John Mulligan, interview by author, August 25, 1999.
60. Glenn Bolger, interview by author, August 13, 1999.
61. Terry Nelson, interview by author, August 12, 1999.
62. Ibid.
63. Eliza Newlin Carney, "Campaign 2000: Winner Take All," *National Journal*, March 19, 1999.
64. Adam Clymer, "Dilemma for Democrats in Clinton Plans," *New York Times*, July 3, 1999, p. A8.
65. Michael Grunwald, "Gephardt Works Tirelessly to Take Back House," *Washington Post*, July 12, 1999, p. A1.
66. Karin Johanson, interview by author, August 12, 1999.
67. Patrick Kennedy, interview by author, November 1, 1999.
68. Background source.
69. Glenn Bolger, interview by author, August 13, 1999.
70. Jane Ann Morrison, "In LV, Kennedy Rips Extremists," *Las Vegas Review-Journal*, August 11, 1999, p. 1B.
71. John Mulligan, "Who Has the Power?" *Providence Journal*, November 14, 1999, p. A1.
72. Patrick Kennedy, interview by author, November 1, 1999.
73. Darrell M. West, *Checkbook Democracy: How Money Corrupts Political Campaigns* (Boston: Northeastern University Press, 2000).
74. Mark Weiner, interview by author, September 7, 1999.
75. Patrick Kennedy, interview by author, November 1, 1999.

CHAPTER 15

1. Larry Berman, classroom visit, Brown University, November 19, 1998.
2. Background source.
3. Kriste Goad, "Patrick Kennedy Asks Democrats to Work for Change," *Memphis Commercial Appeal*, June 20, 1998, p. A13.
4. Tony Marcella, interview by author, August 31, 1998.
5. John Mulligan, "GOP's Santa Throws Himself in Front of the Kennedy Juggernaut," *Providence Journal*, October 15, 1998, p. A1.
6. Larry Berman, classroom visit, Brown University, November 19, 1998.
7. Ibid.
8. Patrick Kennedy, remarks as reported on Web site, www.InsidePolitics.org, July 27, 1999.
9. M. Charles Bakst, interview by author, August 6, 1999.

10. Patrick Kennedy, interview by *Providence Journal* columnist M. Charles Bakst for WLNE-TV feature, October 14, 1994.
11. Jack McConnell, interview by author, August 24, 1999.
12. M. Charles Bakst, interview by author, August 6, 1999.
13. Ibid.
14. Scott MacKay, interview by author, August 10, 1999.
15. Canon, *Athletes, Actors, and Astronauts*; Richard Fenno, *Learning to Legislate* (Washington, D.C.: Congressional Quarterly Press, 1991).
16. Bob Hohler, "The UnKennedy," *Boston Globe Magazine*, June 6, 1999.
17. U.S. House of Representatives Financial Disclosure Statement for Calendar Year 1995, May 15, 1996.
18. Amy Keller, "The Roll Call Fifty," *Roll Call*, January 20, 1997, p. 1; Laura Jereski, "Shirtsleeves to Shirtsleeves," *Forbes*, October 21, 1991, p. 34.
19. Ted Kennedy Jr., interview by author, September 1999. Also see Matt Bai, "A Dynasty in Decline," *Newsweek*, June 23, 1997, p. 30.
20. Karin Reed, interview by author, July 30, 1999.
21. Scott MacKay, interview by author, August 10, 1999.
22. Mark Weiner, interview by author, September 7, 1999.
23. Tony Marcella, interview by author, November 15, 1999.
24. Matt Labash, "Patrick Kennedy—The Man and the Myth," *Weekly Standard*, June 7, 1999, pp. 24–29.
25. Bob Hohler, "The UnKennedy," *Boston Globe Magazine*, June 6, 1999.
26. M. Charles Bakst, interview by author, August 6, 1999; Karin Johanson, interview by author, August 12, 1999.
27. Patrick Kennedy, interview by author, November 1, 1999.
28. Patrick Kennedy, interview by *Providence Jour-nal* columnist M. Charles Bakst for WLNE-TV feature, October 14, 1994.
29. Frank Davies, "Kennedy Supporting Cuban Boy's Citizenship," *Providence Journal*, January 17, 2000, p. A1.
30. Garrett Bliss, interview by author, May 13, 1997.
31. Russell Garland, "No Longer a Newcomer," *Providence Journal*, October 16, 1996, p. A1. Also see Larry Berman, interview by author, August 31, 1998.
32. Ariel Sabar, "Kennedy Joins Effort to Pass Gun-Control Measures," *Providence Journal*, January 4, 1999, p. 1.
33. Background source.
34. Tony Marcella, interview by author, August 31, 1998.
35. Garrett Bliss, interview by author, May 13, 1997.
36. Chris Black, "Rep. Patrick Kennedy Marks a Milestone," *Boston Globe*, July 14, 1997, p. A7.
37. Ted Kennedy, interview by author, June 22, 1998.
38. Scott MacKay, interview by author, August 10, 1999.
39. Drummond Ayres, "She's Got Momentum, And the Name Too," *New York Times*, July 15, 1999, p. A18.
40. David Von Drehle, "Camelot's Future: The Kennedy Generations," *Washington Post*, July 25, 1999, p. A1.
41. Background Source.
42. Ray Rickman, interview by author, July 29, 1999.
43. Bob Hohler, "The UnKennedy," *Boston Globe Magazine*, June 6, 1999.
44. *10 News Conference*, WJAR-TV, January 9, 1994. Also see James O'Neill, "Mirian's Dr. Kevin Vigilante to Run for Congress," *Providence Journal*, January 8, 1994, p. 8A.
45. Sarah Francis, "How Big Is That Algae Bloom?" *Rhode Island Monthly*, August 1997, pp. 74–76.
46. Barbara Tannenbaum, interview by author, December 21, 1995.

Index